Catalytic Coaching

Catalytic Coaching

THE END OF THE PERFORMANCE REVIEW

Garold L. Markle

QUORUM BOOKS
Westport, Connecticut • London

Library of Congress Cataloging-in-Publication Data

Markle, Garold L., 1956–
    Catalytic coaching : the end of the performance review / Garold L.
Markle.
       p. cm.
    Includes bibliographical references and index.
    ISBN 978-0-313-36083-1 (alk. paper)
    1. Supervision of employees.   2. Mentoring in business.
3. Employees—Rating of. I. Title.
    HF5549.12.M365   2000
    658.3'125—dc21   99–36599

British Library Cataloguing in Publication Data is available.

Library of Congress Catalog Card Number: 99–36599
ISBN: 978-0-313-36083-1

First published in 2000

Quorum Books, 88 Post Road West, Westport, CT 06881
An imprint of Greenwood Publishing Group, Inc.
www.quorumbooks.com

Printed in the United States of America

The paper used in this book complies with the
Permanent Paper Standard issued by the National
Information Standards Organization (Z39.48–1984).

10

Contents

Figures

Preface: Deming's Riddle

> If your performance evaluation system does more harm than good, just quit
> doing it. You don't have to have an alternative to make an improvement.
>
> —W. Edwards Deming[1]

I had been harboring doubts about the utility of my company's highly touted
performance evaluation system for several months before I heard him speak. It
wasn't until I stopped to listen to Dr. W. Edwards Deming, however, that the
wheels fell completely off my wagon.

During the 1980s Dr. Deming began receiving long-overdue international recognition and acclaim for his lead role in fathering the modern Quality movement. His famous "Fourteen Points for Organizational Transformation" were
being used by our prestigious *Fortune* 100 company to help it come to grips
with wonderful concepts like "functional interdependence," "process reein-
geering" and the "elimination of waste."[2] The work of Phillip Crosby, Joseph
Juran, Bill Conway and other Deming disciples was being used to drive a new
spirit of empowerment and teamwork throughout the corporation.

These were exciting times. They helped free all of us from our traditional
mental shackles and enabled us to look at the way we did work from a totally
different perspective. We examined everything that Dr. Deming said for wisdom
and insight. It was as if his famous Fourteen Points had been etched in stone
during a private visit on the highest mountain. All except one, that is. At this
company, point number twelve was taboo.

Point number twelve ran in direct opposition to our highly prized performance
management system. For this corporation, challenging any aspect of the annual
rating and ranking process was tantamount to treason. After all, the top execu-

tives were chosen and cultivated this way. To suggest that the evaluation system was logically flawed seemed to be questioning our whole strategy for "separating the grain from the chaff" in addition to the mission-critical "pay for performance" philosophy that served as the glue holding our entire system together.

Point number twelve was discreetly eliminated from all postings and discussions. The rest of Deming was great. Apparently he had just one big blind spot. We learned to fast-forward the instructional videos past this portion of his agenda. Senior management didn't contest his ideas on the subject. They just elected to pay them no heed. It made me curious. What exactly was Deming trying to say with point number twelve? And why did it make everybody so uptight and nervous? In point number twelve Deming states that an organization wishing to transform itself must "remove barriers that rob people in management and in engineering of their right to pride of workmanship. That means, inter alia, abolishment of the annual or merit rating."[3] If that assault on the status quo was not direct enough, in the accompanying material labeled "Seven Deadly Diseases" he added more fuel to the fire. He lists Deadly Disease number three as the "personal review system, or evaluation of performance, merit rating, annual review, or annual appraisal, by whatever name, for people in management, the effects of which are devastating."[4]

Deming stated that these common organizational practices are destructive and prevent companies from achieving the ultimate goal of transformation. It is a testament to the unique power of Deming's other ideas that senior management even considered using his material at all. It exposed the executives to countless unwanted discussions, which they did their best to quickly silence.

When I first gained exposure to these radical new concepts I was on the "fast track." I had received a succession of good ratings and rankings and was promoted rapidly and repeatedly because of it. I was clearly a net beneficiary of the company's rigorous evaluation process. It was working well for me.

Over time, however, I became more and more conscious of the damage these systems seemed to be doing to the people and organizations around me. I began noticing how much the majority of employees and supervisors seemed to dislike the annual review process. Even those who did well seemed to have contempt for the conflicting messages being sent. The reward system clearly encouraged internal competition and gamesmanship while management was openly preaching the critical need for teamwork. The more I studied and learned, the more disillusioned I became with the whole quit.

Perhaps the worst part of the situation was that I, by being in the Human Resources (HR) function, had to serve as an "enabler" of the process. I was a "pusher." As an HR manager I had to *sell* this practice to others. I couldn't just participate as an individual and gripe about it with colleagues, I had to try to convince employees and supervisors that the evaluation system was a good idea. Some I literally had to force to participate.

The problem, once discovered, seemed to be everywhere—not only with our organization but also with every other company in our industry. Indeed, it appeared that literally every large company I was aware of was utilizing some form of performance evaluation process. Everyone seemed to give people grades. Some used forced ranking and some did not, but all tied ratings to pay. Bottom line, we were all singing from the same hymnal and the HR function was leading the choir.

Despite my company's quick and complete dismissal of Dr. Deming's words of advice, I soon began to feel he might be right. On the other hand, I also learned why those in authority at my company were so reluctant to take his recommendation seriously.

In 1993 I was very fortunate to be able to see Dr. Deming in person and witness his response to a pointed question on this subject. "Dr. Deming," the seminar participant queried, "It's clear that you're not fond of performance appraisals or performance ratings. What do you propose that we do in place of them?"

I will never forget Dr. Deming's response to this question, or the way that it made me feel. He said, "If your performance evaluation system does more harm than good, just quit doing it. You don't have to have an alternative to make an improvement."

His logic was impeccable, but as an HR professional it left me feeling very empty. Surely there was something positive about the old system that could be salvaged. Abandoning current practices with no substitute sounded like anarchy. Highly successful companies like mine were conditioned to such discipline over decades. Deming's anarchic prescription gave us visions of chaos and disorder.

In subsequent dialogue, Dr. Deming made it clear that he did not have a solution to all the issues or problems he raised. He thought that there should probably be a better way, but did not view it as his responsibility to tell us all the answers. "That is your job," he would say to a perplexed inquirer searching for a constructive alternative. Dr. Deming was a statistician and management philosopher. He gave logically pure answers, whether they were practical or not. He did not apologize for leaving practical matters to the practitioners.

And so, unconsciously at first and consciously later on, I accepted the challenge. Being a practitioner who now saw the problem, I set off to understand it at a deeper level. I joined others in the search for a constructive alternative.

This book largely chronicles that logical journey. It should prove very useful to those interested in pursuing a similar course. It builds a business case for the complete overhaul of traditional performance management systems conceived in an evaluation paradigm and advocates replacing them with an entirely new method conceived in a coaching paradigm.

"Catalytic Coaching" will be introduced in this book as an integrated system of performance management designed to facilitate a constructive partnership between a manager and employee. It is built around frank, open and constructive feedback and a shared desire for each individual to achieve his ultimate potential. When performed properly, it should turn the time invested in this formal activity from a much-dreaded, time-consuming, non-productive, compulsory act into an activity of value, merit and empowerment. By helping the individuals working within a corporation constructively face their performance challenges and live up to their maximum potential, it can help the entire organization in its quest for growth and profitability.

Catalytic Coaching ultimately solves Deming's riddle. It satisfies management's need to have formal dialogue about performance built into the infrastructure of work. At the same time, however, it carefully heeds Deming's warning not to do more harm than good. My hope is that you will find this book to have articulated the problem in a way that is compelling while offering a solution that obtains that delicate balance.

Acknowledgments

The list of people I must thank for assisting me in producing this book is a long and distinguished one. Without the energy, guidance, encouragement and wisdom provided by these special people this task would have never been undertaken or completed. They should share any credit or recognition for the work that it accomplishes.

From Right Management Consultants I must thank Elaine Bailey and Kathleen Mooney for encouraging me, almost forcing me, to sit down and begin writing.

From the former Louisiana Land & Exploration Company I am indebted to C. A. Zackary, H. Leighton Steward, Rick Plaeger, Linda Jones and Dennis Legendre for helping me shape the prototype of this program.

From the University of Michigan School of Business I owe a debt of gratitude to Professor Dave Ulrich and fellow instructors and classmates in my Senior HR Executive Workshop. Nancy Swanson of Northwest Airlines and Angela Koo, formerly of Dairy Farm in Hong Kong, were among those that were most helpful.

Going back a bit further, I must acknowledge the tremendous education and growth opportunities presented to me at both Exxon and Shell. The investment each corporation makes in developing its people is truly a benefit to all of society.

In developing my consulting and speaking business, I truly appreciate the mentoring and sponsorship of Larry Hart, a more seasoned consultant and Chair for The Executive Committee (TEC). I also appreciate Gary Anderson, Celeste McAllister and Paula Matthews of TEC for helping me become both a speaking and coaching resource to this very vital international organization of CEOs.

I am very grateful to the rich insight provided by my friend and colleague

Carlos Quintero of Sales Effectiveness, Inc. Carlos is a brilliant thinker and strategist. He also serves as an excellent role model in how to effectively coach a colleague. He helped significantly to shape the book with special impact on the structure and content of Part IV.

In addition to guidance and support from business colleagues, several other friends and associates have made special contributions—Virginia Benzier, Dennis Gardner, Jack Mead, Ed Gaine and Mark Belokonny are among those that deserve special recognition.

Closer to home, I am delighted to acknowledge the unwavering support I received from my family. My children, Shanna, Carissa and Garrett, have helped me practice coaching and being coached outside a work setting. My father, Roger Markle, gave my book its first and most thorough reviews. My mothers, Dorothy Markle and Kathleen Coursen, have headed the cheerleading squad and waited eagerly for me to finish this quest.

Finally, it is to my wife, Gail, that I owe the greatest debt of gratitude and to her that I dedicate this book. In addition to being the graphic designer for the figures contained herein, Gail is my life-mate and personal catalytic coach. To her I hope to always be a work in progress.

Catalytic Coaching

Chapter 1

Introduction and Overview

> One of the most frightening and degrading experiences in every employee's
> life is the annual Performance Review.
> > —Scott Adams, creator of "Dilbert"[1]

People hate performance reviews. This would appear to be almost a universal
law of modern business. Whether you call them evaluations, appraisals or counseling sessions, employees seem to have developed a great distaste for the ritual
of having their yearly contribution summarized and categorized in one 90-
minute meeting. Most managers dread giving this annual dose of medicine almost as much as employees dislike receiving it.

Despite these strongly held feelings, it was recently estimated that more than
70 million U.S. workers receive annual performance reviews.[2] William Mercer
Inc., in a 1995 survey of 218 companies, found that almost all managers and
technical/knowledge workers were subject to yearly evaluations. Over the last
several decades the practice of giving people formal evaluative feedback on their
perceived performance has become established as a dominant personnel practice.

The introduction of performance reviews can be traced back to Lord and
Taylor Co. in 1914. This appears to be the inception of the "traditional" model
that requires managers to fill out forms once a year rating employees on how
well each individual accomplished an assigned list of business objectives. A
summary of this evaluation or appraisal is then given orally to each employee
in a face-to-face meeting. The review session customarily ends with communication of the impact of past performance on the individual's base salary.

To be sure, performance management systems have increased in sophistication
over time. Appraisal forms are much more complicated and involved than they

used to be. Standards of measurement have changed to include more categories as they focus on behaviors and competencies in addition to just objective results. Ratings in some systems have been adjusted to include input from teams, peers, direct reports and even customers. Elements of the communication ritual have been refined with additional formal discussions being added at more frequent intervals throughout the year. Form completion has entered the computer age with some companies even putting them online. And countless hours have been spent training managers to be better at giving feedback, conducting interviews and counseling their employees.

As a result of all this modernization, companies are adjusting and supplementing their performance management processes almost continuously these days. Mercer's 1995 study also indicated that more than 70% of the 218 companies surveyed had either changed their evaluation process in the last two years or had plans in place to do so. It is not at all uncommon for companies to make wholesale changes in their performance management systems two or three times in a ten-year period.

In 1996, when Chris Lee assessed the current state of this bedrock personnel practice, he still reported that "a performance appraisal can be the single most demoralizing event in an employee's work year."[3] Despite all the attempts to get beyond the traditional model, Lee concluded that performance management, even in its more sophisticated incarnations, appears to be better at reducing surprises than eliminating pain.

Lee's observations are reinforced in a 1997 survey conducted for the Society of Human Resource Management, which discovered that only 5% of HR professionals were "very satisfied" with their performance management systems.[4] Likewise, a 1998 survey of 152 companies summed up their findings by stating that performance management "receives a tepid welcome throughout the organization." They describe respondents at all levels as "apathetic, at best" and in another survey by the same organization report that performance management "was one of the most commonly mentioned problem areas in need of attention" for the calendar year 1998.[5]

EXPLANATIONS AND RECOMMENDATIONS

This book will argue that fundamental problems exist with traditional performance reviews and virtually all performance management systems because of the basic paradigm on which they are constructed. Attempts to correct these problems within the existing paradigm have been and always will be ultimately futile. Real progress cannot be made until the paradigm is first understood and then replaced.

In defending this point of view, we will attempt to do five things.

• Define the previous paradigm and pinpoint its root problems
• Explain why companies struggle trying to improve it

- Establish a clear business case for replacing it
- Introduce a new system based on a more functional paradigm
- Fully explain how to make the new system work

INTENDED AUDIENCE

This book was written for three target audiences. First, are leaders in organizations who have influence over people-development systems. That would include presidents, CEOs and other senior executives, as well as those who control the Human Resource or Personnel function. Members of these groups should find within these pages motivation to change existing systems and a detailed proposal on how to do it.

A second target audience is managers and supervisors who have a need or desire to help their assigned people develop under their guidance. This book should serve to give solid advice on how to effectively function in the role of coach. Even if they are not able to eliminate or change the existing performance management infrastructure within their companies, supervisors and managers who digest this work should be able to use many of its ideas to operate more effectively within whatever system currently exists. Adopting many of these new practices should greatly increase their effectiveness in communicating about performance and development issues with their direct reports.

A third target audience is employees participating in an organization that is using coaching to help them develop. Members of an organization undergoing a change to the method of people development outlined in this book will find it particularly relevant.

CATALYTIC COACHING DEFINED

The new system as set forth in this book is called "Catalytic Coaching." The term, as we will use it, has both associative and technical meaning. The idea of coaching, of course, is taken from the field of sports. Coaching is a technique for helping others reach peak performance and ultimate potential. It is usually associated with the idea of teaming and fits well with the culture many organizations are trying to create.

John Whitmore, in his book *Coaching for Performance*, describes the essence of coaching as embracing an approach toward learning that emphasizes active employee involvement: "Coaching is unlocking a person's potential to maximize their own performance. It is helping them to learn rather than teaching them."[6] In *The Heart of Coaching*, Thomas Crane describes the use of coaching in a business context as "a healthy, positive enabling process that develops the capacity of people to solve today's business problems."[7]

Many are familiar with the term "catalytic" in connection with chemistry. It also has a more general meaning, however. The dictionary defines "catalytic" as an activity that causes or promotes "a reaction between two or more persons or forces precipitated by an agent." The agent, generally referred to as a "catalyst," is defined as something "that promotes or speeds significant change or action." These ideas effectively combine to convey the image of Catalytic Coaching as a process which purposefully promotes or speeds significant change among people.

More specifically, as it is used here, Catalytic Coaching will be defined as *a comprehensive, integrated performance management system built on a paradigm of development. Its purpose is to enable individuals to improve their production capabilities and rise to their potential, ultimately causing organizations to generate better business results. It features clearly defined infrastructure, methodology and skill sets. It assigns responsibility for career development to employees and establishes the boss as developmental coach.*

The Catalytic Coaching model will be introduced in Part III of this book, wherein the process will be explained in detail. For a quick preview of the model and to get a feel for its flow, you may examine Figure 7-1 in Chapter 7. As a means of introducing the concept and giving you an initial impression where we are headed, let's quickly discuss how Catalytic Coaching differs from most prevailing performance management methodologies.

WHAT MAKES THIS APPROACH DIFFERENT?

Catalytic Coaching can be distinguished from traditional performance management systems in three fundamental ways. It changes what is done, how it is done and the roles of those who do it. Figure 1-1 provides a summary comparison of design features and clearly highlights eleven of the key differences.

Content Changes

Catalytic coaching involves no competitive rating or ranking of employees. They are assigned no aggregate labels or grades at the end of the process. Instead, mangers, functioning as coaches, provide employees feedback on perceived strengths and areas for improvement in light of stated career aspirations. The coach helps each employee construct a development plan aimed at improving contribution in the current job and increasing potential for other opportunities when those are desired.

Catalytic Coaching breaks the direct connection between salary treatment and an assessment of annual performance. "Pay for performance" practices are explained as having an indirect impact on base pay. Catalytic Coaching sessions focus on performance improvement without trying to justify salary treatment. Financial recognition of superior contributors is dealt with in other ways.

Figure 1-1
Comparison of Features: Traditional Performance Review vs. Catalytic Coaching

	PERFORMANCE REVIEW	CATALYTIC COACHING
PROCESS		
Time Focus	Past	Future
Average Length of Feedback Form	4-7 Pages	1 Page
Responsibility for Development Plan	Management/HR	Employee
CONTENT		
Use of Summary Grade or Label	Yes	No
Use of Competitive Ranking	Sometimes	Never
Tie to Salary Treatment	Direct	Indirect
Emphasis on Employee Input	Incidental	Pivotal
ROLES		
Primary "Customer" of Process	"The File"	The Employee
Role of Boss	Evaluator/Judge	Coach
Role of Employee	Recipient of Feedback	Empowered Career Craftsman
Role of Human Resources	Process Policeman	Coach² (Coach of Coaches)

Process Changes

A review, by its very nature, is focused on the past. Catalytic Coaching is focused on the future. No attempt is made in coaching sessions to account for all activities that have taken place in a calendar year. Instead, emphasis is placed only on past issues and behaviors that have likelihood of impacting future performance.

Administrative burden is dramatically reduced for most companies converting to the Catalytic Coaching method. In traditional systems, the number of pages a manager must complete on an employee varies widely. Many require the supervisor to provide up to ten or twelve pages of input, with the majority somewhere between four and seven. Catalytic Coaching requires one page to be completed by the supervisor on each employee.

Ownership of the traditional review process is with senior management and the HR department in most companies. In contrast, the employee is defined as the owner of the Catalytic Coaching process. Each employee has ultimate responsibility to prepare and implement his or her own development plan. The manager serves as a resource and facilitator.

Role Changes

Catalytic Coaching differs markedly from conventional performance management systems in the way it assigns responsibility for behavioral change and career development. Too often in classic systems employees become passive participants in a process designed primarily to rate or rank them in order to try to justify a salary increase.

The approach outlined herein changes responsibilities for almost everyone involved in the performance management process. A boss abandons the futile role of *critic/judge* and becomes a *facilitator in the employee development process*, functioning like a *coach*. Employees, who take the quest for achieving high performance seriously and invest in the process both emotionally and intellectually, are converted from *evaluation subjects* to *empowered craftsmen of their own careers*. The burden of responsibility for career management falls on the shoulders of those with the greatest vested interest. Other aspects of the system are converted to support them.

HR professionals become *coaching consultants* instead of *process policemen*. No longer must they hound managers to make them fill out and submit their forms. By dramatically reducing the burden (to one page) and making the experience both positive and productive, most of the longstanding challenges associated with having to force compliance go away.

Labor attorneys get a *reduction in workload* once a Catalytic Coaching system has been set into place. They also get involved much more in *problem prevention* as sensitive issues surface sooner and the number of discrimination and wrongful discharge suits subside.

CATALYTIC COACHING DELIVERS

Catalytic Coaching is presented as a replacement for, not an addition to, traditional performance evaluations. It will be argued that performance management systems built around the principles of Catalytic Coaching are superior to traditional (evaluation based) systems in producing the key deliverables:

- positive behavioral change
- motivation to work hard
- retention of key contributors
- internal promotions and succession
- prevention of and protection against lawsuits

In addition, organizations that have tried this new system claim it reduces both time and cost required by the annual review process at the same time that it greatly increases the outcomes listed above. Implemented correctly, it can help transform both individuals and their corporations.

PHILOSOPHICAL ORIENTATION

Three important philosophies help define the approach taken in this book: an attitude toward people, perspective on Human Resources, and systems orientation. These should be made explicit at the onset of our journey. We will review each briefly before concluding this chapter with a detailed preview of the road ahead.

Attitude Toward People

Catalytic Coaching is about helping people grow. It's about bringing out the best in people at work. It sets forth a specific methodology for creating and managing a comprehensive and strategic people-development system to help drive a business toward prosperity.

The term "people" is used quite frequently throughout this book. It implies something quite different than "human resources," "human assets" or "intellectual capital." Even the terms "employee" and "associate" convey too much sterility.

It is important to recognize both the joy and complexity of work done by people. Too often we lose sight of the human face of our workforce by using fancy terminology that reminds us of their financial value. It is possible to create development systems at work that both recognize and profit from the humanity that the term "people" implies.

Before you conclude that the author advocates warm and fuzzy idealism, however, please be aware the terms "strategic" and "business" in the opening paragraph of this section were chosen very deliberately as well. Rest assured that the systems outlined in this book promote activities that are designed to impact the bottom line for a company. The irony is that only by treating human assets as people can we have ultimate impact on profitability.

Philosophy of Human Resources

In his book *HR Champions*, Dave Ulrich conveys a clear message that HR professionals must design and implement systems that are better focused on delivering results and adding value.[8] He observes that HR practitioners frequently spend too much time concentrating on what they *do* and not enough on what they *deliver*. In no area is this more apparent than in discussions surrounding performance management systems.

Most HR practitioners, for instance, begin justification for traditional performance management systems by speaking of the critical role they play in providing performance feedback. Process models (when they exist) typically end when the completed and signed evaluation form is placed in the employee's file.

The viewpoint in this book is more utilitarian. A performance management system is defined as useful to the extent it promotes specific desired outcomes that are important to the success of the business. Catalytic Coaching is built on a model that does not end with messages being received or with the implementation of an action plan. The process ends with business impact.

In addition to looking at impact, one must also look at cost. The approach taken in this book might be described as a form of "HR Lite." Using the beer analogy, the desired objective is all the taste with fewer calories. Another way to look at it is to regard these, and all people-development systems, as if they were burden to an organization—items carried with the team on a mountain climbing expedition. Some items are worth bringing on the trip. In fact, some are critical—a tent, for instance, or food, water, dry clothing. Other items make the trip more enjoyable or meaningful, like a camera or a photograph of a loved one. On the other hand, if the trip is long and the mountain is steep, each item needs to be closely examined for its value. Weight must be a consideration.

Too often HR and Legal functions seem to be forcing an organization to take items on the journey that have dubious value. Most classic performance management systems are the equivalent of a 20-pound, battery-powered TV/VCR. We try to sell the hikers on the idea that a motivational video shown at base camp just below the summit might provide a wonderful psychological lift. All the while they keep looking at us like we're crazy. "Can't we just bring a book or cassette?" query the heavily burdened travelers.

Catalytic Coaching aims to capture more of the positive impact intended by most performance management systems at a substantially reduced level of burden. Bureaucracy is held to an absolute minimum.

Systems Orientation

Literally dozens of books line the shelves these days dedicated to the topic of coaching. Almost all of them are written about how to acquire coaching skills. Coaching is positioned as a critical competency for the modern organization member. More seem to be arriving every day.

This book was written for a different purpose. The focus is more holistic. It attempts to make a business case for a performance management system that uses developmental coaching principles at its foundation. The challenge taken here is not so much to help create individual competency in coaching skills. Rather it is to assist in the design and implementation of an integrated people-management process in which coaching skills can realistically be expected to operate. Said another way, the emphasis is not on how to teach supervisors to coach. It is on how to create an infrastructure that institutionalizes coaching.

Because of its systemic orientation, this book deals directly with issues that other books fail to address. Those who teach coaching as a skill seldom dwell on critical interface issues with already existing, deeply entrenched performance management systems. They treat coaching as a technology useful to change behavior without regard to the processes used to evaluate performance and determine pay increases. They fail to investigate the inherent overlap and conflict that almost always exists when an organization has an annual performance evaluation process that rates and ranks people to determine promotions and salary treatment.

The business impact of coaching activity can be affected dramatically by the presence or absence of evaluation practices that are linked to pay and promotion. From a systems perspective, for coaching to have impact, no formal process affecting distribution of rewards can afford to be ignored. Because of these systemic concerns, the aim of this book is not to *add* coaching on top of traditional responsibilities for performance management. The goal is to *replace* evaluation-based systems with one that is equally structured, but coaching and development-based.

THE PATH FORWARD

Part I of this book attempts to put the performance review in perspective. It helps define the prevailing paradigm and clarify the dilemma that we all intuitively know exists. It explains why the practice of rating and ranking undermines the effectiveness of systems designed to develop people. It describes the inherent bankruptcy of attempts to pay for performance. In short, it helps explain why many have come to regard the evaluation of human performance as industry's poorest performing personnel practice.

Part II explores strategies that have been taken by companies to try to improve the effectiveness and efficiency of traditional performance management systems. It reviews strategies that are incremental or evolutionary in nature. It reviews those that are more radical or revolutionary in nature. And it explains why most of these strategies have been ineffective in resolving the true problems posed by the prevailing practice. It introduces the concept of measurement as a way to clear out some of the fog and put systems to a test.

Part III introduces the Catalytic Coaching model. It presents both a bird's eye view of how the process works and then takes the reader through a thorough step-by-step discussion of how to implement it.

Part IV covers ancillary issues. It defines the infrastructure, competency requirements and commitment needed to make Catalytic Coaching work. It discusses money matters and how to handle salary administration once performance labels are removed. It describes how specific programs work in concert with Catalytic Coaching to form an integrated people-development system. It describes important skills training and gives specific advice on how to coach a variety of special cases. And finally, it outlines the type of commitment that leaders should embrace to generate maximum benefit from the coaching process.

In addition to the text outlined above, we have also attended to more pragmatic matters. In the various appendices, we have included sample forms that can be used to manage this kind of process. We've also included several examples with forms completed. Many of these run parallel to work discussed in various parts of the text. Our purpose in presenting this material is to give you something to benchmark and pattern other work after. Forms and procedures ideally need to be customized to fit exact circumstances. To the HR practitioner these model forms and completed examples can be invaluable.

One final note before transitioning to Part I. Sprinkled throughout the book are illustrative stories that we will call "tales from the front." In every case these extended examples are based on actual incidents involving real people. To preserve the anonymity of the people and companies involved, however, no real names are used and minor facts have been changed.

Likewise, because examples of company programs and practices are sometimes not flattering, a decision was made to not reveal the names of any companies cited. Again, slight modifications of company descriptions were sometimes used to protect both innocent and guilty. In all cases, every effort was taken to preserve the integrity of the data cited.

Without further delay, let us begin our journey. We start our first section in search of an answer to the question: "How bad can it be?" Setting the issue of popularity aside, what's really so wrong with performance evaluation systems as they're being practiced today? With all the pressing issues facing businesses, how can we justify prioritizing the time and energy it takes to change such an omnipresent institution of organizational life? When we do take the time and energy to change one, why do we always seem to end up with the same problems? These questions and more will be addressed in Part I.

Part I

Problems with the Prevailing Paradigm

The improvement of understanding is for two ends: first, our own increase
of knowledge; secondly, to enable us to deliver that knowledge to others.
—John Locke, *Essay Concerning Human Understanding* (1690)

The statement "people hate performance reviews" contains truth that traverses
companies and specific practices. That is because all performance reviews share
a common philosophical and theoretical framework that defines them as an ar-
chetype or paradigm.

The vast majority of contemporary performance management systems are
built on an evaluation-based model. The prevailing paradigm can be defined
operationally as any performance management system that includes at least one
of three practices: the assignment of grades, normally through a process of rating
or ranking, and/or a direct link between perceived contribution and salary administration (usually referred to as "pay for performance"). It is these practices
that both define the prevailing paradigm and help create its inescapable problems.

No matter what other features a system includes (360° Feedback, peer review,
focus on core competencies, etc.), if it contains even one of the three defining
elements, it is part of the prevailing paradigm. Like a lone anchovy in the middle
of a large pizza, the potency of any of these practices is so strong as to permeate
and flavor all that surround them.

For our purposes, "rating" will be defined as the practice of assigning a
competitive grade, label or number to an employee's annual performance. Common labels include terms like "Outstanding," "Meets Expectations," or
"Needs Improvement." Sometimes systems feature the use of numbers or letters

instead. The Mercer study, referred to earlier, indicates that more than 74% of all performance management systems include the use of some kind of overall grade or numeric score.

"Ranking" is the practice of placing names of employees on a list in perceived order of contribution. This is done to afford a clear and precise calibration of relative perceived value. The appeal of ranking is its aura of scientific rigor. Ranking insures symmetry and precision. No one can argue when a line is drawn between the 90th and 91st percentile separating the winners from those in second position. Nor does one have long to debate should it become necessary to trim out the deadwood. Once prepared, the list is always present to be used in helping determine successions and layoffs. To the engineering, scientific and financial minds that created this practice, it takes quite a bit of convincing to persuade them to change. The alternatives all seem so artificial and arbitrary.

While ranking seems to be waning in popularity, the Mercer study reports that it is still practiced at 20% of the companies they surveyed. In addition, we will take the position here that limiting the number of individuals who can receive each performance grade is a form of ranking. (Restricting the number that can be labeled as "Superior Contributor" to 10%, for example.) Many of the same principles apply. Defined in this manner, a much larger fraction of organizations, perhaps even a majority, can be described as practicing employee ranking.

"Pay for performance" or "merit pay" will be defined here as the practice of attempting to link base salary adjustments and/or bonuses directly to perceived performance. In 1993 Towers Perrin reported that that 95% of the companies they surveyed claim to have "merit pay systems."[1] The Institute of Management and Administration reported a slightly smaller number in 1998, perhaps signaling a gradual shift away from the practice. Their statistics reveal that 81% of the companies they surveyed utilize performance management systems that influence employee pay. [2] Shift or no shift, it is clear that the practice of linking pay to performance remains firmly entrenched as the dominant paradigm.

The chapters in Part I take a process perspective to argue that the core practices of rating, ranking and pay for performance both define the prevailing paradigm and ultimately undermine its effectiveness. Most of the problems people associate with traditional performance management and the annual review ritual stem from these three practices.

Chapter 2 will begin our analysis with a look at performance management from a process perspective. We will begin by offering a model of a generic or "traditional" performance evaluation as it is conducted commonly today. We will then attempt to uncover the outcomes traditional systems have been structured to achieve and the inputs they use to achieve them. Finally, we will discuss lessons learned from talking to the various customers the system is designed to serve.

Chapter 3 will feature a discussion on the problems caused by rating and ranking. We will review the inherent tendency to promote internal competition and gamesmanship and to focus on grade justification. Lost are efforts to promote teamwork, system optimization and employee development.

Chapter 4 will deal with the challenges posed by tying pay directly to performance. We will discuss the dilemmas faced by people being told to do one thing while being paid to do another. We will also explain the impossible task of sustaining the mythology that working hard and performing well entitle the worker to big salary increases.

As Part II will later show, it is critical to understand the core components of the prevailing paradigm and the problems these practices create if one is to expect to make meaningful systemic change to the practice of managing human performance.

Chapter 2

Traditional Performance Evaluation: Bureaucracy at Its Best

> At a time when many corporations are engaged in unrelenting searches for ways to improve operations and reduce costs, there is one aspect of organizational life that has largely escaped scrutiny: Performance Appraisal. Perhaps this is because performance appraisals have become an unquestioned fact of life in most large organizations. As with most unquestioned facts, a critical examination can prove beneficial.
>
> —Fred Nickols, Executive Director, Educational Testing Service[1]

This chapter will attempt to outline the basic components of a traditional performance evaluation (review or appraisal) system and break it down into logical parts. We will provide a generic nine-step model and explain how it typically works. Then we will study the process in more depth by focusing on inputs, outputs and customers. We will argue in this chapter that the traditional system represents a long-standing ritual that is more concerned with activity than results. In the end, we will find few customers that appear to be happy with the traditional way of managing human performance.

Before we begin this detailed process examination, however, it might be prudent to start this chapter with a discussion of an important principle. The concept of "amnesty" will be reviewed in order to help establish the proper mindset for this investigation.

AMNESTY

Practitioners of Quality Management use the concept of amnesty when uncovering systems and processes that are flawed, ineffective or inefficient. Amnesty acknowledges the value of the practices currently being used and the improvements they made when they were put in place. At the same time, it allows us to consider the possible need to change.

Amnesty is based on an underlying assumption about human behavior. It assumes that most people, most of the time, do the best they know how to do. If, using new logic and insight, we can come up with a better way to do things, that is a reason to celebrate. Placing blame on those who designed or practiced less efficient means of operation in the past is of no value. They were doing the best they knew how at the time they introduced the systems that we now see as deficient.

Technological Apprehension

More than a few senior executives working in the 1990s were reluctant participants in the technological revolution. When personal computers started infiltrating professional ranks in the 1980s we quickly dismissed them and then made up excuses to delay having to learn to use them. After all, a manual typewriter had served us well through college. Why change?

Many of us were quite surprised when we discovered how much using a PC increased our freedom of thought and expression, let alone the boost it eventually gave to our productivity. Those who eventually made the change can probably no longer remember why we avoided it for so long. Our children and grandchildren couldn't even begin to understand. Amnesty says: "It's okay. It doesn't matter. Let's move on."

It is in this spirit of amnesty that Part I of this book is presented. The many intelligent, hard-working academics and practitioners who designed and perfected the performance management systems of the past should be admired. Their contributions have brought us this far. They've helped define the people development infrastructure in some of the most highly effective organizations the world has ever known. We all have benefited greatly.

Nonetheless, it is just possible there could be a better way. Perhaps with new insight, this same intelligence and hard work can lead us to even higher levels of achievement.

A Mouthful of Foot

Thank goodness I knew about the concept of amnesty when I first started redesigning performance management systems. I'll never forget my first big presentation on the subject to my boss, the Vice President of Human Resources.

I had finally figured it out—why our current system of performance evaluations was a complete failure. After 30 minutes of presenting irrefutable logic on the error of our ways, I glanced over at my boss. He sat there in silence with eyes glassed over.

When I asked him what was the matter, he slowly, quietly replied. "Gary, I am the one who introduced this system. It was the first thing I did with the company when I entered here ten years ago. It's one of my proudest accomplishments. Before I came here, we had nothing.''

In my youthful enthusiasm, armed with the righteousness of my ideas, I had forgotten completely about the pride people take in their work . . . and the importance of knowing the history of an organization's systems.

Fortunately, I was able immediately to talk to my boss about the concept of amnesty and to give some quick recognition for the tremendous milestone that he had achieved a decade earlier. Even more fortunately, he was a quality individual who did not hold a grudge or throw me out of the room for my incredible lack of diplomacy. He was able to see the logic of the argument I was presenting him and, above all else, he wanted to do the right thing for our people. In this case, amnesty worked both ways. I will be forever grateful.

Reciprocal Agreement

Because of this experience, and many others, I am well aware of the tremendous investment and contribution that someone or some group of people has had in the performance management and evaluation systems currently operating in almost every company. I hereby encourage any and all of you to accept this offer of amnesty. There is every reason to believe that the systems you have in place represent the best thinking available at the time they were constructed.

At the same time, I ask you to offer me similar courtesy. The intent, as I point out what I think are inherent problems with traditional systems, is *not to place blame*. The purpose is to *provoke new thinking*. If a statement is made that is too strong for your situation, describes a problem which you do not think is real or one you have successfully overcome, please extract from the dialogue that portion that you think is relevant for your situation and accept in advance my apology. Rest assured, we all are limited by our awareness.

THE PROCESS PERSPECTIVE

One of the foundation principles set forth by the Quality Management school is that "all work is accomplished by process." In other words, work is a series of actions with a beginning and an end. There are system *inputs* and *outputs*. And for each process there is a *customer* or perhaps *multiple customers*. Ultimately, making that customer happy is the key to long-term success.

Using these basic principles, the process perspective has helped us redesign the way we do everything from manufacture cars to make pizzas. This methodology has prompted service providers of all kinds to talk more regularly with the people who pay for their services. It has caused us to greatly modify what we do and how we do it in every major aspect of business.

Many in Human Resources and senior management are familiar with these principles from seminars we have not only attended but also helped teach. We use them to assist teams in saving money and streamlining operations. We use them to ask provocative questions and logically sort out better answers. We seldom use them, however, to analyze traditional HR practices. It is time to change that. It is time to use these techniques on the long-standing institution of the annual performance review.

TRADITIONAL MODEL

Figure 2-1 shows a flow diagram of a generic nine-step process. It assumes a multi-layered hierarchical organization consisting of employees, supervisors, managers and senior management. It also assumes the presence of a human resource function as well as legal oversight.

Someone in Human Resources typically starts the process by alerting the organization that it is time for the annual process to commence. In some cases this begins with employees providing input to their supervisors on work they have done that year. Many systems skip this step.

The next step is for a supervisor to complete some form of formal evaluation on the employee. This usually entails filling out several pages of input about an employee's perceived contribution over the previous twelve-month period. Forms range anywhere from one to fifteen pages with the majority requiring between four and seven pages of input. Most require rating an employee against a series of five to twenty performance standards. Often these are expressed in behavioral terms such as:

- Takes Personal Accountability
- Influences Others
- Builds Organizational Capability Through People

Other times they are listed as skills or attributes:

- Openness to Change
- Willingness to Accept Responsibility
- Technical Expertise

Ratings for these behaviors or skills are most frequently established using a scale with between three and seven gradations. Here are some examples of scale descriptors currently being used by various companies:

- Needs Improvement/Meets Expectations/Exceeds Expectations
- Unacceptable/Needs Improvement/Effective/Very Effective/Outstanding
- Needs Much Improvement/Needs Some Improvement/At Standard/Strength/Towering Strength

Figure 2-1
Traditional Performance Evaluation Process

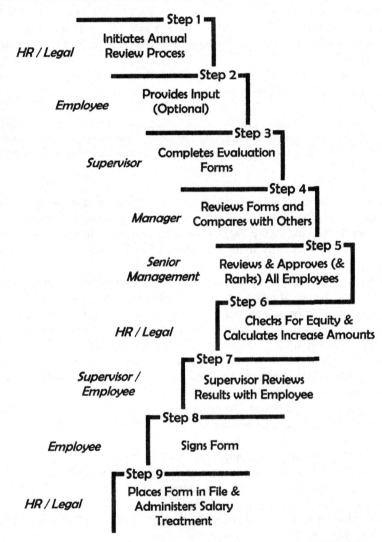

Step 1
HR / Legal   Initiates Annual Review Process

Step 2
Employee   Provides Input (Optional)

Step 3
Supervisor   Completes Evaluation Forms

Step 4
Manager   Reviews Forms and Compares with Others

Step 5
Senior Management   Reviews & Approves (& Ranks) All Employees

Step 6
HR / Legal   Checks For Equity & Calculates Increase Amounts

Step 7
Supervisor / Employee   Supervisor Reviews Results with Employee

Step 8
Employee   Signs Form

Step 9
HR / Legal   Places Form in File & Administers Salary Treatment

Most systems, including the classic model outlined here, require the inclusion of an overall rating that summarizes performance for the year in one letter or grade. The Overall Performance Rating usually employs the same rating scale as utilized for the individual skills or behaviors. It is the one measure that is most important in influencing subsequent salary treatment and affecting pro-motability.

Steps Four, Five and Six are cascading reviews of the work done at lower levels. Managers look at all the forms submitted by their supervisors and check them for agreement and equity. In some cases, when they are personally familiar with the work of an evaluated individual, they may provide specific input to be incorporated on the evaluation forms. They may also encourage a supervisor to change labels or grades for individuals they perceive to have been rated unfairly or inaccurately.

The literature is rife with information about the perils of easy grading. Jonathan Segal describes this phenomenon succinctly:

As a general rule, supervisors give their subordinates inflated performance appraisals. Poor employees are evaluated as marginally competent, marginal employees as satisfactory, satisfactory employees as above standard and good employees as deserving a throne next to God.[2]

Because of this recurring problem, companies frequently resort to the task of reducing grades of some employees in order to meet a standard distribution, or bell-shaped curve (see Figure 2-2). In an effort to curb rampant "grade inflation" companies frequently limit the number of employees that can be given the top grades. For example, it is quite common to limit the number of employees receiving the top grade to a number like ten percent. In other words, no more than one out of every ten employees can be rated "Outstanding" in a given system. Twenty percent might be allowed in the second tier, 30 in the middle group and so on. The theory here is that talent is distributed normally across any population. Percentages are imposed to force supervisors and managers to make hard decisions about which employees deserve the most reward and recognition. Managers are instructed that it is there responsibility to help separate the grain from the chaff.

To insure that managers are being fair and impartial across organizational boundaries and to continue the equity check on the higher level performers (including the managers themselves) functional or executive management gets involved. They typically concentrate on the their direct reports first and then overview those below them. Again they check for perceived equity and to insure compliance with distribution rules. In addition, it is at this level that ranking activities are most aggressively coordinated.

In an effort to make sure that relative contributions are clearly delineated, some organizations take the next step and require groups of subordinates to be ranked against each other. This involves taking groups of employees of similar pay grades and listing them in order of perceived value to the company. Doing this insures that there will be no confusion about where the "Outstanding" achievers stop and the "Very Effective" contributors begin. The point at which percentiles change over the boundary figure is where one grade begins and the other ends.

Ranking normally requires Human Resources to help senior management facilitate some group interaction process to insure that everyone has a fair chance

Figure 2-2
Common Forced Distribution Rating System

to represent their people. It can be a challenging process to facilitate as well as to participate in. We will speak of the implications and impact of ranking and rating in more detail in the next chapter.

Following the senior management review someone in Legal or Human Resources typically is charged with checking results of the process for discriminant impact. In this step the test is to see if any protected classes (i.e., minorities, females, people over age 40) did more poorly than should be expected. They do one final review to see that all rules have been followed and then load the information in the system for processing the salary increase budget.

In the traditional system pay is linked to performance through the Overall Rating. The grade assigned the employee is supposed to influence the amount of an annual increase and, in some cases, the number of months between increases. The logic here is that the better performers should get bigger base salary increases more quickly than the poorer performers. We will discuss this practice in much more detail in Chapter 4.

Step Seven is the actual performance review itself in which the supervisor provides a synopsis of his appraisal orally to the employee. He typically goes over highlights from the evaluation form and attempts to justify the Overall Rating. In some systems he is required to give the employee a copy of the review form, in most he is not. The supervisor talks for most of the meeting and normally encourages only clarifying questions. Once the Overall Rating is communicated, however, the supervisor typically stops talking and asks the employee for reactions.

Since both employee and supervisor know that the Overall Rating has been through several stages of review, there is not much to talk about. Even if the employee has a problem with his grade, the chances of having it changed are very slight. The employee normally accepts the feedback and grade and waits for one more important piece of data. At the conclusion of the interview the supervisor informs the employee of the amount of his base salary increase.

Many systems like to formalize the documentation process by having an employee sign the last page of the evaluation forms saying that a review was conducted and he was informed of the information it contains. The final step in the process is for the signed form to be placed in the employee's personnel file as an official company document. Human Resources must also make sure that the appropriate salary adjustments are made on the communicated dates.

In Part II we will discuss common enhancements to the traditional system (soliciting evaluative input from peers, 360° formats, competencies, etc.). As far as a base model system is concerned, however, the one listed above is a good generic starting point. While it may not represent every system fairly or accurately, it should serve as a good reference point for the traditional way of doing things.

PERFORMANCE EVALUATION AS PROCESS

While almost every seasoned HR professional knows intimately how to administer performance evaluations, few have broken the activity down into logical components from a quality or process perspective. Despite all the complaining, no one usually asks you to. HR professionals are trained in quality principles to help others re-engineer their processes, but seldom get around to using these techniques to examine significant elements of our own work. We are the typical shoeless cobbler's kids Dave Ulrich refers to in *Human Resource Champions*: "Too often, human resource professionals are the cobbler's unshod children: they design systems, give advice, and help others, but they fail to apply HR principles to themselves."[3]

At some point, however, it becomes interesting to experiment with the concept of shoes. The remainder of this chapter is the result of using Quality principles to examine the traditional performance review process.

CRAFTING FOOTWEAR

If the ritual of performance evaluation is to be studied as a process, then there must be a beginning and an end to this activity. More specifically, it has to have *inputs* and at least one *output*. It also has to have a *customer or customers* and a clear *purpose*.

When studying a system or process from a quality perspective, you are normally instructed to start at the final stage. Literally, "begin with the end in mind. Where does this process end? What is it designed to produce?" That's where we will begin our logical journey.

PROCESS OUTPUT

Most struggle when asked to define the desired output of their performance evaluation process. Are you trying to produce happy employees? More informed supervisors? Comprehensive personnel files?

After some deliberation and conversations with colleagues, most looking at traditional systems will conclude something like this. The final output, the way things are being operated, is most likely *the completed evaluation form* that is placed in the personnel file following the briefing with the employee. (That is clear from the diagram in our previous section.) Once the form is filed, everyone has usually signed off, the review has been conducted and a salary increase has been communicated. This is the clear end of process for the traditional system.

Part of the task in quality management is to find process outcomes to measure. For measurement purposes, we can define the output in a traditional system as a filed review form. After all, the job of a system administrator is normally to shepherd completion of all forms in advance of some very tight deadlines. As long as all the forms are processed and employees are given their performance discussions before a certain calendar date, the systems administrator is regarded as having done a good job.

BUSINESS PURPOSE

Knowing what the process produces is interesting. A completed form in a file. Great. Wonderful. The next question that immediately comes to mind, however, is "Why?" or "So what?" Why is having a completed document in a file a worthwhile activity? From a business standpoint, what purpose does it serve?

Think about it. If you owned a company, how much would you pay to have a completed form stuffed in a file somewhere? How many hours and how many dollars is that worth to you? Surely that is not what makes this performance evaluation process worth paying for?

As simple and straightforward as this sounds, these questions prove hard to answer. Ask around and it quickly becomes clear that everyone involved in the process seems to have slightly different understandings about what it is supposed to achieve.

Try searching for the business purpose of an evaluation system by asking managers and supervisors why they conduct annual performance reviews. The overwhelming consensus on this question will probably not make you feel any better. After a few stabs at a diplomatic answer, the honest answer comes out. "Because you guys in HR and Legal make us," is the most honest and most frequent response you will probably receive.

If you push them harder for possible things that the system is designed to accomplish, they usually can help generate a list such as this:

• Justify Salary Treatment

• Reward/Reinforce Good Effort and Results

• Change Behavior

• Document the Files: Protect the Company from Lawsuits

- Identify Training Needs
- Feed the Development/Succession Planning System
- Determine Promotability and Retention Value

This answer is certainly appears more comforting and reassuring. We'll poke a few holes in it later, but at least it may give the impression that we are not wasting our time with a totally worthless system after all.

PROCESS INPUTS

Now that we know the primary output and the many business purposes of a traditional performance management system, the next step is to consider things that go into the process. What inputs trigger the commencement of the perform-ance evaluation cycle? What other inputs are critical along the way?

Once you determine the process output, the inputs flow more freely. Main inputs are the oral and written comments and observations of the supervisors and managers familiar with each employee's work. HR representatives, and sometimes lawyers, give counsel to those directly responsible for completing the form. Inputs are also obtained from other supervisors and managers for use in developing relative ratings and/or ranking. Before the process concludes, in-puts also include comments and reactions from the employees being reviewed.

CUSTOMERS

Perhaps the most interesting and enlightening issue to pursue in this quest of quality is to specify the customers of the performance evaluation process. Ex-actly whom are we trying to serve with a performance evaluation system? Who are we completing these elaborate assessment forms for? Pose this question to several senior managers, HR representatives and a number of long-term em-ployees. The answer is invariably a long list. In priority order it will probably include:

- The Employee Being Evaluated—To explain salary treatment and provide feedback to reinforce/reward/punish behavior and discuss career progression.
- The Supervisor/Manager Who Completes the Form—To demonstrate he/she has eval-uated performance in an objective manner and protect him/her in case the employee complains or has problems. Some might say it also helps the supervisor look good by maximizing employee contributions.
- Upper Management—To identify high potential candidates and "trim out the dead-wood."
- Human Resources—To justify salary treatment, set training and development curricu-lum and identify the best candidates to move up, over or out.

- The Legal Department—To protect the company from expensive litigation.
- The Shareholders—To make this a more profitable company.

In summary, everyone appears to be a customer of the process but each customer seems to have slightly different expectations. Yet, all of the expectations appear to be important and good.

The Acid Test

For those of you who know the quality process well, you know the next step in this process of inquiry is the real kicker. Once you have identified process customers, you must ask them how your system is working. You must take a survey or otherwise gather facts to determine their level of satisfaction with the process. In short, you must identify how well your system accomplishes its goals—in the eyes of its customers.

The next step on the journey of discovery is to do the unthinkable. To ask employees, managers and supervisors of your company what they think of your evaluation process. How is it meeting their needs as customers? The best way to get an answer to this big question is to meet with groups of customers face to face.

Employees as Customers

When you get a group of employees together to discuss the performance evaluation process, start the meeting with an interesting icebreaker. Ask them this: "What do you think of first when you hear it's time to receive your annual performance review?"

I have held dozens of meetings with individuals ranging from file clerks to vice presidents and everyone else in between. The response varies only slightly across groups. The three most common responses always seem to be some form of the following:

- "Oh no. Not that again."
- "Another trip to the Dentist."
- "Money."
- "The annual 'Exercise.' "

To be sure, there is usually some contrarian in the crowd who smiles and says that when its time for his review each year he cheerily proclaims: "Great! Here's my chance to learn how to improve my contribution to the company." Others normally receive this kind of statement in the workshop with rolling eyes and chuckling. Some feign convulsions or attempt to induce vomiting.

When you ask them to elaborate, employees use words like "demeaning" and "negative" to further describe their feelings. Most claim to remember only two things from their yearly evaluation: their performance rating and the amount of their increase. All else is considered supporting data meant to justify those two key decisions. It is soon forgotten.

Ask them if they use the information gathered in the annual ritual to help improve their performance for the next year. Watch as they greet this question with silence and sideways glances. While some supervisors seem to make the process more meaningful, the value that comes from the forms that Human Resources requires them to complete is deemed by most to be a political necessity that produces modest value at best.

Supervisors/Managers as Customers

When meeting with managers and supervisors, add a second icebreaker. Rephrasing the first question slightly, ask: "What do you think of first when you hear it's time to *conduct* annual performance reviews?" The most common responses are surprisingly similar:

- "Oh no. Not that again."
- "Tons of paperwork."
- "Waste of time."
- "The annual chore."

You'll probably get the occasional response that is politically correct. Something like: "Opportunity to help my staff improve." That is rare, however. The vast majority of supervisors and managers speak of the large amounts of time and energy they invest in the process with little to show for it in the end. They complain to their HR representatives every year about the burden this system represents to them.

Upper Management as Customers

Most CEOs, COOs, CFOs and other top executives in a company profess to be supportive of the prevailing performance evaluation system. They require their direct reports to participate in the process of completing evaluation forms on each of their people. When it comes to following the procedures themselves, however, they frequently elect not to participate. We'll explore this whole phenomenon in greater detail in the next chapter.

Despite the fact that they frequently elect not to complete the official forms on their own direct reports, some senior executives claim to value the exercise. They require form completion from direct reports because they value having consolidated lists breaking individuals up by performance ratings. Rank lists are even better. This method of dividing a large organization up into bites, and thereby separating the "horses" from the "mules," is normally deemed as useful for dividing up booty and assignments. Besides, the system must be a good one. It produced them didn't it? Why mess with success?

The HR Perspective

Human Resources normally views the process as successful if all the forms are completed and submitted on time. Success equals on-time compliance. Real thought and energy being invested in the review process by a supervisor is seen as gravy. They serve as process policemen or "regulatory watchdogs" as Ulrich describes them. It may be unsatisfying, but in most companies it's an important function they've served for years. In some ways, it's job security.

Most HR managers are very frustrated with the performance evaluation process. They see the inconsistent message coming from upper management and it cascades down from there. "It's like herding cats trying to get these guys to cooperate each year," a frustrated HR Director told me. "If I didn't make it mandatory to turn in the forms in order to process a salary increase, I wouldn't get 30% participation in this program."

Legal Review

When you begin your search for meaningful feedback, prepare to be surprised by what you learn from customers in your legal department. Surely, they should be pleased that you're doing this. Pages and pages of tedious assessment completed on each employee would certainly seem to be enough to satisfy even the most data-hungry of lawyers.

In fact, you will find the opposite. When you really start asking good questions, you discover that more often than not a performance evaluation system serves as a greater liability than asset to a company trying to protect itself. Check the roster of wrongful termination or affirmative action suits against a company and you will find Exhibit A *against* the company in many, many cases is a performance evaluation completed before the employee was deemed worthy of termination.

To be sure, the company may present into evidence the most recent negative performance evaluation; and occasionally it may have two. Most frequently, however, those forms will be countered with several from years previous that at best "damn with faint praise" the employee who was terminated.

"The supervisor just didn't get tough enough and use all the options on the form" a lawyer will complain as he tries to build his case defending the company against the weak performance review. In theory this is true. The forms would and should induce greater honesty and frankness. The supervisor should have cited the real shortcomings that he noticed in those early evaluations. In practice, however, it seldom happens. Instead, the supervisor remains optimistic and fails to really lower the boom with a bad evaluation until he is ready to cut the cord completely.

Most corporate attorneys are not happy customers of the traditional evaluation process. Ask yours if it is helping more than hurting as it is currently being utilized. You will most likely find the same.

The Shareholder as Customer

To be honest, we have not really done a lot of work assessing shareholder happiness with the performance appraisal processes practiced at most companies. Our assumption is that most shareholders are looking at more global measures of productivity and are interested in systems that support producing gains in the value of the company stock. To the extent the systems practiced at a company contribute to profitability and growth, they will be valued by shareholders. Their motives are typically quite straightforward and clear. More on this subject later.

Finally, a Satisfied Customer

After days and hours of discussions with unhappy customers, there is one you can normally count on to say a kind word or two. The Compensation Manager for most companies is satisfied with the output of the performance evaluation process as normally practiced. Admittedly, he doesn't require much to be happy. Nonetheless, his needs are typically met.

Here's a typical situation. As long as the Compensation Manager receives a letter grade (or number) within twenty days of someone's salary change date, he can plug it into the computer and generate a recommended salary increase. Since the prevailing paradigm features a system that typically satisfies this requirement, the Compensation Manager's needs are met.

LEARNINGS FROM THE PROCESS PERSPECTIVE

In the final analysis, what we have here seems to be a process with many objectives and even more customers. Most of the customers are not happy with the results of the process and probably wouldn't continue to use it, if they were not required to do so.

To most modern workers, performance appraisals are just another example of Catbert's handiwork. Catbert, for those of you not fully conversant with the world of "Dilbert," is depicted by cartoonist Scott Adams as "the evil HR Director." Catbert seems to delight in imposing illogical systems on his employees to rob them of their humanity and spirit. The performance evaluation is just one tool from his debilitating arsenal. Two of its major components, rating and ranking, will be reviewed in detail in the next chapter.

Chapter 3

Rating and Ranking: The Curse of Competition

In practice, annual ratings are a disease, annihilating long-term planning, demolishing teamwork, nourishing rivalry and politics, leaving people bitter, crushed, bruised, battered, desolate, despondent, unfit for work for weeks after receipt of rating, unable to comprehend why they are inferior . . . sending companies down the tubes.

—W. Edwards Deming[1]

The practice of grading annual employee contribution was described in earlier as a defining feature of the prevailing paradigm. Almost all performance management systems include some kind of rating or ranking procedure whereby employee performance is judged against certain standards. Ultimately and inevitably these systems put employees in competition with each other.

"Rating" was defined previously as the practice of assigning a competitive grade, label or number to an employee's annual performance. We discussed the common labels used in the process in Chapter 1. In Chapter 2 we reviewed a model for the prevailing practice that demonstrates how rating typically occurs.

"Ranking" was defined earlier as the practice of placing names of employees on a list in perceived order of contribution. While it is less popular, the practice has a long and storied utilization in many industries and companies. The mechanics of the ranking process were also described in the context of the traditional model in Chapter 2.

In this chapter we will review the process of assigning grades and labels with an emphasis on the impact it creates. We will explore how rating and ranking activities cause unavoidable problems that color the entire employment relationship. Rating and ranking will be shown to foster internal competition that is detrimental to a company's best interest. These practices destroy human spirit, encourage gamesmanship, fail to produce the results they promise and undermine teamwork and quality efforts.

KILLING THE HUMAN SPIRIT

Perhaps the best way to begin to understand the damage done by a performance management system is to look at one very closely. We will start this investigation with the examination of a system that many have considered a prototype. It was benchmarked by companies in a variety of industries for many years. I got to know this system from the inside as both administrator and customer.

The earliest portion of my career was spent working for a corporation that was famous for its management development programs. Like other elite *Fortune* 50 powerhouses, this company was proud of its ability to attract the best and the brightest. They were even prouder of their track record for identifying future superstars, from the very inception of a career—individuals capable of being groomed to serve at the organizations highest levels. They had a very elaborate system of performance rating and evaluation that identified these "high fliers" within two years out of college. Those few who made it on the fast track had a tremendous ride ahead of them.

This was a big corporation—one with thousands of employees to choose from. They hired from the best schools in the country and recruited nothing but winners. This mindset produced an interesting parable employees were told soon after entering the company. It had to do with an orientation session that used to be given for newly hired college graduates.

In years gone by they had gathered together large assemblies of new hires in one common area. The leader of the seminar would ask all those with 4.0 cumulative grade point averages to please stand up. Several around the room rose from their chairs. He asked them to remain standing and be joined by anyone who had served as president of a campus social organization (fraternity or sorority). Several more rose. He went further to request those who had achieved Phi Beta Kappa honors to stand and join the others. By the time he finished with the valedictorians and salutatorians almost everyone in the room was on their feet. Usually some overachiever was standing on his chair.

This oft-repeated story was probably rooted more in fiction than fact. Nonetheless, it served to get the point across to prompt recruits that this company had the good fortune, financial strength and growth plan to attract a tremendous array of high achieving individuals. Their cup literally overflowed with talent.

And what did they do with all these high achievers? They put them in competition with one another. The real competition had just begun. What they wanted to find were "the very best of the very best."

The main mechanism to "separate the grain from the chaff" in this company both then and today is the performance evaluation process. The annual ritual consists of supervisors completing an eleven-page form analyzing the individual and rating him/her against a number of criteria deemed critical to success with the company. These "core competencies" included such things as Communication Skills (both oral and written), Analytical Ability, Problem-Solving Capability, as well as a couple of big categories called Quantity of Work Produced and Quality of Work Produced.

Each competency had a detailed description of exactly what it meant to be highly blessed or lacking in this particular attribute. Individuals were then rated against these criteria with examples cited for why they were given the score they received on each item. Additional pages were included that broke all this information down into finite detail.

The process culminated in a performance label and numerical score. Each individual was rated either "Outstanding," "Very Effective," "Effective," "Marginally Ineffective," "Needs Improvement" or "As Good as Fired" (or something like that). To make sure that the labels were used carefully and really meant something, they were distributed by a ranking system that insured that no more than 10% of the population could be labeled "Outstanding." No more than 20% could have their performance labeled "Very Effective", and so on.

Without this requirement of a forced distribution of grades it was determined that supervisors would be too lenient. They would engage in "grade inflation" and we would ultimately find more than two-thirds of the population rated above average. To the engineering and accounting minds that dominated our senior ranks, this made no sense. Tough decisions simply had to be made to determine *relative* contribution and value. Successful business leaders made tough decisions every day. It was deemed mission-critical to know who was performing better than whom.

Life was good for those who made it to the first performance tier. Nicknames for the "Outstanding" performers included "Waterwalker" or member of the "God Squad." Those who could achieve and stay on that elusive plateau were truly on the fast track. Raises came faster and were larger. Promotions came quickly with rapid changes in assignments. Eventually the name for consistent members of this group would be "Boss."

The "Very Effective" group was limited to 20% of the population. When times were prosperous, there was still plenty of "good stuff" left over for this group. They were much more than solid citizens. These were the "Almost Stars." They got scraps left over by the Waterwalkers, but they were plentiful. Raises, promotions and plum assignments were still available to many of them. There was still hope.

If you were labeled with 30% of the population in the third tier ("Effective") and still had hope for advancement, you needed to make sure you rose from this status the following year. Two in a row and your career was in the deep freeze. Raises and promotions came only sparingly, although you were not likely to be on the top of the list for layoffs or downsizing. That was reserved for your teammates below.

To be labeled "Marginally Ineffective" in this organization was a very dangerous status. And yet, by definition, 25% of the population each year had to have that label. If times were good, you had an opportunity to try to improve your rating next year. If times were bad, it was a subtle signal to start reading the want ads.

Most of the remaining 15% were rated "Needs Improvement." There was no strict quota for how many had to be labeled "Unacceptable." The majority of people who received the last label were given that status almost posthumously. Some were even terminated before they actually received their formal review in writing.

Despite a tag name that seems rather innocent (after all, who among us doesn't need to improve some aspect of their job?), "Needs Improvement" performers were on very shaky ground. The organization was sending them a clear signal that they were not performing at a competitive level. Someone rated this way should expect no promotion and probably no salary increases for very long periods of time. These 15% were the dregs of the system.

The ritual for determining performance ratings was very rigorous. Each year a supervisor would complete the worksheets on her direct reports and then bring this material to a meeting with her comrades. With senior management supervision, they would then force rank individuals against one another. To make the numbers meaningful, large groups were formed spanning across disciplines. Based on level and location, Engineers might be compared to Accountants and Lawyers and HR professionals. They normally started at the top and picked the top performer first. Then they switched to the bottom and selected the worst performer. Finally, they met in the middle and separated the good from the not as good. In the end, they had a list of at least 50 employees (preferably 100 or more) that fit a perfect bell-shaped curve.

For most managers and supervisors ranking was a frustrating and painful process. It was especially difficult for the newcomer, or the staff manager, or the lower-ranked manager, as they had the hardest time securing the prized slots for their constituents. Even with an official from the HR department in attendance at each meeting, the power players always seemed to prevail. The highly ranked, well-positioned managers and supervisors frequently came home with more than their share of high rankings for their favorite direct reports. They typically fought amongst themselves for control of the game.

In the battle for positioning, it was quite common to have strong disagreements over ranking issues. The fight for the top few spots was usually most intense. Hurt feelings, bruised egos and silent vows for revenge were the unfortunate fallout of the more contentious ranking sessions.

For those not privy to the passion play taking place behind the scenes, the end product that emerged from this process was a clear and concise rank-ordered list. Sometimes the list had to be merged with another list to get an even bigger population—one that better justified the forcing of a bell-shaped curve. But in the end, the final product usually seemed to have a degree of face validity. In general, those at top of the list were perceived by the majority to be pretty strong performers. With notable exceptions, those at the bottom were normally regarded as less valuable in their contributions and/or potential for advancement.

Despite the brutality, the evaluation process effectively fed the management development and succession planning systems with strong, competitive people. Complaining about the exercise was not deemed worthy of merit. "No pain, no gain" was the implied mindset. They considered that this is simply what must be done to build a world class company.

I won't try to kid anyone. Like many others, I came to this organization because of the reputation it had for building leaders. Not only did I want to be the beneficiary of it, I wanted to learn how it worked and use the process to develop others. I was proud that an HR function was so vital and strategic to the business plan of this major corporation.

And just as I hoped, I was put on the fast track and became the beneficiary of the early identification system. I worked hard, did well and was suitably rewarded. Raises, promotions and increases in responsibility came rapidly my way. And within a few years I got to be part of the system that made me. I gained responsibility for the management of the rating and ranking systems. I got to peek behind the curtain and work with the wizard. And that's where my perception started to change. Here is what I found.

It makes sense that those who fair poorly in a competitive environment might not necessarily think the system equitable or fair. That is understandable. Nobody likes to lose—especially former valedictorians, Phi Beta Kappa recipients or fraternity/sorority presidents. Telling one of these individuals that they have been rated "Effective" or "Meets Expectations" can lead to some pretty intense, heart-wrenching discussions. If that's what it takes to build a great organization, however, perhaps these sacrifices are necessary.

On the flip side, however, one would think that someone leaving a performance discussion with an "Outstanding" performance rating would be delighted with this system. After all, the rewards should soon be heading her way. She was now christened with success. Her future was golden.

Euphoria is seldom the emotion expressed, however. Once the newly anointed gain perspective and recognize how the game is played, they began to think through the logic of the system. How many people are in their rank group? How close to the cut-off point for the next grade are they? For some people losing one spot on a rank list would mean changing their evaluation label from "Outstanding" to "Excellent." Even a minor slip up can cost them their coveted slot and all the associated perquisites and status.

More questions torture the top performers. If they aren't number one, who has to die or leave the group for them to move up the rank list? Who are their biggest threats from below? What kind of assignments should they take that will allow them to hold on to their lofty status? What assignments should they avoid because they are too risky?

Perhaps you've noticed something about people with perfect grade point averages throughout college. Few did it by accident. Most took the issue of grades *very* seriously—sometimes at the expense of what they were supposed to be learning, sometimes at the expense of any number of other life activities. For some of them, it was more important what grade they received than what they studied or learned. In the same way, people with the top ratings in companies promoting internal competition between employees are seldom there by accident. Most are highly focused and driven to gain and maintain elite status.

If someone stumbles onto a top 10% rating the first time, she soon develops a strategy to retain this status. The label/grade almost has to become the focus of energy for an individual to remain on top. Competition is simply too fierce. Political survival skills are absolutely critical.

Another interesting thing about people with an "Outstanding" rating is that it is almost impossible to make people who receive them happy. If they are not rated number one, they want very much to be. The secret obsession of those most alert is to identify and pass those ahead of them.

Even more ironic, the person achieving the top slot in an entire rank group (which in some systems can contain 50 to 150 people) is typically scared to death about being promoted to a new group where the competition is tougher and the top slots are already staked out. It sometimes takes even the most competitive performers two to three years to get back to the elusive "Outstanding" classification in the higher peer group. To the ultra-competitive this is very frightening. Upward movement needs to be well choreographed and timed.

Even if they do not move up in rank groups, there are always dozens of anxious climbers right behind them. Number ones have to regard every potential interaction as an opportunity to slip up or lose ground. Peers are clearly seen as competitors instead of allies. Only the naive buy the line about everybody being "teammates." Those rated number one use healthy paranoia to get and stay on top.

Meanwhile back at the ranch, we have the "Also Rans." All the second tier folks want to talk about is what it takes to elevate to the first. "Five people ahead of you have to die" is not a comforting thought. The third tier group resent their label: "Effective." How demeaning! These are people who are used to being standouts! They are winners, or at least they were. If they hang out down here for very long they will have to change how they see themselves entirely.

Those rated below "Effective" are usually scared, or resigned to their fate. If they are satisfied with their status in the company, they go home on time and quit trying to do extra work. Why should they bother? They are typecast as castaways. They are only drones. Let the others fight it out over queen status.

Tale from the Front: William Tells

Thirteen years after the fact a network administrator named William continues to tell in vivid detail of an evaluation session he had with his manager. In that meeting William's boss informed him that he had been rated "Effective" using the system described above. While 70% of the organization had to be rated with this label or worse, it was considered the kiss of death for someone who aspired to high office.

His manager went on to say that while William would probably have a lifetime job with the company, he would "probably never really have a career." That was reserved for better performers. William's destiny was slated for lateral growth.

On that day William began making plans for his departure. As soon as a suitable position was available, he resigned to take a Director level position with another company. The corporation never shed a tear. It simply moved another former winner down the list to fill the new vacancy in the list of "Also Rans."

Provocative question: How do you take an organization populated only by winners and convert them to nothing but losers or paranoids? At this company and many others like it, the answer is simple. Just put them through the annual rating and ranking system.

Cheryl's Story

Cheryl, a new supervisor in an energy company, got a good feel for the true Darwinian nature of ranking-based performance evaluation systems in her first year on the job. One of her direct reports was a safety engineer named Bradley who was about fifteen years her senior.

Bradley was a safety engineer who had risen to the supervisor level in the line organization before being moved aside at mid-career. He was a hard worker and had been doing the safety job for about five years. Beside the fact that Bradley was occasionally abrasive and talked too much, he did a very good job as safety coordinator and had helped the company set some outstanding, internationally recognized safety records. The company's safety programs literally served as benchmarks for the industry.

Because he had once been a second-line supervisor and had not been demoted when moved into the safety position, Bradley had a salary classification level that was higher than normal for the job. In fact, he was classified at the same grade as Cheryl, his boss. They were actually ranked competitively against each other. (Sounds fair, doesn't it?)

Bradley's rank group also included some of the most competitive and high-performing people in the company—dozens of them. Because of this, Bradley was an easy one to place near the bottom of the 110-person rank list. Compared to others with significant upward potential, he was easily expendable. In the end, Bradley wound up being ranked sixth from the bottom. (Remember, someone has to fill those spots.)

Because of this low ranking, Bradley had to be given a performance label that corresponded. (Performance labels were tied to ranking and distributed on a bell-shaped curve as well). This action forced Cheryl to try to document justification for using a "Needs Improvement" performance label. Try as she might, Cheryl could find few legitimate things for Bradley to significantly improve. He had made no serious errors and had completed most of his work on time. Nonetheless, it was her job as supervisor to try to explain to Bradley why his perilous position and insulting label were justified.

Cheryl and Bradley talked and argued for six hours. At first Cheryl really hoped she could convince Bradley of the logic behind such a system. She could not. Her discussion was not constructive. It was not fun. It was a truly miserable, unhealthy, unproductive experience for both of them.

ENCOURAGING GAMESMANSHIP

One of the most significant forms of collateral damage that comes from traditional performance evaluation systems is the quality of feedback that is passed along to the top performers in an organization. This is particularly prevalent in organizations that either rank or have forced distributions to their ratings. This activity can be described as a "zero sum game." Roughly translated this means that in order to have winners there must by definition be losers.

In a zero sum game there is a finite list of those who can be labeled winners. With performance ranking or rating based on a bell-shaped curve, that ratio is determined mathematically. Out of 100 employees only ten can be in the top 10% and thus receive an "Outstanding" rating. More natural divisions in perceived contribution are subjugated to the discipline of a mathematical approach. For the sake of "objectivity" numbers take precedence over other possible groupings.

As long as the forced distribution rule is enforced, it doesn't matter whether a company officially practices ranking or not. They are in effect ranking when they draw a line at a given percentile and force performance ratings into groups. The impact is much the same.

On the one hand, this makes perfect sense. A large research company abandoned the bell-shaped curve following a series of layoffs. During a two-year period they had laid off almost every employee that was rated in the bottom three rank groups. Theoretically, they had purged themselves of all below average and many average performers. It seemed cruel and inhumane to now reinvent this lower class by forcing the high-performing survivors now doing double duty back onto a bell-shaped curve. The managers complained bitterly at the thought of having to do this.

As a result, they eventually created an organization made up of 77% above-average performers. And, ironically, the business was still performing well below expectations. They were losing money steadily for years. Something seems wrong with this picture. The "Nice Guy Approach" doesn't make sense.

On the other hand, different companies faced with the same dilemma retain system integrity at whatever cost. In contrast, we might call this a "Damn the Torpedoes Approach." When downsizing occurs, they stick to their original course and continue full speed ahead using a bell-shaped distribution for allocating performance grades.

Companies that go through significant restructuring and downsizing still force survivors onto the same brutal curve. After much internal debate, a division of a telecommunications company elected to continue the practice of meeting a normal performance distribution curve even after downsizing by approximately 55%. In these kinds of situations, people can experience drops in performance ratings from the top 20% to below average in the course of one year. Meanwhile, they may be doing more work of a higher caliber than ever before. Darwin would have been proud.

Because of the competitive process used to divide up scarce ratings, the manager of a high-performing employee is reluctant to put down anything in writing that could be perceived as negative or more than a superficial performance issue. As described previously, the typical process calls for groups of managers to get together to force-rank their populations into a larger pool. Even if they are not ranked, when performance labels are allocated based on a restricted basis, the same exact logic applies.

A competing manager can use any written flaw or negative distinction about your employee to lower her on the list to give room for his own employee to take a higher spot. Therefore, very little negative information is included on an evaluation sheet of someone regarded as an overall good performer. It could cost her the rating she truly deserves.

Consequences of this action can be far reaching with long-term consequences. They can also be very costly to the employee. Here is a common example of the kinds of problems this practice creates.

The Story of Jane

Jane is an engineer for a construction company. Pam is her HR Director. A highly coveted management position came open. It required someone with a mechanical engineering background and experience of a certain kind. It also required strong leadership skills and the ability to work effectively in a team environment.

Having participated in the ranking session and reviewed all the paperwork on the engineering group for several years, Pam was excited at the prospect of Jane becoming the first female manager for the division. Jane had been described routinely in the annual reviews as a bright young engineer and recently secured her third consecutive rating in the top twenty percent of her engineering peer group.

When Pam began lobbying for Jane with the three principal decision makers, they looked back at her with concern. "Are you kidding? Jane? She couldn't handle that job," one of them said. "She has a fundamental problem with assertiveness. She's not very good at working with difficult people. No way she could lead a tough group like that." They all nodded in agreement.

Not to give up easily Pam remind them that Jane had been rated "Very Effective" for three years in a row. She had also been recently given a large performance bonus and there had never been mention of Jane having an assertiveness problem anywhere on her evaluation sheet. "I don't care what the forms say," another manager testified. "Jane's had this problem for years. She's nowhere near ready to handle that job. I'm not sure she ever will be."

"Does Jane know that?" Pam queried.

"She hasn't been bold enough to ask," the third chuckled in reply.

Upon checking out the situation further, Pam ultimately determined that the managers looking to fill the open position were unbiased about Jane's true current capabilities. They were not really using her sex, race, age, etc. to disqualify her. They wanted to promote someone they felt confident would succeed.

The frustration Pam had is that Jane's bosses had not been honest with her about where she truly needed work. Had they confronted Jane three years previous about her lack of assertiveness, perhaps she would have had time to demonstrate progress.

Because the issue of assertiveness was only mentioned casually to Jane and never made a part of her formal review, she had assumed that it was not that significant. Had she known that skill deficiency might one day cause her to be bypassed for promotion, she might have reacted differently. Bottom line, they had not given Jane a chance to prove whether she could step up or not. By trying to protect her performance rating and maximize salary treatment, the whole system had unwittingly sabotaged Jane's career potential.

As frustrated as people in Human Resources might be by managers and supervisors who engage in this kind of costly and shortsighted "gamesmanship" they need to consider the ultimate source of the problem. It is the HR-provided system that often induces managers and supervisors to make unhealthy choices. Unless you change the system, you should not realistically expect future results to be any different.

FAILING TO PRODUCE RESULTS

Observational humorists like to begin their commentary with an opening line that queries: "Did you ever notice . . . ?" Here's one for the die-hards who believe in the sanctity of the performance evaluation process. "Did you ever notice that at the top of many organizations they don't do performance evaluations?" We have to this phenomenon in the last chapter. The practice seems to be very widespread.

In many organizations the top operating officer will not personally utilize the performance evaluation system he imposes on those below him. The CEO, COO or President seldom feels compelled to complete the forms describing her direct reports in terms of communication style, leadership skills, team participation and so on. As a result, the most critical individual contributors in a given system are frequently those with the least amount of formal feedback.

When someone is bold enough to quiz one of these individuals as to why they fail to follow their own rules, the response typically involves three excuses. First, they are extremely busy. Second, they feel, because of the constant intimate contact they have with their direct reports, that their direct reports each understand precisely how they are doing and where they stand in the boss's eye. Third, employees at this level should be able to tell by the size of their annual bonuses the clear message about perceived value and contribution. If the top officer humors the inquisitor further, he might finish with a justification that reminds you that these are very senior people we're talking about who have learned over the years exactly where they have shortcomings.

Bill's Short-Term Solution

Karen, an HR Director for a financial services company, encountered this problem with her CEO (Bill). In a moment of sheer frustration Bill called Karen for assistance in dealing with the performance of his personal secretary. Bill needed help in changing his assistant's behavior or he wanted her moved from under his direct supervision. When Karen asked Bill if he had completed the five-page annual evaluation forms on his poor-performing secretary for the past two years, he confessed that he had not. In his defense, he used the general explanation outlined above. He was busy, they talked almost every day, she should know where she stands, etc.

When Karen reminded Bill that his secretary had only four years with the company and two years with him, he grew quieter. Bottom line, confronting his secretary about her shortcomings was not a pleasant subject to Bill and he preferred to avoid the confrontation. And, frankly, he did not feel the forms the company used at the time to evaluate people were of much use. He wanted to change her behavior, not affect her salary or damage her entire career by saying something negative on the formal review form.

The difference between this CEO's dilemma and that of other managers is only one thing. He could get away with skirting the performance evaluation system. Who was going to mandate that he participate? The VP of Human Resources had tried to get Bill (his boss) to complete evaluation forms several times, but Bill elected not to. At some point the VP of Human Resources made a decision not to press the issue. They did their best to work around the absence of completed forms.

One problem here is that when the big boss doesn't participate, it becomes a symbol of organizational status to his direct reports to do the same. Those with the biggest stroke try to follow his example. For those who do not have the status to avoid using the forms, visibly dragging their feet becomes a way to show relative power.

In an energy trading organization, the Chief Financial Officer made it very clear that compliance with this annual ritual need only be superficial. The process was not deemed worthy of much real thought time. Bottom line, he knew who the good and bad contributors were in his organization and the fancy HR-driven evaluation process was of nuisance value only. Following his lead, his strongest direct reports, likewise, complied with the letter of the law and abandoned the intent. The forms were completed and submitted with little thought or analysis.

It would be easy to blame this situation on unenlightened executive management. Most HR people experience resistance to performance management practices, in one form or another. Most senior executives seem to come to the top jobs strong-suited in general business skills with particular technical strengths in marketing, public relations, finance, engineering, manufacturing or whatever. They often start out short-suited, however, in people skills or in seeing the value of the developmental systems that Human Resources supplies.

It is easy to go along with this logic. It makes sense. It is easy. It puts the blame on others. It is out of their control. There is nothing they can do if the top boss does not want to cooperate. They don't have to change.

On the other hand, have you ever wondered if perhaps there could be more to this story? Perhaps the real reason these smart business people do not follow the recommended processes for evaluating and discussing performance with their direct reports is because they do not find the process to have value.

Look at the forms you use more closely and critically. Begin to think about using them to describe people at the Vice President level and above. When you do, key words will likely jump into your head, like "demeaning" or "insulting."

Despite the fact that even senior executives sometimes have major shortcomings to address, the prospect of using conventional evaluation forms to convey this information is not a positive one. Putting things on paper in this manner could make it harder to give critical business leaders the kind of salary treatment and/or promotion opportunities that they truly deserve. In short, close inspection of your forms and process may reveal the true source of the problem. It may have less to do with lack of support from the person at the top than with the woefully inadequate process that we have given her to work with.

Here is a wager. If the system were worthwhile, the CEO would use it. For example, if the performance management system truly facilitated meaningful change in behavior and motivated recipients to work harder, she might use it twice a day. Most CEOs, CFOs and COOs spend their time on things they think have impact on the business. The more projected impact, the more time they invest. They are rewarded handsomely in most cases for making these judgments.

Most have correctly surmised that their current systems will NOT facilitate meaningful changes in behavior in their direct reports. Most systems will NOT leave evaluation recipients wanting to work harder. They take a lot of time and often produce the opposite of intended impacts. Hence, you won't be able to force executives to spend time using these forms. In most cases, they're probably making a good call. Others lower in the organization might do the same, but they're just not powerful enough to get away with it.

Edward's Surprise

Exit interviews are almost never fun, but they are frequently very interesting. One intriguing exit interview was with a mechanical engineer named Edward. It seemed Edward was leaving the company for greater opportunity. Not an uncommon reason given during exit interviews. Only problem was, he was currently working for one of the most profitable corporations in the world that was going through an enormous expansion program. And Edward was ranked the number one engineer in a group of 135. It didn't seem to make sense that he was leaving for a lateral position as an engineer for a smaller company.

As he talked, the interviewer learned some interesting things. First and foremost, Edward's primary motivation for leaving was not money. In fact his new position paid only a little more than he expected to get from his next scheduled increase with his current company. He was leaving for promotability—future upward movement potential.

When the interviewer asked him to reconcile his decision to leave with the fact that he was so highly regarded by his present company, Edward was puzzled. In fact, based on all the negative feedback he was constantly receiving from his well-meaning, but tough-minded boss, Edward thought he was doing only slightly better than average. He had no idea of his lofty ranking until one of his bosses was given permission to share it with him after the resignation was announced.

It was not clear whether Edward was more surprised or frustrated to hear the news of his high standing with the company. On the one hand, he knew that people in the top ten percent of their rank groups had usually made it to the "fast track," and the number one slot held a special feeling of promise and speed. On the other had, the fact that he had absolutely no clue about where he stood until he had committed himself to another organization made him angry. "What a stupid system!" was his way of summarizing the situation.

Edward never seriously considered changing his mind once his resignation was announced. He knew his reputation would be tarnished forever for having considered leaving. He had also given his word to the new company. The five years he and his first employer invested to make him the best in his class left with Edward as he started his career afresh with a new employer.

UNDERMINING TEAMWORK AND QUALITY

When parents became frustrated with their children in America in the 1950s, it was quite common to use spanking as a method to get them to behave. The mere threat to "take you over my knee" or "get the belt" was often just as effective in getting youngsters to sit up straight and stop horseplay.

Then along came Dr. Spock who taught people that corporal punishment for kids was a bad idea. He argued that spanking was potentially damaging to a child's self-esteem, etc. He suggested things like "Time Out" and other techniques that get the child's attention without the pseudo-violence.

Once parents learned of the potential damage they were doing and were introduced to some reasonable alternatives, many abandoned the practice of spanking. Most American parents today look at spanking as something to avoid except in the most extreme circumstances. Given a new perspective, spankings now seem more like "beatings" than a loving way to correct behavior.

That is how a growing number of people have come to view performance evaluations, with the same revulsion. They understand the motivation and see that occasional positive results can ensue, but doling out performance grades based on a fixed distribution concerns them deeply. Dr. Deming was our Dr. Spock. We now believe it is very, very ineffective to rate and rank people in an attempt to get them to improve.

As described earlier, many began gaining enlightenment with the arrival of the Quality movement and its focus on the importance of teamwork. Dr. Deming became a beacon of light as he discussed the importance of system optimization. He said that an organization was a system of interdependent functions. Individuals were the smallest unit of production. He described a need to "subordinate" individual goal achievement in order to "super-ordinate" performance of the whole.

In a famous example, he described the need for "interdependence" as existing on a continuum. On the low side were organizations that did not depend as much on the collective to be effective. He cited a bowling team as a group having a low degree of interdependence. Each member merely did the best he or she could. Scores were added together in the end and that became the team score. Bowler A had limited impact on the scores of Bowlers B, C or D, and vice versa.

On the other side of the continuum, not all the way to the high end, he described an orchestra. An orchestra is highly interdependent. In other words, to be a good orchestra, members of the group had to work together very carefully. They could not have the best trumpet player and the finest flutist compete for attention of the audience. Each had parts. Some were given solos, but those were clearly structured to be part of the overall piece. When all is said and done, the best orchestras were those that worked together the most elegantly. Individual excellence was not the key determinant of quality.

Here is the punch line. Dr. Deming contended that "a modern organization" (meaning any of us banded together that call ourselves a business) is even more interdependent than an orchestra. In other words, setting up systems to maximize individual performance may help create a good bowling team, but it would probably produce a very unsatisfactory orchestra. People need to be incentivized to work together in teams and groups with the purpose of maximizing organizational performance. Internal competition between individuals in the same organization is simply and clearly a bad idea.

A culture that revolves around rating and ranking individuals has a challenge producing effective teams. In this environment, another word for teammate is "competitor." Your peers and colleagues are the very ones you are compared against. And unlike in most schools, only so many can get the A's. You must think twice before helping a colleague do something that helps her look good. Remember, rating and ranking are about *relative* and not *absolute* performance. By definition, helping a peer or colleague works against your own best interest.

As we've discussed earlier, the real players know how the game works, and they use this knowledge very carefully. When asked how they feel about teams and teamwork, they are loud, proud supporters. They are in the front row for all the team pictures. But behind the scene, they are always on their guard. Teams are merely a means to an end. The end is "self-promotion." Literally.

"We'd Drill Different Wells"

Perhaps the best way to illustrate the inherent problems with systems built around internal competitiveness is to recount another real-life work experience. This one was reported by Jerry, the head of Employee Relations for a large, independent oil and gas company.

Jack, the executive in charge of offshore exploration and production operations was frustrated. He had tried for two years to get his group of senior managers to function like a high-performing team, but he could not get them over the hump. Jack invited Jerry, who was regarded as the resident expert in the teaming process for the company, to work with his leadership group to see if there was anything that he could do to help.

Jack was relatively new to the team. He had been brought in to turn around a bad situation. The offshore division was on a long dry spell between major discoveries. If he could not help them make a profit soon, rumblings were that the company would be forced to abandon their deep-water activities and close the offshore office. Some felt that the company could not be successful in the offshore (where potential for large discoveries was highest), the entire company would not survive. To say the stakes were large would be an understatement.

One key area of frustration for Jack was with the budget process. This was an annual ritual that required months of preparation. It involved almost every geologist and geophysicist in the division taking turns making presentations on the areas they had studied for months. They came in, one after another, to make recommendations on their three to five best prospects for finding oil and gas in their assigned areas.

A senior group of the top thirteen managers listened to all the presentations. When they were done presenting their 50 to 75 prospects, a decision had to be made on which seven to ten prospects to drill. The output of the yearly two-day marathon meeting determined the drilling schedule for the whole year and in large part the economic viability of the most costly and /or profitable business unit in the company.

Jerry's task was to help this core group of thirteen senior managers work more like a team. To the great frustration of Jack, the general manager, this was the situation:

In the end, after all is said and done, they will not make a decision based on consensus. They argue with each other to impasse and always make *me* decide where to drill. Frankly, I don't know the areas near as well as they do. I just got here and am not an expert in the offshore. I really need this group to take ownership of the problem and help decide where we need to concentrate our limited resources. Surely a group decision would be better than any individual decision I can make.

Two months before the commencement of the annual budget process, Jerry began his quest to help convert this group of hard working, well-intentioned individual contributors into a high-performing team. Everyone knew what was at stake.

They began with a standard two-day seminar about the fundamentals of team-work and then set aside one half-day a week to study team process and begin integrating new practices into their routine meeting style. About the sixth week things began to get interesting. They started having frank and open discussions about what kept the team from taking ownership of the decision-making process for the budget.

This is when Jerry discovered that *he himself was the cause of the problems the group was having in operating like a team.* Despite the fact that his office was more than 800 miles due west, it was Jerry's fault they were compelled to sub-optimize their performance. This revelation did not come without a great deal of high volume discussion. When Jerry pushed them to the wall, asking over and over again why they would not make team-based decisions on where to drill, this is what they finally told him: "You don't pay us to be team players. You pay us to be great individual contributors. And unless you are going to change the way you treat us and reward us, we have to be martyrs to behave differently than we are today."

Here is the explanation in more detail. It starts at the level of the geologist or geophysicist. Each is assigned a geographic area and given a goal to come forward with five drillable prospects per year. Three is okay, four is good, but five is the ideal, six or more is not necessary. Five good ones will put you in excellent standing when it comes time for your annual review. Geologists and geophysicists rise and fall on the rank list each year based on their ability to "generate prospects." Literal hero status was reserved for those who generated prospects that led to discoveries.

Discoveries can take years and involve dozens of people, but the geologist/geophysicist and his team leader (manager) are lionized for their parts in generating income for years to come. A mythical status of "oil finder" goes to those who can do this more than once. Legend has it that a bronze bust of the latest and greatest "oil finder" is on constant display in the Chief Operating Officer's plush downtown office.

Along with the prestige of being labeled an "oil finder" goes other niceties. Big raises, promotions, cash bonuses, and stock options, too. As they were proud to tell all concerned, this company "pays for performance." Performance for this group was pure and simple: To do well they must find and produce oil and gas. Everything else was secondary.

But let's get back to the melodrama. How does all this well-intentioned and logically based all-American reinforcement system affect the company's annual budget process? Here's what they told Jerry.

After working for almost a year on an area assigned to him by management, a geologist or geophysicist is required to make a presentation to a group of superiors that displays his accomplishments. Based on his personal goals that means coming up with a minimum of five prospects for commercial drilling. More importantly, if he aspires to higher office or more than an average increase, he must find oil. And since it is impossible to discover oil where you do not drill, his chances for success increase with every prospect he can convince management to drill.

Over time an informal "hog law" made it customary to limit the number each individual strongly pushed for to three. In other words the template for presentation went something like this. "I have combed through my assigned area X for the last year and discovered five viable prospects. I am here today to give a strong recommendation to drill my top three prospects."

And so it went. Creating the annual budget was a series of presentations following that exact process. Fifteen individuals came forward in a row and made their pitches. "These are my top five; we should drill these three." A manager on the senior team who helped her direct reports prepare for this ritual represented each presenter. She also had a stake in any drilling success. After all, someone who could manage a group of multiple "oil finders" was an even more valuable commodity than an individual oil finder.

When all fifteen presenters had made their case, the general manager would turn to the senior team and ask what they thought. Each had, in turn, synthesized their groups down to five prospects with three strong recommendations to drill. The same ritual ensued now at a higher level. "After careful analysis, I put forward to you my five top prospects with a strong recommendation to drill the top three." When all were finished, there were 36 "strong recommendations."

When Jack asked for synthesis and compromise, he found instead impasse. He needed a maximum of ten or eleven prospects to drill and he could get them to agree on no less than three times that number. They just kept repeating: "My top three prospects and any seven others." When they tried to narrow it down further, the managers just got angry and started saying negative things about each other. The whole situation deteriorated until Jack adjourned the meeting in frustration and made his best guess alone. Because the group could not decide, he was forced to do it for them.

This type of decision making had other negative consequences. When Jack's boss questioned his proposal for which wells to drill and sought clarification from any of Jack's team, he instantly sensed the lack of consensus in the proposal. This made it harder for the offshore group to compete for scarce drilling dollars that were being divided up across the whole company. The same money could be invested in domestic onshore ventures, foreign ventures, or even in refining or R&D.

The infighting and gamesmanship continued throughout the year. Everyone positioned himself/herself to have better advantage for the coming year. In the truest sense, colleagues on the senior management team were seen as competitors. They collected dirt to use against each other during the coming year's budget review. They remembered who took advantage of them and they competed fiercely, if silently, for positions of advantage.

The funny thing about all of this is that everyone knew what was going on. They just didn't know how to stop it. In the end, they pointed their fingers at Jerry and said it was his fault. After all, it was the Human Resources department that gave them the evaluation process and the pay and bonus systems. When Jerry asked them what the company could do to change the dysfunctional way they were behaving, they told him the honest truth. ''Unless you change the way you recognize and reward us, I don't think anything ever really will change. At best you'll just drive negative behavior further underground.'' Here is what they said needed to change if Jerry really wanted them to think and act differently.

First, abandon individual bonuses and go to some form of profit sharing. Include everyone, they said, not just the senior managers. Support staff can make or break the group's ability to perform and should be recognized as legitimate members of the team.

Second, abandon this arbitrary quota system for finding prospects and discoveries. Quit making people out to be heroes who were fortunate enough to be assigned a good area. Let individuals move and flow to where the really high payoff areas seem to be.

Third, evaluate people on how hard they work and their contribution to the team, instead of how well they position themselves in connection to a discovery. Understand that discoveries are the work of lots of people and that individuals [are neither how talented nor never do it alone.]

Fourth, recognize that all of them have career aspirations and some will work very hard for the chance at advancement. Help them achieve their potential without all the temptations to optimize their own situations at the expense of others.

As Jerry listened to all this he became almost physically ill. Here he was, the great guru of teamwork in his company, sent on mission to help an underperforming group learn the many benefits of working together synergistically, and he discovered that their biggest obstacle was of his own creation. The HR systems that the group was forced to operate under were dragging them down. The "pay for performance" policy that headquarters senior management were so very proud of was incentivizing the wrong behavior.

The full horror of the situation was summarized to Jerry in one incredible phrase: "If you change the way you reward and reinforce us, we'd drill different wells."

They explained by saying:

If we're all tied together and success of our division is the first and foremost thing that is measured and rewarded, we'd make different decisions on where to drill. We'd participate more openly and honestly in the decision-making process. In addition, it could make this a happier and more productive place to come to work.

While the majority of you reading this book are probably not in the oil industry, the same logic applies to other businesses as well. These extremely intelligent people worked 60 hours a week fighting against incredible international business forces. The pressure to cut costs and maximize the chance of bringing in new business was off the chart. And yet, the silly rules that were used to create the illusion of winners and losers significantly influenced the most critical business decisions the company had to make. Everybody knew it, they saw the damage it was creating, and yet they couldn't stop doing it—even if it meant losing their company and their jobs.

To anyone who has ever thought of Human Resources as a necessary evil, an administrative burden that is incidental to the business, this real-life story should encourage you to reconsider. Whatever you call this stuff, it represents the rules of the game. Change the rules and people play differently. Change the way people play and you impact the odds of winning or losing. And isn't that what most companies really were created to do—win?

In the next chapter, we will examine in more detail the way in which monetary rewards intertwine with the rating and ranking process to alter and affect the game.

Chapter 4

Pay for Performance: The Big Lie

Managers who complain that their workers are not motivated might do well to consider the possibility that they have installed reward systems which are paying off for behaviors other than those they are seeking.
—Steven Kerr, Chief Learning Officer for General Electric Corporation[1]

Using money to manipulate behavior gets us in all kinds of trouble. We dig a hole for ourselves when we promise what may not come true.
—Peter Block[2]

Perhaps the biggest misstatement oft repeated in corporations today is the expression: "We pay for performance." At least the way this expression is typically translated, it simply does not and cannot work. This chapter will discuss the modern mythology of "pay for performance" and its role in complicating and undermining the performance management process. It will reveal why attempts to tie the evaluation of annual contribution directly to base pay proves problematic over time. It will also demonstrate how the illusion of pay for performance along with the reality of individual bonuses frequently work against a company's best interest.

THE "AMERICAN WAY"

When a company official talks to a glassy-eyed recruit about the firm's pay for performance philosophy, it is usually with his right hand covering his heart and the American flag waving in the background. After all, what is more noble or patriotic than the concept that you get rewarded for what you do. "At ABC

Corporation, those who work hard and deliver the goods are amply rewarded,'' the recruiter is proud to say. Since most eager young entrants into the workforce have every intention of working hard, this is welcome news. Their minds race with visions of rapid and continuous upward growth in both salary and status.

When queried about how this system works, the official will explain briefly about he annual review cycle and its direct connection to the salary system. Performance labels are usually briefly discussed, but the more complicated subject of allocating grades based on forced distributions and/or competitive rankings is glossed over whenever possible. The candidate will learn about all this in time.

After all is said and done, the overall impression management leaves with both potential and actual employees is that the pay for performance system is designed to give better performers bigger raises. When employees come to their review each year, those who view themselves as good performers typically look forward to at least one part of the interview—the part at the end where they are advised of their big, fat salary increase. For the young up-and-comer, this can frequently be true. But if she sticks around for a while, the deal changes. The implied contract is voided. Perhaps a typical example can best illustrate this point.

A SAD TALE: THE STORY OF HARVEY

The first year Harvey came to work for GoodStuff Enterprises, he was pretty green. Nonetheless, he worked hard and made an excellent first impression. Harvey's boss, Mr. BigBucks was very pleased by Harvey's willingness to work an occasional Saturday or Sunday to keep up with the torrid pace.

Mr. BigBucks called Harvey in after the first year and told him what a wonderful job he'd done in getting his feet on the ground at GoodStuff. ''Because of your hard work and excellent first year performance, Harvey, I'm giving you a 5% raise,'' Mr. BigBucks stated. Harvey was very pleased. He told Mr. BigBucks in response, ''You haven't seen anything yet, sir. Wait till you see how hard I work next year!'' And with that Harvey planted his nose firmly to the grindstone and went back to work.

Continuous Improvement

The second year was superb for Harvey. He became more knowledgeable about GoodStuff Enterprises, their products and customers. He spent loads of overtime at the office, at least one weekend day a week. And Harvey's production record showed it. He couldn't wait for his next annual review.

As it turned out, he was right. Mr. BigBucks lauded praise over Harvey as he informed him, ''Harvey, because of your fine work and excellent performance this year I am giving you a 7% raise and promoting you to Department Supervisor. Congratulations and keep up the good work!'' To say Harvey was pleased would be a big understatement. He was ecstatic. "Mr. BigBucks," he said, "You haven't seen anything yet, sir. Wait until you see how hard I work next year!"

And so it went for the next several years. Harvey kept working hard and doing well and Mr. BigBucks delivered with excellent performance ratings, promotions and big salary increases. After five years Harvey was promoted to Department Manager, reporting directly to Ms. Godly herself.

It was during the seventh year that the equation seemed to change rather mysteriously for Harvey. Ironically, it was the year in which he had had his best performance ever. He was on his third year in a row of breaking performance records for his division. His department was functioning like clockwork. And aside from the fact that he was spending an average of 80 hours a week at the office, everything was perfect. Harvey had his sights on a new sports car that he was going to buy with the big raise he anticipated. Last year he was given 9%, and he hoped for even more this year.

Dimininshing Returns

When Ms. Godly sat down with Harvey this year, she was not quite as animated as in year's past. She went through the performance review rather slowly and emphasized what a great job Harvey had done on all his projects. She noted the wonderful records that he continued to set. She gave Harvey an "Excellent" rating, as she did for the last several years. After a few mumbled words and phrases about "the system" and "wish it were different" she notified Harvey that his raise this year would be 5%. That was good, she said, "when you consider things like inflation."

Harvey was shocked and disappointed. He was counting on a percentage increase of at least what he received the previous year. "Is there anything I can do different or better?" Harvey asked, trying to recapture his positive state of mind. "No kid, you're doing just fine," said Ms. Godly.

"Well, you haven't seen anything yet," said Harvey, as his long-established optimism and determination kicked back in. "Wait until you see how hard I work next year!"

Harvey was true to his word. For the next twelve months he literally lived at GoodStuff. In fact, for a Christmas present his wife bought him a cot for his office. She also gave him a family portrait "so you can remember what we look like," she said, trying to show her support. Despite tough business conditions, Harvey broke his previous performance records one more time.

Harvey was exhausted on the day of his annual performance review. He had worked literally 100 hours the previous week to close out his books and lock in the record marks. Ms. Godly did not appear to have slept very well either when she entered the room for the review. She went painstakingly through the evaluation form, noting Harvey's many accomplishments and thanking him for his fine work and effort. When it came time for the discussion on salary, however, there was a long silence. When Ms. Godly started mumbling about "the system" again, Harvey's hopes sunk. His increase this year would be 3%. "Just about even with inflation," Ms. Godly noted, trying to give the message the most positive spin she could muster.

Harvey was stunned. He was too tired to think clearly. Instead, his mind kept flashing on all the sacrifices he had made that year for the company. He thought of all the missed ball games and recitals. He remembered falling asleep at dinner on a night out with his wife. He left the meeting in silence.

A Change in Tactic

When he arrived home, his wife could tell immediately that the news was bad. "How much?" she asked quickly. "Three percent," he mumbled as he slumped into the couch. "Three percent!" she screamed. "Three percent! After all you do for that company, they give you a three percent raise?" She was silent for only a moment. Then she continued. "I remember when they used to value you at GoodStuff Enterprises. I remember when they used to give you big raises and promotions and treat you with respect. Mr. BigBucks used to take care of you. Mrs. Godly either can't or won't." She continued, "You need to find another job. There must be a company out there somewhere who will treat you fairly. This is a disgrace! Ms. Godly and GoodStuff can go jump in the lake."

The next workday Harvey brought home his cot. He started working regular hours and even took an occasional lunch break. "Why kill yourself for these guys?" he told his colleagues. "It doesn't pay."

What Happened to Harvey?

Those who know the way typical compensation systems really work may be able to identify the roots of Harvey's dilemma. For those who don't, let's review some basics.

Harvey works for a company that bases its salaries on the market. Almost all companies do. That means, in essence, that they target a salary for each job type based on what others in the area, region or country pay for similar jobs.

As illustrated in Figure 4-1, the average salary for an entry-level accountant working in Atlanta, Georgia, might be $25,000 per year, with the top earners in this bracket making $30K and the bottom $20K. An entry-level engineer might be slightly higher; an entry-level Human Resources analyst slightly lower. An second level accountant with three or four year's experience might average $30K and Accounting supervisors might have a median income of $40K.

Companies will normally determine average pay (midpoint) and calculate a range around that figure that they will operate within. A typical salary range is 20% on either side of the "midpoint" or average. Based on data they purchase

Figure 4-1
Sample Salary Ranges

	$20K	$25K	$30K	$40K	$45K	$50K
Accountant I	I_____I_____I					
Accountant II		I_____I_____I				
Engineer I						
Accounting Supervisor			I_____I_____I			
Engineer II						
Accounting Manager				I_____I_____I		
Engineering Supervisor						

from consultants or gather in surveys, organizations determine exactly how much they need to spend on any given type of employee.

In other words, the best marketing analyst in a company should normally not be paid more than 20% above what companies in the reasonable recruiting area pay for experienced marketing analysts. To pay more than the market requires systematically would lead to noncompetitive labor costs. There simply has to be a ceiling for how much a company can or should pay for any given craft.

There are also internal equity issues. For example, the newest marketing analyst should probably not make less than a mid-level secretary. The highest paid mechanic, taking into consideration normal overtime, should not make more than a mechanical supervisor with more than two years of supervisory experience. These are the kinds of rules and comparisons that must be made if a salary system is to have any type of logic or integrity.

In addition to imposing salary ranges on various jobs, most comprehensive salary systems have provisions for moving people along in their salary range. Over time, as an individual stays at a given salary level, she should move along the range toward the top. Salary systems are typically designed so that when an individual is low in their range, they have the opportunity to get larger increases. While merit can assist the individual in moving along the range, once you get high enough things must slow down, or . . . you will go over the top, which is not permitted.

Harvey's dilemma, as illustrated in Figure 4-2, was that he moved fast in the beginning, but then eventually slowed down. That is because he ultimately be-

Figure 4-2
Harvey's Salary History

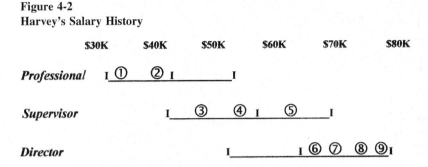

Annual salary in each work year indicated by circled numbers.

3% average annual range movement.

came stuck on a salary level and stayed there. Because he was a superior performer, he ascended to the upper limit of the range quicker than many others
might have, but . . . once there, barring the possibility of a promotion to a higher
salary grade, he had nowhere to go. Until Ms. Godly or one of her colleagues
left and created an opening, Harvey was stuck.

Lack of Knowledge Hurts

Unfortunately for the characters in our story, they didn't understand how the
system worked. Part of this was Mr. BigBucks fault, for he gave Harvey some
misleading information early in his career with GoodStuff. When he told Harvey
that the big raise was "because of his hard work and excellent performance,"
he was only telling a half-truth. At the time it was very convenient and served
to stoke Harvey's fire. However, in the long run it became a problem.

A key reason Harvey received such big increases in the early years was because he was so low in his salary range. In short, Harvey was paid below average
for the market. A good salary system will very quickly help correct this problem.
Good performance helps, but his high potential and low pay rate did most of
the work. When he finally got to the level of Department Manager and slowed
down for a few years, he crossed the midpoint of his salary range and began
approaching the "cap." Much to the chagrin of both Harvey and his new boss,
the system slows down even for the best performer as he approaches the top of
the range.

Here's something both seemed to miss, however. Assuming the company has
benchmarked Harvey's job correctly, even with his last small increase Harvey
should be among the highest paid individuals in his position in his market. If
he looks externally for comparison, the data should confirm this fact. Ironically,

back when Harvey was getting the biggest increases, he was probably furthest from being paid competitively to the market.

The trouble with most salary administration systems that claim to base themselves on a pay for performance philosophy is that they encourage people to concentrate on the wrong thing. People get focused almost exclusively on the amount of their annual increase. That is the symbol of how much the organization values them. "When I get a big increase it shows that they value me and appreciate my contribution." This is both naive and wrong. And it doesn't serve us well in the long run to tell them this.

Harvey's story is about a system that fails to live up to the illusion that the administrators created for it. It demonstrates a lack of understanding on the part of the individuals who designed the system and those responsible for promoting it. While potentially viable for some people for a few years, it is impossible to sustain over time. The system administrators in this case chose to operate the system according to design, but spoke of it in a way that was not realistic. The inevitable eventual outcome is disappointment and disillusionment.

In the next example the individual involved took the opposite approach. He forced the salary system to comply with his message about performance. Unfortunately this strategy also poses some serious inherent complications.

A RUNAWAY TRAIN

The Chief Operating Officer (COO) for a large advertising agency decided to disregard the salary system as it pertained to his personal secretary. He did not have the heart or stomach to advise her that she was at the top of her salary range. When she did a great job in supporting him, he gave her a big annual increase, year after year. When he retired, she was making more money in base pay than half the engineers and two-thirds of the accountants in her company. And she was paid overtime. Working an average of less than 50 hours a week, she literally took home over $75,000 a year. The COO left it up to his replacement to freeze her salary for the rest of her career and continue paying her substantially over the highest market rate.

No system can sustain increases of this type. It is simply not competitive. And it is not the salary administration system that needs to be changed. What needs to be changed is the way we talk about salaries and salary increases. We cannot continue to sell the illusion that the annual increase is the reward for good performance.

THE REAL INDICATOR OF PERCEIVED VALUE

Peter Block, in his book on stewardship, discusses many additional problems associated with pay for performance mythology. He talks about it as a "divine right of kings" which promotes the class system and serves "as the glue to a command-and-compliance culture."[3] He also recognizes that it sends a message about direct incentives for annual contribution that is not sustainable over time. Simply put: "We do not have enough money to actually purchase behavior from people inside an organization."[4]

The true measure of how much an organization values an employee, as designed by the compensation system, is the total compensation package that that individual receives. The amount of an increase is but a footnote.

One of the grave errors in tying a compensation system too closely to the evaluation system is that it feeds the illusion that has just been discredited. All the ritual and pageantry only serves to detract from the real message of total pay. An annual base salary increase should be nothing more than an adjustment to keep someone's pay competitive with the market.

Better performers should expect to have advantages in several areas:

1. Retention, when times are bad;
2. Promotion on the Career/Professional Ladder, more quickly than poorer performers;
3. Promotion on the Supervisory/Managerial Ladder, when opportunities arise; and
4. Selection for Choice Assignments, again based on opportunity.

Depending on the mechanics of the compensation system they are under, a better performer may also get slightly larger increases slightly faster than poorer performing peers . . . *for a while*. Eventually and inevitably, however, their total compensation should be competitive for the position they are filling and the experience they bring to the workplace. Rather than try to sell the concept as "pay for performance," we might be wise to change it to "pay for contribution" or "pay for market value." At least these concepts focus on something closer to reality.

WHEN WORDS AND MONEY COLLIDE

Reductions in motivation and increased disillusionment are natural offspring of a system that over time cannot live up to what it advertises. The results may be even worse, however, when organizations develop reward systems that can. The effective use of annual bonuses and lump sum awards for executives, senior managers and sales professionals can often have unintended side effects. They can drive behavior in a way that works against the company's stated values and best intentions. Good incentive systems can often produce very bad results.

Ron's Game

Ron was a regional director responsible for a real estate development company. Late February one year business conditions were so poor that senior management was forced to call for a dramatic reduction in the company's capital budget. Since Ron was responsible for more than two dozen people and had an annual budget of more than $100 million, it was assumed the recent news of a 30% cutback would have dampened his spirit.

Roger, a staff manager from another division, ran into Ron at the gym one day. When Roger asked Ron how his group had received the bad news, he was shocked to hear Ron's reply.

"My staff is just fine," Ron reported with a big grin. As he looked both ways to confirm that there were no eavesdroppers, he whispered: "Look, Roger. By the time I get the official notice that we have to cut our budgets, I'll have either spent or signed contracts committing my entire budget for the year." With his colleague sitting in stunned silence Ron continued: "Look, they don't pay me to sit in my office. They pay me to develop property. I can't do that without construction, and I can't do construction without a budget. Let the slower departments worry about cutbacks and budget cuts. We're spending ours." After a brief pause, he concluded: "Hey, you just tell me the rules of the game and I'll figure out how to win."

Hearing this open declaration of rebellion made Roger's blood run cold. He could not believe the self-centered audacity of the individual making this statement. While Roger was not naïve enough to think that gamesmanship like this was not going on in other places, he found it incredible that a peer would be so bold as to discuss his scheme publicly. And this person was on the short list for even higher office.

To make a long story short, it turned out Roger was the one who did not understand the true system at work. Ron not only got away with his ruse, he had a very successful year and was rewarded with the largest bonus he'd received to date. At the crossroads with pay and words diverging, Ron chose pay and was much the richer for it. People of principle, like Roger, who reacted to the words and what they thought was the right thing to do for the greater good, could only learn from their mistakes.

It took Roger a long time to truly understand that his friend Ron was, indeed, only doing what he was being incentivized to do. The problem was with the reinforcement system and not Ron personally. Change the rules and Ron would change his behavior. He said as much.

The Super Salesman

Another example of words and money colliding was brought to my attention by a lawn products salesman named Keith. It was October one year when I noticed Keith was spending much more time than usual around the house. For the first nine months of the year Keith seemed to live on the road. The sudden change in pattern was both odd and interesting. When I asked Keith what was going on, he proceeded to provide another reward system gut check.

Keith works for a large national company that sells lawn mowers, power trimmers, edgers, etc. He has a territory that covers the better part of two states. And while the newspaper was talking about how his company was having a very bad year, Keith himself was having a very good one. In fact, as of early October he was quite confident that he was going to exceed his annual sales targets by approximately 10%.

Keith had enough sales accounted for by October that he was going to max out his yearly bonus. He felt no compulsion to earn any more. In fact, he lectured me on the folly of such a practice. "You know, of course" he said, "they use the previous year's achievements to set next year's targets. The saps that are blowing by this year's targets are only making it harder on themselves for next year."

I asked Keith for more information about how his company was doing as a whole. He replied that they were doing quite poorly and might be in the red for the entire year. Layoffs and consolidations were likely if business didn't improve. They had just held an emergency meeting to motivate people to generate more revenue.

But my friend saw through this game. To him personally it made more sense to stockpile his sales to hit the books in January instead of November. He'd already capped out the present year's bonus. He didn't want them to change his targets substantially, and putting off booking of his sales would give him a quick start on his next big bonus check. It was the only smart thing to do, and Keith was a smart guy.

Keith wouldn't be tricked into sacrificing his own livelihood for the some trumped up "higher cause" (like survival of the business). He was a consistent superior individual contributor and wanted to stay that way. He could only snicker while those that "overachieved" last year struggled to meet their goals this year. He knew that they were the ones most likely to take the fall when consolidations hit.

And Keith's words proved prophetic. When the overall business continued to languish through year-end, the company reorganized and some of his colleagues lost their jobs. Keith's territory, however, just got bigger. Thank goodness he had those extra sales stashed in reserve so he could start the next year out at his usual excellent pace. Not to mention that he also maintained his four handicap.

THE ALIENATION OF CLAUDE

Let's examine another example of a person's career counseling being mishandled because of an evaluation system built around allocating financial reward. This case involves a pilot by the name of Claude who works for a company still practicing a traditional evaluation-based performance management system.

Claude flies cargo planes for an air freight company. He's been with them for close to twenty years. When asked about his performance management process at work, Claude responded: "It's a joke. In the end, it doesn't really mean anything."

Claude went on to explain that his company rated him on a five-point scale in five different performance dimensions. He reported that he had been given fives (the top rating) in each category for several years. He was given almost no counsel on performance issues he needed to improve. As a function of these top-notch evaluations, Claude felt he had generally been treated a little better than others with respect to salary administration. One day, however, things took a sudden turn for the worse.

Claude applied for promotion to fill a senior management-level position. He knew several others that had applied as well. At least three had about the same level of service that he did. There were also a few more junior candidates that were perceived as "favorites" to those making the decisions.

Claude's manager gave him some insight into the process. It seems several of the individuals who had applied for the job also had all fives, or very close to all fives, in their ratings. Senior management did not feel comfortable making the decision to fill the position based on those grades alone. In fact, the key decision maker let it be known that he thought most of the grades were "inflated" and presented a distorted view of reality. To resolve the situation, he forced a "re-rating" of the individuals for promotion purposes.

When one of the less senior "favorite" candidates won the promotion, Claude and some of his senior colleagues felt violated. In fact, Claude was downright angry. His explanation of what happened involved expressions like "suck-ups" and "backstabbers."

Claude made it a point following this exercise to inform his boss whenever he felt like he observed someone who was "playing" the system for promotion. He also started talking openly about what he wanted to do when layoffs came again and he would face an inevitable invitation to exit.

Hearing this kind of story makes it difficult not to wonder whether anyone in Claude's organization was aware how severely the company had demoralized this man. After all, Claude was not a poor performer. He was consistently rated at or near the top of his class. His feedback was always superlative. Clearly, they could not have intended to do this to him. What possible good could it serve? The most probable explanation was that this was system-related collateral damage.

While I do not truly know the inside details of this specific case, I can make a pretty good guess as to what took place. My bet is this. Claude is *very* good at being a pilot. When asked to rate him against standards for his current job, he sets the curve. Since the annual review process is about justifying salary treatment, each year they rate Claude against the same standards and he excels.

When considering Claude for a managerial assignment, however, different standards are imposed. Based on these standards Claude does not set the curve. In fact, he might have a couple of obvious deficiencies. And frankly, the two perceived "favorites" probably grade out better. The problem is, no one has had the responsibility to speak of these things to Claude. They probably didn't want to risk demotivating him. Ironically, by avoiding this difficult discussion that is exactly what they did.

Void of any other explanation, Claude is left to fill in the blanks for why this travesty of justice occurred. Had he been a minority or female or approaching retirement age, the "because I'm different" defense would provide an easy out. They were biased because of his lacking the preferred status. And of course, there is nothing Claude could do to change these realities.[5]

Had Claude spoken up at a meeting or said something controversial, perhaps that would be his way of giving meaning to his dilemma. As it was, Claude and his senior colleagues developed a theory about "favorites." You had to be a "suck-up" and spend all your energy pleasing the boss to get ahead. Since he and his senior colleagues had too much integrity to do this, they became victims and were powerless to change.

In search of a plausible alternative explanation, let's imagine for a second, that Claude and his colleagues were truly not the best candidates for the management position. Let's theorize that despite the lack of time in grade at the pilot level, the individual chosen to fill the senior management slot possessed more of the skills that the company truly believed would allow him to be more successful. If this was the case, the company did, in fact, select the right person for the job. Unfortunately, however, they deeply alienated at least one valued employee (if not three) in the process. What could they have done differently?

To begin with, at some point they simply must sit down with Claude and discuss his perceived strengths and weaknesses with respect to a job to which he seems to aspire. Evaluating Claude for twelve years running based on the same static standards is not helping him grow to his potential. By attempting each year to justify the highest possible base salary increase for Claude (4% instead of the 2.75% received by the average worker), they may be killing Claude's chance at promotion. Only by being honest with him about his perceived strengths and shortcomings with respect to the higher-level jobs can they truly give him a chance to grow.

For instance, in the closed-door session that cost Claude his opportunity for advancement, they undoubtedly spoke about him pretty plainly. What did they say? Does Claude lack initiative that the best candidates more readily display? Does he struggle with making formal presentations? Do the best in class evidence more charisma or charm? While these criteria may have no impact on Claude's current position as a pilot, they may have everything to do with his potential for advancement to a senior managerial level. And it is the performance management system with its focus on salary increase administration that dictates Claude be told nothing negative on paper.

The solution to Claude's problem is the subject of this book. To give people like Claude a true chance at development and promotion a company must put a system in place that facilitates dialogue about growth. It must get information from employees about positions to which they aspire and conduct discussions with them about what they must do to be competitive for this kind of opportunity. They must learn to say *to* Claude what they more freely tell others *about* him. They must stop grading him, stop evaluating him and start coaching him. They must give him feedback relative to his perceived capabilities versus his desired future.

In this specific instance, they may also have to help the employee redefine reality. Many people, including perhaps Claude, don't really want some of the jobs they ask for. They apply for promotional opportunities because it seems to be the thing to do. They don't really want to do some of the things the job requires, but they want the money or the status or the feeling of moving forward in their careers. Sometimes the managerial ladder seems like the only true game in town.

When someone like Claude (an outstanding pilot) expresses interest in a position that management perceives he may not be ideally suited for (senior manager), someone needs to seriously talk to him. They need to discuss with him what campaigning for the coveted job implies. Many times the individual will rethink his position and withdraw his application. Not because he is intimidated by the subtle ''signal'' that he won't get the job, but because he truly understands that he is probably better suited to something else.

Those that ''stay the course'' and want to ''swim upstream'' at least learn what they are up against. Given time and enough determination, they just might make it. They might literally transform themselves into that to which they aspire. To do this, however, they need outstanding coaching and a true desire to change and grow. They need a development system that does more than try in vain to ''pay for performance.''

THE ROCK AND THE PITCHER

No matter what other activities a performance management system includes, if it features and advertises a direct link between performance evaluation and pay, predictable and unavoidable conflicts will occur. Most people will nod their heads in agreement and learn to pay homage to whatever value statements senior management passes on to them. Then they will do what they are paid to do.

Communicating that teamwork is a core corporate value elicits a head nod. Many will participate. Few will openly argue against it. Preaching about system optimization and maximizing organizational effectiveness by breaking down departmental barriers, etc. gets a another nod and perhaps a slight yawn. Charts and graphs are posted on the walls showing business unit performance versus goals. People will monitor company progress and hope for god results, especially if some form of gainsharing (even a small amount) is tied to the information on display.

Making a culture built on a platform of continuous improvement gets a head nod. So does the extended interpersonal implication that peers, customers and subordinates can give important feedback on how to do jobs better. People participate on peer reviews or 360° Feedback surveys, when requested. Managers try to get something positive out of what is sometimes a painful experience.

All other initiatives move aside, however, if it is communicated that annual pay is directly impacted by the evaluation of individual contribution. If evaluations determine the size of a salary increase, who gets promoted, and who is protected in the event of a downturn, all other issues and initiatives are subordinated. The organization is paying for individual achievement above and before all else. All other initiatives and value statements are placed in appropriate context somewhere down the line.

The conflict between money and talk is an unfair contest with a consistent winner. Perhaps Sancho Panza said it best when describing what inevitably occurs when a rock collides with a water pitcher. "Whether the rock hits the pitcher, or the pitcher hits the rock, it's going to be bad for the pitcher." In the same way, money wins most every time.

Part II

Moving Forward Through the Fog

We can chart our future clearly and wisely only when we know the path which has led to the present.

—Adlai E. Stevenson

The complaints from employees and managers about traditional performance management systems described in Part I have not gone unnoticed in industry. Far from it. In response to negative customer feedback companies have struggled with how to improve the prevailing paradigm. Unfortunately, most do so without fully coming to grips with what it is about. Because they lack insight into the design features that define the paradigm and render it ineffective, most change initiatives are moving forward in a fog. Most efforts to change have resulted in making systems different rather than better.

With the insight that comes from clearly defining the prevailing paradigm, we can learn from the change efforts that have been attempted. Part II will give a brief history of change initiatives that have received most prominence. We will discuss the most popular fixes that have been put in place and the typical pluses and minuses that seem to follow with each.

Companies that have made attempts at change seem to have adopted one of four different strategies: "tweaking, supplementing, tossing or substituting." Two of these strategies may be thought of as *evolutionary* in nature. In other words, they represent attempts to salvage the traditional system either by making minor adjustments (tweaking) or by adding on additional features and procedures (supplementing). Chapter 5 will discuss evolutionary change strategies. Chapter 6 will review the other two tactics that appear to be more *revolutionary* in nature. Abandoning the traditional model with no direct substitute (tossing) is one radical option a few companies have chosen. Replacing the traditional performance review with a completely different process (substituting) is the fourth and final strategy.

The purpose of Part II is to put in context previous attempts to improve the performance management process. It will help the reader better understand why a new, more effective model is needed. It will also help lay the philosophical foundation for the Catalytic Coaching Model that will be set forth in Part III.

Chapter 5

Evolutionary Change Strategies: One Step at a Time

It is errant to imagine that evolution signifies a constant tendency to increased perfection. That process undoubtedly involves a constant remodeling of the organism in adopting to new conditions; but it depends on the nature of those conditions whether the direction of the modifications effected shall be upward or downward.

—T. H. Huxley, *The Struggle for Existence in Human Society* (1888)

When companies attempt to improve a traditional performance management system without eliminating the practices that define the prevailing paradigm, they can be described as adopting an evolutionary change strategy. Operationally defined, an evolutionary change is one that attempts to improve a system while retaining the practice of grading individual performance and tying evaluation results directly to salary administration. This chapter will review two types of evolutionary change tactics: tweaking and supplementing. We will start our discussion with a review of the most commonly adopted fix: tweaking.

EVOLUTIONARY CHANGE STRATEGY #1: TWEAKING

Organizations that make minor adjustments to a traditional performance management system in an effort to improve its performance are engaged in what might be called "tweaking." This strategy could also be described as "fine tuning" or "adjusting." Using a tweaking strategy implies that an organization feels that the performance management system itself is worthwhile, but might be improved with minor changes. Tweaking involves *operating within the existing paradigm* to bring progress from small changes. Changes that involve more significant or substantive modifications are not considered tweaking. These will be discussed later in this and the subsequent chapter.

Of the four change strategies, tweaking is the least confrontational and least controversial. Possibly for these reasons, it is the most popular. Tweaking is frequently initiated due to negative feedback from either employees or managers. Sometimes a senior executive simply senses that the system is ineffective and requests change. Quite commonly tweaking will be conducted with Human Resources leading an ad hoc team of concerned employees through an upgrade exercise. This practice assures participation from the rank and file and helps promote acceptance once changes are determined.

Because they almost always operate within the framework of the existing paradigm, these groups normally conclude with some kind of revitalization program in tow. Recommendations typically involve making adjustments to the forms that are used or the manner in which the information is gathered or processed. More specifically, they usually involve modifying assessment items, changing scales and labels, and enhancing procedures for completing forms.

MODIFYING ASSESSMENT ITEMS

A common form of tweaking involves the number or type of the items used to evaluate performance. These changes are typically prompted by a perceived disconnect between the behaviors or attributes on which performance is assessed versus those which are perceived to be important to driving business success. As companies go through cultural change and implement different types of initiatives this misalignment can become more obvious.

Most culture change initiatives emphasize the importance of the way work is done (process). This can cause problems in systems that put the primary emphasis of the evaluation on what gets done (results). Companies that make priorities out of teaming practices or quality principles often feel uncomfortable not including items in the annual review cycle that ask for an evaluation of work process.

Using the theory that what gets measured gets done, they seek to influence behavior by including items that emphasize things like health and safety awareness or even honesty and ethical business behavior. They promote cultural change initiatives directly by requiring people to be rated on how well they accept feedback, seek divergent views and embrace change.

The underlying assumption here is that people are dissatisfied with traditional performance management systems because we are not measuring the right thing. Change what we measure and the system will be more effective and better received.

Most tweaking initiatives involve adding categories to rate people on. For example, an oil services company put together an all-star ad hoc team to upgrade its evaluation system. Following several weeks of work, they came forward with a new form for assessing performance that they felt took them a big step forward. They went from asking five basic questions about annual contribution to asking a combined total of 32. Eight questions were listed as pertaining to "Role," fifteen were listed under "Working Together," and ten were grouped under what they called "Actions."

"Role" items retained the individual impact perspective that was closest to the original form. It looked at the quality of individual contribution, delivery of results, personal initiative, etc. The fifteen "Working Together" questions concentrated on issues like *willingness to collaborate with others, sharing information*, and *ability to keep a secret*. It also included questions about *safety, health* and *environmental stewardship*. Finally, the "Actions" section included questions on *communicating openly, receiving constructive criticism* and *maintaining high moral and ethical standards*. The 32nd question called for an *overall assessment of the individual's commitment to the company's principles and impact on business results*. Each item was to be scored on a scale of one to five, with an option to not participate if the item did not apply.

Those familiar with the discipline of instrument development and the science of testing might have many questions for those that designed a form like this. For instance, is each item of equal importance? Does the fact that there are six questions under "Role" mean that individual contribution is less than half as important as "Working Together," which has fifteen? And why are health and safety listed under "Working Together" while moral and ethical behavior are listed under "Actions"? Why is there an item about achieving business results under "Actions," when it would seem to fit more appropriately under the "Role" category with other items about individual achievement?

The answers to these questions are not important for our purposes. Despite the fact that the assessment tool would not have held up well to informed analytical scrutiny, those that developed these forms were well-intentioned, high-performing customers of the process. They were just trying to make the act of assessment better match what they perceived to be reality. Besides, no one really looked at the 31 individual items anyway. All that really got used was the answer to item number 32 (the overall rating), and that hadn't been substantively changed from the original form that the group had modernized and replaced. The essence of the traditional paradigm was left intact.

CHANGING SCALES AND LABELS

In addition to modifying the performance items that are assessed, another common form of tweaking involves changing performance descriptors and scales. While the trend seems to be to increase the number of items being assessed, many companies have taken the exact opposite tact when it comes to the categories to grade them. The general trend seems to be to reduce the number of categories to describe behavior. Usually this involves converting to three big buckets ("Meets Expectations," "Exceeds Expectations," or "Does Not Meet Expectations") rather than what had traditionally been five-, seven-or ten-item scales. The justification for category reduction most typically used is that it is hard (and very subjective) to distinguish shades of gray.

For every trend there are exceptions, however. Those who have used the "three bucket" approach for a number of years sometimes get the opposite kind of feedback from process customers. They are led to believe that one of the major sources of dissatisfaction in their systems is the failure to provide enough room for differentiating performance. They may respond by moving their system by going in the opposite direction. They change their scales from three grades back to five or seven or nine items. Since neither state truly resolves the problem, those residing in either camp eventually eye the other as a possible improvement.

In addition to problems with the number of categories for grading performance, there are problems with the actual grades themselves. Often people attach negative feelings to the performance labels that are assigned to them. Employees in companies that use words or phrases for descriptors frequently develop disdain for the labels themselves. The majority, relegated to the middle of the pack, often develop the greatest frustration. Being called "Effective" or "Meets Expectations" or any other version of "average" does not reconcile well with their desire to see themselves as winners.

One solution commonly used is to convert verbal performance descriptors to numbers or letters. Numbers seem to be the most common, but they are used in many different ways. In some companies, a high number is good. In others it is bad. Many seem to use a four-point scale (like in college), but some use decimals and others do not. Some also invert the grading scale so as to break the association with academe (i.e., 1 is best and 4 is worst).

A senior group of engineers and technical experts, after meeting on their own initiative part-time for the better part of three months, tried to address problems they perceived with the performance evaluation system. At the conclusion, they formally submitted a 30-page proposal to their HR Director recommending their idea for change. They suggested that the company alter the current grading system by converting grades from one to three decimal places. In that system a 4.0 was considered the top score, followed by a 3.5, 3.0 and so on, down to 2.0 at the practical bottom (1.0s were usually terminated before review time).

The scientists were very upset about the existing system and felt that by changing the scale in that manner it would lend an air of sophistication to the process. They conjectured that the additional decimal points would resolve some of the frustrations about perceived arbitrariness and subjectivity that people were feeling. It might also better demonstrate incremental progress from year to year. For example, a person receiving a 3.438 one year might improve to a 3.614 the next and this might give her a sense of progress. In the current system these numbers would probably be rounded off to 3.5 in each year.

The HR Director, sensing that this change might only exacerbate the issue, declined to make the recommended change. The illusion of objectivity would probably not pass muster. She feared people might begin fighting for every single rating on the form. As it was, the few employees who currently argued did so most frequently over only the one key (overall) rating. And since they were not changing the number of individuals that could be allowed into any given performance category (only 10% 4.0s, 20% 3.5s, etc.) the numbers would still ultimately have to be rounded off based on a forced distribution for the purposes of salary administration. The proposed change would not have dealt with the real problems created by the system.

ENHANCING PROCEDURES

The third type of tweaking that we will explore has to do with changing procedures for form completion. Tweaking procedures typically involves three types of modifications: who is completing forms, the manner in which forms are submitted or processed and the way grades are ultimately determined.

Changing Who Completes the Forms

One of the most popular forms of tweaking that has surfaced in recent years is commonly referred to as "peer review." Peer review typically involves getting evaluative information from others besides just the direct supervisor of the employee. In its strictest interpretation, peer review involves getting data from an employee's colleagues at her same grade level. In actual practice, however, companies sometimes include input from multiple customers (sometimes even external) in what they call peer reviews.

The use of peer review is intended to recognize the complexity of modern work environment and reinforce the notion that pleasing just one person is no longer a sufficient method of operating. Peer reviews help reduce the perception that grades are determined only by one person, but they can also serve to dilute critical feedback that is coming from a boss.

Modifying the Method of Gathering and Processing Data

Increasing the number of raters puts tremendous pressure on what is normally an already taxed infrastructure of data collection and processing. Implementing peer review, for example, can increase the number of forms that must be completed for the annual review process by six to ten times. When design features like this are modified, companies are often compelled to introduce computer systems that make keeping collecting and transmitting this information more organized. Even without going to a multi-rater format, most companies that attempt to modernize their systems these days try to include some form of automation in the package. While this does not typically change *what* is done, it changes the dynamics of *how* it is done substantially. In some cases this can result in timesaving and efficiency. In others it can result in at least temporary frustration and inefficiency.

A mining company upgraded a performance management system so that raters could give all their input online. Unfortunately, it proved to be a tremendous inconvenience for many of the highest level individuals who had to spend time completing the forms. Most executives of the company had previously done most of their form completion while traveling. They used a diskette that walked them through a series of 110 questions and the associated comments. When they were done, they shipped the diskette off to the central HR department, which compiled it and loaded it all in a master program.

Because of the new system, they could no longer complete evaluations while traveling. It was, of course, impossible (or at least unrealistically expensive) to attempt any kind of connection via modem while on a plane. Compounding the problem was the fact that those who completed the forms in outlying offices, scattered around the world, had to stay online for an average of over an hour to do even meager justice to the evaluation. This proved to be very expensive for those getting online from hotel rooms in Asia and countries with weak infrastructure.

To make matters worse, there was no easy way to save an evaluation that was halfway completed. Since it was also quite common for those connecting via modem to get knocked off inadvertently, losing all input that had been submitted to date, the executives quickly tired of this enhancement. As a result, many ended up printing out multiple copies of the evaluation form and penciling in their data. Then they turned this over to their secretaries who had to resubmit it using the executive's online account.

Even when technological changes provide actual efficiencies, they do not change the essence of an evaluation system. It is important to remember that this form of tweaking, at its best, is invisible to the main objective of the process.

Changing the Way Grades Are Determined

The final procedural tweaking that we will discuss involves modifying how overall ratings are determined. Companies sometimes see this as a way to improve an unpopular or ineffective appraisal process.

We have already reviewed the decision on whether to force a distribution of grades to meet a bell-shaped curve. Whether this is done through competitive rating or full-blown rating process, the effect is the same. The key becomes where to draw the imaginary line between individuals and groups and how flexible are you in making that determination.

A certain HR organization recently engaged in serious effort in the task of upgrading their evaluation process. People were disturbed about the "cliffs" that seemed to exist between those rated in each of five performance groupings. Drawing the line between an "Outstanding" contributor and one who "Exceeds Expectations" exactly at the 90th percentile was not perceived as equitable. In some cases a more natural split between levels of contribution seemed either slightly one way or the other.

Despite the expert's recommendation, the COO decided on the only solution that made sense to him. Develop a salary system in which every single increment on the continuum had an impact on career and salary. Use the ranking system already in place to its fullest extent. Get rid of the cliffs and make it continuous. A 93rd percentile would be better than a 92nd. A 62nd would be better than a 61st. Indeed, the change did eliminate the problem with cliffs. Unfortunately, it only amplified the amount of internal competition that was taking place and made gamesmanship and individual positioning the undisputed way to succeed.

Other forms of adjustment include changing the weighting of individual items that are being evaluated—creating a form of algorithm for determining the overall grade. This amounts to following the example set forth by the science/engineering group referred to earlier, without resorting to three decimal points of accuracy.

Another technique is to experiment with the mechanics of how overall ratings are assigned. A typical enhancement is to have a team of managers listen to presentations on each subordinate and then validate a boss' recommendation. Since the method of determining consensus can affect the ultimate outcome and modify a supervisor's suggested rating, changes in those procedures must be approached very sensitively.

IMPACT OF TWEAKING

After all is said and done, tweaking can be shown to have both positive and negative impact on employee perceptions of the performance management process. Because it fails to address the fundamental nature of the prevailing paradigm, however, tweaking tends to have little actual impact on the accomplishment of key business objectives.

Aside from minor enhancements in procedures, tweaking can generate a positive response in two major ways. First, if a cross-functional team is involved in suggesting the changes and helping implement them, it can lead to more employee buy-in. Even if the changes leave the paradigm intact and result in no net positive impact on the business, the fact that they were permitted to try to make improvements will normally count for something.

The second potential benefit would come from a perception by employees that the company is at least trying to "walk the talk." By attempting to listen to complaints and address them, they are modeling behavior they normally ask others to follow. Admitting that this critical process may not be perfect also affords them some credibility. It demonstrates a commitment to the notion of continuous improvement.

On the negative side, are two major issues—the amount of time and energy it takes to develop a plan of change and the disillusionment that inevitably comes from realizing that tweaking does not and cannot ultimately resolve underlying problems with the traditional system.

The process of tweaking can consume substantial resources. Unless an outside firm is used, the wasted resources are mostly time. It can take a good deal of time and energy to develop even the most modest suggestions for changing a performance management system. Coming to consensus with a large, disparate group on a subject of such subjectivity is not achievable overnight. This is made much worse when groups are improperly chartered or boundary conditions are not made clear from the start. If they don't know which changes are out of bounds, there will be inevitable clashes and wasted energies.

Even when boundary conditions are made clear from the onset, any group trying to address improvement of a performance management system is bound to have at least one member who wishes to challenge the assumptions. Groups that flounder or come up with suggestions that cannot be implemented can impact attitudes of all employees negatively. No one likes to work on a solution that cannot ultimately be put into practice.

The biggest problem with tweaking, however, is that eventually the same problems that existed before will resurface. As long as the system continues to include the practices that define the traditional paradigm, these problems are inescapable and inevitable. Following an initial surge of positive energy and optimism, within a minimum of two salary cycles, people will begin to sense the same and potentially some new problems. Without changing the paradigm, the same underlying issues remain. The system does not really produce behavioral change. It does not promote teamwork. It does not motivate employees to work harder, etc.

It is easy for disillusionment to set in after people realize that nothing has really changed. They are still being graded and labeled and forced to compete against each other. Most disheartening, especially for the brave team that struggled to make improvements while operating within narrow parameters, it appears impossible for the system to be any other way.

EVOLUTIONARY CHANGE STRATEGY #2: SUPPLEMENTING

"Supplementing" will be our way to describe attempts to improve an existing performance management system by adding new practices without making any fundamental changes in design. While tweaking attempts to modify and improve what is currently being done (by changing who has input on ratings, grading labels and scales, etc.), supplementing introduces new features or tools that might give extra insight or impact. Rather than change an existing process, supplementing adds an ingredient.

Supplementing is not normally as systemic in conception or intent as tweaking. Supplementing normally occurs when someone in the organization, usually in Human Resources or executive management, feels that new features should be added to the existing performance management system. A team is less frequently used to validate this need or facilitate implementation.

There are two major supplements that have received widespread attention in recent years. The first has to do with what are commonly called "competencies" (or "core competencies" in some settings). The second has to do with the practice of 360° Feedback. They are considered supplements because they each deal with giving performance feedback but are typically introduced on top of existing systems. Some attempt to use these initiatives as replacement strategies over time, but in most cases they remain add-ons to the traditional system potentially indefinitely. In the discussion below, we will define each approach, give typical examples of how they are used and discuss the pros and cons of each approach separately.

COMPETENCIES

The 1995 William and Mercer survey indicated that more than 60% of all companies conducting performance evaluations now include the assessment of competencies.[1] For many this has been a recent addition (or supplement) to the traditional practice of judging annual contribution.

"Competencies" are normally defined as skills, capabilities or behaviors that are valued by a corporation for people in certain jobs. Since not all jobs require the same competencies, organizations sometimes elect to define a set of skills that apply to each general type of job. Frequently managerial and supervisory jobs are assigned different competencies than professional jobs, and those are different than administrative support jobs or wage jobs, etc. Some companies go so far as to break these down even further by specific craft or area of expertise.

"Core competencies" are those competencies that a company feels should apply to everyone that works there. These help define the culture and are seen as related to successful implementation of the strategy the company takes to the market.

For example, in most companies managers and supervisors might be expected to have competency in delegation and employee motivation, while those without people reporting to them are not. A salesperson might be expected to have intimate knowledge of the market for his specific products. But everyone should have "core competencies" such as achieving results, acting with honesty and integrity, and operating safely.

Lists of competencies can be long and the process to develop them tedious. Some companies may select more than 100 competencies it expects various employees to develop and cultivate. They normally do this by taking a larger generic list of possible competencies and selecting those that fit the company and its business needs. Frequently this is done with the help of consultants or a specially trained internal resource.

Often an internal group of employees is used to select the competencies and fine-tune the way they are worded. Without effective facilitation, this process can take weeks and months to complete with significant energy invested in subtle changes in words and phrases. Oddly enough, once the final list has been determined and precise wording has been accepted by all, the list of chosen competencies frequently appears very generic. It could easily apply to many other companies across all kinds of industries.

Competencies in Action

A major airline added assessment of competencies to their evaluation process a few years back. They kept the basic structure of the appraisal intact but chose to supplement it with a review of 36 core competencies for all individuals and 13 more for managers and supervisors. The supplemental book used to complete the annual competency assessment for each covered employee is 22 pages long. The annual review sheet was modified somewhat to accommodate the highlights from this exercise. The original five pages of evaluation remains, however, and the overall rating that dominated the activity stayed essentially unchanged.

A Canadian-based automotive company introduced a set of 30 competencies to help employees understand more precisely what they meant by three of the four areas that they included in their annual performance evaluation. They included ten competencies each on what they call *technical expertise, leadership and teamwork skills*, and *business skills*. Interestingly, they made the use of this four-page form optional and chose not to attempt to generate competencies for one other key area of the evaluation: *attitude*. They also elected to have both employees and managers appraise competencies on a five-point scale. On the formal appraisal form itself (that is tied to salary administration) managers are asked to utilize a three-point scale. Employees are only invited to make comments in reaction to their managers' evaluation.

THE 360° FEEDBACK PROCESS

While the addition of competencies to the assessment repertoire has received much fanfare and attention, it pales in comparison to the hoopla created by the introduction of the 360° Feedback Process. At their root, however, they are really just variations on the same theme.

The 360° Feedback Process can be easily interpreted as a logical extension of competency assessment. After determining the 30 to 130 behavioral descriptors (competencies) a company feels its people should embody, it merely introduces a discipline with which to gather and process that data.

The defining element with regard to 360° Feedback is where evaluation data comes from. In a conventional assessment it is almost always from the boss down to the employee. In a 360° Feedback Process data comes from all angles: up down and sideways. The 360° Feedback Process includes data gathered from peers and direct reports along with both the boss and employee's opinion. It offers an opportunity to see contribution measured from a variety of different perspectives. For some, it can be an intimidating experience; for others an epiphany.

By submitting to a comprehensive inspection from direct reports, peers and a boss, people open themselves to hearing things that for long years have gone unsaid. When facilitated effectively, they can utilize these new insights to address areas for improvement that have the potential to help them make performance breakthroughs.

The 360° Feedback Process in Action

A Hong Kong–based consumer goods company uses a 360° Feedback Process to provide information about both individual and group competency. They view it as a way to increase "objectivity" and "accuracy" of an assessment (by including more and different raters). They use it to promote self-awareness and enable people to benchmark themselves against others in the company and in other industries. They introduced it as a developmental tool without a direct connection to pay, and although they originally implied they were going to make a direct link, they have not yet felt comfortable in doing so. Their data suggests that only 6% of the companies in Hong Kong have tied 360° results to pay.

That same experience seems to be true here in the states. Most companies are slow to convert their 360° systems from a focus on development to impacting pay. The primary reason is that they are nervous that tying pay and promotability directly to the survey instrument will change the quality of the feedback provided. In other words, people may be more reluctant to say what they truly feel if they think that it might impact their boss or colleague so directly. Some companies can be seen sending a very curious mixed message about the importance of culture change. They threaten to tie 360° survey results more directly to salary administration if managers don't take seriously the command to become more sensitive and caring.

Why Has the 360° Feedback Process Been So Popular?

The 360° Feedback Process has been warmly embraced by many companies that began using it in the late 1980s and early 1990s. Perhaps its greatest advocates have been those at the top of the organizations. Many CEOs and senior executives cite this process as the most valuable learning tool they've experienced since achieving officer status. For some it is a literal revelation. Some senior executives are so moved by what the 360° process did for them that they instruct the HR department to mandate participation by all their direct reports and then cascade this experience all the way down the company. Some are willing to spend hundreds of thousands of dollars to do it.

Where Does 360° Feedback Fall Short?

Because of its widespread application, popularity with senior management and idealistic conceptual foundation, finding negative things to say about the 360° Feedback Process is controversial. Nonetheless, as a supplemental strategy to enhance a performance management process it has at least two major problems. These are inefficiency and complexity.

To say that the 360° Feedback Process is time consuming would be a massive understatement. For example, a typical manager will have, let's say eight direct reports, one supervisor and six peers complete feedback forms on her, plus she must complete one on herself. Forms usually run between 50 and 150 questions with additional space to write in comments. Since most administrators emphasize the importance of the written comments, completing a 360° Feedback form is much more time consuming than just checking off a bunch of boxes.

Normal time to time to complete a form will range from 45 minutes to two hours per individual. For the sake of argument, let's assume that one hour is average. At this rate, each survey requires roughly sixteen hours of input. Add to this a two-hour orientation meeting, three-hour initial counseling session with a trained consultant, one-hour clarification/debriefing sessions with direct report groups and the boss (and possibly peers), a 90-minute follow-up session with the consultant and ongoing stewardship meetings with the boss.

In total, a rough estimate of thirteen hours for the participant directly and between 30 and 60 hours for his evaluators would probably be considered par. Multiply that number by the total population undergoing the 360° process and you will begin to see what a substantial investment in time and money this process represents. When blanketed across a large organization with direction to repeat the process annually, the numbers can be huge.

Second efficiency problem: turnaround time. Most 360° systems take several weeks, if not months, to complete the feedback cycle. A week or two is allocated for distribution and completion of the forms. Then they must be sent somewhere for scoring. The information is consolidated and presented to a facilitator for review. An initial meeting is scheduled with the participant. Sometimes there is a second meeting a few days or weeks later in which an action plan is produced. Usually at this time the participant has her first meeting with her input donors to review with them what she has learned and what she plans to do about it.

One problem with the delay is that most informants have forgotten what they have said on the feedback tool by the time they sit down to get their recap on the message received. "Did I or didn't I make a comment about his ineffective delegation skills?" or "How did I rate him on communication skills?" are typical questions. Even if they kept a copy of the completed seven- to ten-page survey instrument, many have would take the time to pull it out to make those comparisons.

If the informants have filled out forms on more than just one person, the confusion can be even greater. When you add the complexity of hectic schedules to the complexity built into the 360° Feedback data collection process, sessions that occur three months after the forms are completed are quite common. At that point, who knows how working relationships may have changed?

The third efficiency challenge is very basic. Direct out-of-pocket cost. No one gives away the forms or form processing. Fees range from $50 to $200 per survey. Custom tailoring of forms can add significantly to the initial cost.

An international manufacturing company paid a consulting firm more than half a million dollars and jetted around an internal international team for almost a year to tailor a set of 77 assessment items specifically to suit the company. The horrible irony was that because they made even slight variations in the standard form, they lost the ability to benchmark their scores against those of other companies that had answered the standard questions. It would take years and tens of thousands of dollars in additional consulting fees to determine what their unique scores meant on a relative basis. Even more ironic was the fact that the executives who authorized this extravagance did so because of the incredible insight they felt they received from using the *generic* version of the forms that the HR staff felt compelled to customize.

Once the questionnaire instrument or process has been established, the biggest ongoing expense is time with trained 360° consultants. They are expensive to rent and expensive to have on staff. The market rate on credible external experts with credentials ranges from $500 to $3,500 a day. A hard-working consultant can maybe do six private sessions a day.

But wait, there's more. Perhaps the biggest problem with the 360° process has nothing to do with efficiency or cost. It has to do with its impact on the interaction between manager and direct reports. At the highest levels this is typically the only form of feedback one will receive. Remember, power players avoid conventional evaluation forms. Once they discover the 360° Feedback Process, they often consider this an appropriate substitute. They force this on their Vice Presidents once a year and consider this their primary donation to the coaching process.

But if the boss thinks he or she is sending a clear and unambiguous perform-ance message via the 360° format, that is seldom the experience on the other side. The boss answers a series of a hundred questions and hopes that the general themes will emerge. Granted, a good facilitator helps in this process immeas-urably, but improvement feedback from the boss is often indistinct. By nature of the process, it is blurred in with messages from peers and direct reports. If there is one perspective that demands to be very clear, it should that be from the boss.

Learning the Hard Way

Jerry was the Vice President of Marketing for an international manufacturing corporation. Based on feedback obtained in his first 360° Feedback Process, he developed the following competencies to concentrate on for improvement:

• Knowing the business
• Acquire a more global perspective
• Develop key personnel

This list was determined by input from all levels. There was nothing very alarming or revolutionary about it. It all made sense to Jerry, given his time and tenure with the company and his role as a partner on the strategic business team.

The Ph.D. who functioned as his 360° facilitator helped him develop an action plan that his boss accepted without challenge. It was built around the afore-mentioned basic insights and challenges. It contained seven major action items that were designed to help him make progress in the three key areas.

Four months following a second stewardship session of his 360° Action Plan, Jerry was terminated for a long-standing issue that was never mentioned on this form (or in subsequent meetings for that matter). It seems his boss felt strongly that there was a serious "misalignment" problem. Jerry had ideas and said things that were not always in agreement with the boss, and because of his level in the organization, this was a problem. Because he had long-term aspirations to do other things, the boss felt it more practical to hasten Jerry's "opportunity to pursue other interests" than to try to "align" him. They gave him a package and cut him loose.

This example raises some interesting questions. Wouldn't it have been nice for a key issue like this to have surfaced on Jerry's 360° survey? If it was important enough to ultimately cost him his job, how could it have been missed completely in two iterations of such a comprehensive process? Perhaps the survey did not ask the right questions. As a matter of fact, there was no single question on the form that specifically addressed the subject of alignment or misalignment. Perhaps the most compelling issues were lost in the shuffle with other, less important ones. Whatever happened, the system failed.

A similar experience occurred with two other colleagues who were going through the 360° process for the first time. The first was a company President (Jill) who had to visit her HR VP (Mary) on the day before her 360° consultant was to return for session two. She was supposed to have an action plan ready to present to her consultant. Jill entered Mary's office in a state of agitated confusion.

"Mary," she said as she dropped a three-inch pile of mixed up papers on her desk, "I am so confused. I have all this data and am not sure what the heck to do with it. I have to have an action plan by tomorrow and all I get out of this stuff is a headache.'" Mary spent the next two hours helping Jill synthesize the data into themes so she could put forward a plan.

Later that day, the chief operating officer came to see Mary for a repeat performance. Despite all the time and attention invested by the company, consultant and everyone else to date, both senior executives were still lost in the woods. Thousands of trees but no forest in sight.

The True Value of 360° Feedback

Even though there are some serious concerns about the manner in which the 360° process is frequently used, it can still be an invaluable tool that should be included in every large organization's toolbox. Unfortunately, however, the old expression about the hammer holds true here. I believe it goes something like this: "When the only tool you have is a hammer, all your problems begin to look like nails." In short, it is clear that many have overused the 360° tool and applied it to areas where it is not the best method to gather or explain data.

The true value of the 360° process is in providing a much-needed perspective on what we are doing to those who work for and with us. It is a protected mechanism that allows our direct reports and peers to provide us with feedback on how we work with them. It reminds us that in pleasing the boss, by being extremely task oriented and getting things done, we can do damage to others or be a less-than-desirable leader and/or teammate.

This is where the big revelations typically come at the highest level. The great taskmasters find that their "command and control" management style gets the job done, but at the expense of the relationships with those below and beside them. Few emperors are ever advised that they lack clothing. The 360° process, when done properly, allows this humble message of imperfection to be sent upward. For those at the top who would not want to consciously step on or over anyone, this can help create revelation. It can produce dramatic insight that leads to focused efforts to change and improve.

Based on these observations, we would argue that the 360° Feedback tool is not effective as a primary mechanism for delivering downward feedback. Supplementary, yes, but not primary. A boss doesn't need protection to tell a direct report her flaws. The complexities of the 360° data-gathering methodology are an unnecessary burden. As explained above, the message from a boss is frequently muddled or lost in the shuffle with 360° Feedback. Very simply, there are easier, more effective and more efficient ways to provide downward feedback and coaching. One specific method for accomplishing this objective is the subject of this book. It will be outlined in detail in Part III.

IMPACT OF STRATEGY #2 CHANGES

In a nutshell, supplementing whether through the addition of competency assessment or a full-blown 360° Feedback Process can provide valuable new insights. These can help people change and serve to identify development needs that run across the organization.

The flip side is that these initiatives can be used inefficiently. They can cost lots of time and money to develop and even more to administer in perpetuity. They can also lose their impact over time as feedback becomes redundant. Perhaps most importantly, however, by the very nature of their "add-on" status, supplemental strategies can be rendered ineffective. Who pays attention to a 40-item report when a one-item summary tells them everything they need to know? As long as the traditional model is in force and money is attached to the completion of a standard evaluation form, these supplements will continue to receive only secondary attention.

Breaking from the traditional model is the subject of the next chapter, which covers what we call revolutionary change strategies.

Chapter 6

Revolutionary Change Strategies: Taking Giant Steps

Revolutions are not made; they come. A revolution is as natural a growth as an oak. It comes out of the past. Its foundations are laid far back.[1]
— Wendell Phillips, speech in Boston (1852)

As stated in the introduction to Part II, there are two types of strategies companies have adopted in attempting to improve their performance management systems that are more revolutionary in nature. These strategies involve either abandoning the performance review entirely (tossing) or making fundamental changes in the paradigm (substituting). This chapter will explore some of the ways companies have introduced these more drastic changes and will explore both the pluses and minuses typically associated with each approach.

CHANGE STRATEGY #3: TOSSING

Tossing means simply to stop doing performance reviews. Companies engaged in tossing quit asking managers and supervisors to fill out forms evaluating people on their performance. They come up with another way of determining how much of an increase or bonus to pay to people. They may encourage people to talk about how to improve contributions but impose no centrally controlled or monitored methodology for doing so.

Companies that abandon a formal evaluation process normally do so out of complete frustration. Often it is after several iterations of tweaking or supplementing an existing system in an attempt to get it to be more efficient and effective. When they come to the ultimate realization that the system is not capable of being made acceptable through evolutionary change tactics, they resort to the ultimate form of revolution. They toss out their old system with no clear replacement.

Those who take this drastic step are normally following the advice of quality theorists like W. Edwards Deming or Peter Scholtes who were the earliest advocates of revolution. To paraphrase the Deming quote cited in the preface, doing nothing is better than doing something that has a net negative impact. Tossing an ineffective and inefficient system that people dislike can be seen as an improvement by itself.

Using similar logic, Fred Nickols encourages companies to "scrap" their performance appraisal systems instead of trying to redesign them:

> If you're a change-minded senior executive looking for ways to improve performance, cut costs, or free up resources that can be redirected against important issues waiting in the wings, you might give serious thought to scrapping your company's performance appraisal system. It devours staggering amounts of time and energy, it depresses and demotivates people, it destroys trust and teamwork and, adding insult to injury, it delivers little demonstrable value at great cost.[2]

While this logic is hard to dispute, most companies (especially those with large numbers of employees) usually perceive this strategy as the most bold and dangerous form of change. While it is not uncommon in small companies to go without a formal system of performance management, few large companies feel confident enough to take this step. Fear of legal exposure typically convinces them to they must do something. Nonetheless, some have tried.

Tossing in Action

Examples of companies tossing out their performance management systems follow a predictable plot line. Someone at the top of an organization finally tires of trying to patch a traditional system. They get fed up with the inevitable ineffectiveness and inefficiency. They aren't shown any alternate systems that look better to them, so they just quit doing the one they don't like. They go cold turkey. They wait for signs of chaos and confusion or at least for someone to scream.

Case in point. A division of a major American auto manufacturer got so fed up with its annual review process that they finally abolished it. The task force assigned to fix it discovered so many problems in the way the program was being administered that it felt the task was impossible. In addition to all the bias and error they uncovered, they determined that the process wasn't actually changing employee behavior anyway. Hence, they did not feel their decision to do away with the practice would have any affect on company productivity.

Case 2. A manufacturer of packaging materials became so disgruntled with their entire set of company policies and procedures that they held a rally in the parking lot. Employees built a bonfire and were allowed to burn all of the personnel manuals. While they revised and modernized some of their personnel practices, no one attempted to resurrect the performance management system. As Gina Imperato described it: "The company's well-established approach to reviews literally went up in smoke."[3]

IMPACT OF STRATEGY #3 CHANGES

There are at least three kinds of positive impact that come from a tossing strategy. There are at least as many negative impacts, however.

First, perhaps the most obvious positive is the inevitable reduction in bureaucracy and paperwork. Depending on the system that is being tossed, this can be substantial. Whatever papers are completed informally in a free-for-all condition pale in comparison to those required by the traditional paper-intensive evaluation machine.

Second, also significantly positive, is the reduction of internal competition and gamesmanship. Political positioning that goes hand in hand with the rating and ranking process is no longer consciously or unconsciously encouraged. Assuming there has been no substitution of a new system for dividing up booty, people may be encouraged to work more cooperatively together and optimize performance for the good of the organization.

Third, an unexpected positive, in some cases there might be a reduction in legal exposure. As we've discussed previously, quite frequently a company's own performance review forms from a conventional system work against it in confrontational situations with employees. In this case there will be no required formal record that might work against a company in the event of a discrimination charge or lawsuit.

On the negative side, perhaps the biggest challenge is that many employees may soon begin to wonder where they stand. While some may assume the absence of negative feedback to be positive, this may not always be the case. Others, even your highest achievers, may miss the benchmark insuring them that their performance is at or above par. While most consider the traditional ritual both boring and painful, the majority probably also think of it as a necessity.

That brings us quickly to the second negative: quality control. Some may get better feedback under a totally informal system—fabulous coaching, in fact. But others will get absolutely nothing. And there will be no systematic way to tell who is getting what. In a system that has tossed all aspects of formality, supervisors are operating on their own recognizance. It is a laissez-faire style of management on steroids. Exit interviews may soon become your quickest source of data on the quality of management/employee interaction.

A third problem created by the tossing of the formal performance management process was listed previously as a potential advantage. Legal exposure can work both ways in this situation. By giving up all semblance of control over formal dialogue concerning performance, an organization is rolling the dice. Time will tell whether the lack of forms with damaging information prevents more lawsuits and grievances than the lack of any kind of formal structure creates.

CHANGE STRATEGY #4: SUBSTITUTING

Substituting is a revolutionary change strategy that recognizes that some formal mechanism is needed for performance management, albeit one that is fundamentally different from the traditional paradigm. To be classified as a substituting strategy (and not just supplementing or tweaking) a change initiative must do more than add new features or change from one kind of evaluation-based system to another. Our definition of substituting requires that the paradigm of the traditional performance review must be fundamentally altered. The new process must eliminate all three defining elements of the traditional paradigm:

- Rating: the assignment of competitive grades or labels
- Ranking: comparing relative performance of employees against one another
- Direct links between the performance review and salary administration

Before we talk about companies that would qualify as having practiced a full substitution strategy, let's quickly discuss the many more that have come part of the way.

Partial Revolution

Partial paradigm shifts are not uncommon, but they don't count for our discussion here. Several companies have taken a half step beyond evolution to discontinue the practice of ranking employees. Even in large companies where this kind of practice once was very common, fewer and fewer companies adhere to the strict definition of this practice any more. Whether because of the time it takes to conduct the process or the inevitable conflicts with teaming and quality, many have begun the transition away from ritual. Of the three key components that define the traditional paradigm, ranking is the easiest to abandon and the first to fall victim to paradigm experimentation.

The next step in a partial paradigm shift is typically to drop the practice of rating, or at least using an Overall grade. Sometimes companies simply quit reporting the rating to employees but still supply one to the compensation manager. This practice can help a company advance but can just as often create a setback. Supervisors must grapple with the notion of whether to violate the system and secretly convey the invisible grade to their better performers. Nonetheless, those trying to practice "evolutionary" revolution often cannot bring themselves to make a complete transformation in one iteration. It may take a couple of review cycles for them to go all the way toward abandoning the use of ratings.

The biggest step in revolutionary change comes when a company commits to finding an alternative to the "pay for performance" strategy that almost all clung to at one point in their history. Sometimes companies are able to make the leap with one jump, but often they must ease through revolution in steps. Typically, elimination of the secret rating (label or number) is the last to go. While it is possible that companies could still rate or rank while overtly breaking the link to salary administration, it does not appear to be very common. Those that have come this far seem to have a more holistic view of the process and have made a more complete transition out of the prevailing paradigm.

FULL-SCALE SUBSTITUTION IN ACTION

Perhaps the only meaningful way to talk about the strategy of substitution is through the use of examples. There are many different possible approaches that can be attempted in replacing a traditional performance management system. We will discuss three examples of companies that have set off on their own path, each using a slightly different model on which to move boldly forward through uncharted territory.

Minimizing Bureaucracy

A medical center in Colorado has received a good deal of attention for the revolutionary tack they took to change their traditional performance management system. In 1990 they tossed their system without knowing what, if anything, would replace it. Nine years later, they are still averaging four calls a month from people wanting to hear more about their minimalist approach to performance management.

The revolution began after a team of individuals could determine no viable way to salvage the company's performance evaluation process. Hearing their dilemma, the CEO told them to forget it. If there wasn't a significantly better way to do things, he told them to just abandon the practice completely. And so they did. Almost immediately, however, the company sensed a need for some minimal structure. To accommodate this they came up with what is now referred to as "APOP." APOP stands for "annual piece of paper."

In a nutshell, here's how the process works. Each year a supervisor is required to have a structured conversation with each employee about his or her performance. Prior to the discussion the supervisor presents the employee with a list of open-ended questions for them to talk about together. Questions are directed toward the employee and request information on what the manager can do to help improve the employee's contribution and grow.

Following the discussion, a paper is signed, saying only that a conversation took place. It records the date, time, place and agenda for the meeting—nothing else. No grade is given and no direct link to compensation is attempted. The intent of the APOP system is to put emphasis on ongoing dialogue and constructive exchange of ideas. Formality and bureaucracy is reduced to an absolute minimum.

The program was originally introduced as a stopgap. Because both employees and management seem reasonably content with the system, however, they have tried to hold onto the essence of the program. Over time, however, the radical minimalism of the APOP has been somewhat modified. Features have slowly been added. There is now an employee learning plan that must be completed each year. There is also some additional paperwork that must be completed on individuals based on regulatory requirements. Nonetheless, they have stood tough with respect to the defining paradigm issues. Nine years after introduction there are still no grades or direct links to pay.

Harnessing Technology

If the medical center might be said to have taken a minimalist approach in revolutionizing their performance management system, a defense electronics company might be said to have taken just the opposite. They developed a high-tech solution that requires active involvement with the system to occur on an ongoing basis with formal reviews at least quarterly.

In order to promote continuous and ongoing discussion about progress in goal achievement, they developed a LAN-based computer system to encourage attention being focused on accomplishment of objectives. It encourages employee's to take ownership of their responsibilities by requiring them to develop their own work objectives and submit updates at least quarterly.

Managers are obligated to meet with employees at least four times a year to hear a verbal explanation of what employees report by computer. Their key responsibility is to help make sure employees have what they need to accomplish their objectives. The system does not use any kind of grading or labeling of employee performance. Employees are essentially evaluating themselves, at least in terms of goal accomplishment. There are no direct ties to salary administration in this system. Individual developmental needs are not the primary focus of the system. The predominant emphasis is on generating results for the business.

Teaming Up to Solve Problems

In 1995 a large Information Systems (IS) department within a much larger shipping company implemented a team-based management system. Because of their decision to organize using self-managed work teams, they did not feel comfortable with the conventional evaluation-based system used by their parent. They wanted a performance improvement system that put less emphasis on individual achievement and better promoted teamwork.

After achieving consensus on what defines excellent performance for its work teams, the department required each to begin meeting quarterly to review how it is doing. Every three months members of each team use a five-point scale to rate team performance on 31 criteria. Then they conduct a meeting to discuss the results of the vote and review individual performance as well. Using a variety of techniques, they solicit information on individual strengths as well as things each person needs to work on. They consider this process a form of team-based peer review.

No overall rating for individual performance is included in the team review process. They do not want to take a chance of having feedback distorted or filtered because it is linked directly to money. Pay is dealt with in a separate annual compensation review. Salary increases are influenced by a factor that weighs team performance at 75% and individual development (competencies gained) at 25%. Managerial review insures that both team and individual assessments appear equitable across the organization.

The system is still in place four years after its introduction. Segments of the parent company are investigating whether the system is transferable to them.

IMPACT OF STRATEGY #4 CHANGES

Full-scale Strategy #4 changes are relatively uncommon. Most companies that think they are boldly experimenting with a fundamentally new system retain at least some logical ties to the traditional paradigm. We have cited three examples, and there are certainly many others. Suffice to say that all are a bit unique with no dominant practice having taken hold. As one of the leaders of a Strategy #4 practice stated, "These are uncharted waters we're trying to navigate."

Because of the variety of solutions that have been attempted, the impact of Strategy #4 changes can be summarized in three definitive words: it all depends. The pluses and minuses vary based on the replacement system that is put in place. Nonetheless, if we take the three cases highlighted above as representative examples, we might conclude the following.

Most Strategy #4 changes at least try to increase the amount and quality of meaningful communication that is exchanged. Some do it through technology, others through teams. Still others attempt it through refined mechanics for dialogue. Clearly most seem to have an increase in the amount and quality of feedback as a top priority.

All systems that have broken the direct link between individual performance and salary administration seem to benefit somewhat. Some have tried to reduce internal competition and gamesmanship. The team-based system is a prime example of where words and money are being made more consistent.

The verdict on bureaucracy reduction is a true mixed bag. The medical center's Annual Piece of Paper technology started out to be a huge time-saver. Over time, however, it seems to have given back at least some of the efficiencies gained. While the time it takes to conduct quarterly peer review sessions in the IS group is substantial, they speak of this as simply "what we do." They consider it running the business and do not think of it as an add-on. Nonetheless, because some kind of annual compensation review is still conducted, it must be thought of as at least incrementally more time consuming.

The defense contractor's technology-driven system requires continuous updates and four formal reviews a year. Even with the most efficient systems interface, this would have to be perceived as a net addition of work.

On the delta side, it is hard not to imagine at least some confusion rising on the part of individuals wanting to know "where they stand" after the change in systems. The team-based approach puts so much emphasis on the whole, is it possible that the individual can get lost in the shuffle? Information Systems people are highly coveted in the market right now. Each individual wants to know something about their own future. External opportunities can lure away those who feel they are being regarded as average. Indeed, individual development issues are one of the key concerns the IS group feels they have in fine-tuning their team-based system.

The defense systems company spends countless hours reviewing goal achievement each year. Can this be at the expense of personal development of the individuals? Knowing how you are doing versus your stated goals is great, but does it motivate someone to stick around for the long haul?

Perhaps the most interesting question mark arises with laissez-faire strategy represented by the "Annual Piece of Paper" approach. Are people being given good feedback and developed here? The Annual Piece of Paper strategy sounds very romantic until you start thinking about verbal messages being misconstrued and misinterpreted. How do you know who has been told what? There is no assurance that the message that a supervisor thought she sent is the same as the employee thought she heard. At least in conventional system, something is put on paper that all can see. Having development issues clearly defined and communicated on paper allows a developmental infrastructure (all of management and the HR support systems) to work together to help someone grow.

CLEARING OUT THE FOG

Tweaking tends to makes things different, not better. Effectiveness (as defined by the systems contribution toward accomplishing business goals) is not likely to improve. Supplementing may or may not make things better, but almost always makes them more costly. Effectiveness may get a small boost, but efficiency typically suffers.

Ignoring could only be considered smart if the word if you disregard the lost potential for business impact. It's like keeping money in the bank instead of investing it in the market. You may not lose your nest egg, but it's not likely to grow very fast either.

Substituting is totally dependent on the form of substitution. If the new system is some form of experiment with only partial change in the three major components of the prevailing paradigm expect mixed results at best. If all three are dealt with and the alternative is based on a coaching or dialogue-based model, the likelihood of a positive impact on both efficiency and effectiveness is high. Change in this fashion represents a fundamental re-engineering or reinvention of the prior practice. It requires a shift in paradigm.

ON SHIFTING PARADIGMS

A recent article in MIT's *Technology Review* spoke about a new medical procedure they referred to as "welding wounds."[4] In essence, a group of high-tech surgeons have discovered a methodology for closing wounds using laser light and protein solder. Laser welding is capable of producing faster surgeries, fewer complications and quicker healing. Wounds heal over almost immediately and scars are less visible.

The technology of wound welding represents a paradigm shift. It is not an enhancement of the age-old tradition of sewing a wound shut with thread. It is a completely and totally different approach to a long-standing problem. It uses chemistry instead of mechanics to accomplish its objectives. The end result may look reasonably similar to the untrained eye, but wounds that have been welded have proven to be up to 80% stronger than those repaired with conventional sutures.

In the same way, Catalytic Coaching, which will be outlined in detail in Part III, has taken a completely different approach to the subject of performance management. It may look similar to the prevailing practice to the untrained eye, but on closer examination it will prove to be quite different both in terms of technique and impact. Measurement, the subject of our discussion in the next chapter, is the key to demonstrating those differences.

Chapter 7

Measurement:
Putting Systems to the Test

In everything there lieth measure.
—Geoffrey Chaucer, *Troylus and Cryseyde* (ca. 1375)[1]

As a business person, I am obligated to examine any and all systems in light of the value they add and the resources they consume. Tentatively, at least, performance appraisal systems don't appear to be worth what they cost.
—Fred Nickols, Executive Director, Educational Testing Service[2]

This chapter answers the question, "How bad can it be?" Anyone with a traditional performance management system who has read this far is likely to be asking this question, if not out loud than at least silently. If you concede that traditional systems are unpopular and you agree with the logical problems created by this approach (gamesmanship, sub-optimization, etc.), does that justify the effort and expense it takes to change paradigms? And if you do change, how will you know that you have truly made things better instead of just different?

Measurement is essential in determining the effectiveness and efficiency of a performance management system. This chapter will discuss a simple, practical way to measure any performance management system in order to make data-based business decisions. The information it provides will help you determine whether it makes sense to change systems. It will also help you assess the value of changes once they are made, hold the gains that come from an effective system modification and keep a system running in an optimum state.

THE CASE FOR MEASURES

Much is being written in the literature these days about the need for HR professionals to position themselves as strategic business partners. To do this effectively, Ulrich instructs that we must spend more energy emphasizing the *results we deliver* and less describing *what we do*.[3] We must communicate the value created by our various work processes. HR functions and processes should be regarded for the impact they have on the organization and the net value they add in contributing toward accomplishment of business goals. The only conceivable way to do this is through systems of measurement.

In his book *How to Measure Human Resource Management*, Jac Fitz-enz makes this point clear.

The successful HR directors know that they need to transform their department into a business partner. This requires establishing partnerships with their customers and developing the ability to track the effect of their work on the outcomes of their internal customers.[4]

Fitz-enz argues that you can, indeed, measure what we do in Human Resources. He refutes the "mythology" that this work is too subjective. As founder and leader of the Saratoga Institute, he regularly offers public seminars on the quantitative management of HR practices. This organization has done much to begin establishing a baseline of performance in dozens of critical areas. The institute publishes annually a study that provides benchmark data, broken down by industry, on everything from turnover rates to benefits and training costs.

According to Fitz-enz, the need for increased measurement in Human Resources is not debatable. The only challenge is learning how to do it. "The only real issue in applying measurement to the HR function is: What is worth measuring? Management will accept progress over perfection."[5]

There are a number of good books on the market that advise about the importance of measuring various aspects of the HR function.[6] There are several that give specific advice and formulas for evaluating the impact of individual systems and processes. For example, computing the impact of training and the value of "intellectual capital" have each become more common.

I have found virtually no resource, however, that provides a practical way to assess the effectiveness and efficiency of performance management systems. Which has been written about how to appraise people, but little is about how to appraise appraisal systems. This chapter will provide the foundation for such a system.

PRAGMATISM AND THE BOTTOM LINE

Any discussion of value in a business context must address the subject of money. Sooner or later it all comes down to a universal cost/benefit analysis.

Value is computed by determining what you are getting relative to the money being spent. Once translated to this universally accepted language, decisions can then be made based upon estimated return on investment.

Speaking in financial terms is not a common practice for most HR practitioners. As Ulrich suggests, most are more comfortable talking in terms of services or programs. They become frustrated when challenged to demonstrate the financial impact of a training workshop or benefit policy. To be sure, the connection can sometimes be difficult to approximate. Failure to try, however, often gives the impression that the HR function is a burden to the business rather than a strategic partner focused on helping grow revenue and improve market position.

I approach the challenge of assessing performance management (PM) system effectiveness from the perspective of the practitioner. Whereas academicians may concern themselves with experimental rigor and scientific validation, most of my colleagues in lead business positions want an answer to just a few practical questions.

For example, many want to know: "Is my system doing what it's supposed to do?" Some might have a follow-up question: "How can I know when it's time to change processes?" And those who have recently changed systems in an effort to improve process performance might greatly benefit from knowing: "Has the new system made things any better?"

Figure 7-1 represents a seven-step model that addresses the pragmatic questions articulated above. The remainder of this chapter will be devoted to explaining that model and illustrating its use.

THE PM SYSTEM ASSESSMENT MODEL: AN OVERVIEW

While it is possible for an individual analyst to perform a system assessment by walking through the model without seeking input from others, it is much more meaningful and accurate to gather data from a larger group. It is ideal to gather data from a focus group composed of nine to twelve individuals. When possible, members of the focus group should include the following individuals, although exact participation will vary by specific company needs and availability of personnel:

- Head of Human Resources
- The Administrative Manager in charge of the Performance Management Process (if different)
- At least one significant Line Executive (COO, CFO or CEO preferred)
- Corporate Labor Attorney
- 3–4 Managers/Supervisors with Multiple Direct Reports
- 3–4 Employees who receive guidance but do not complete forms on others

Figure 7-1
Performance Management System Assessment Steps

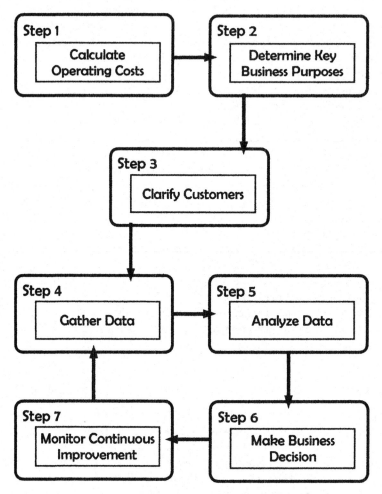

When assembling the focus group, it is critical to include representatives from as many parts of the organization as possible. Participation from the main business functions as well as a blend of Line/Staff, Headquarters/Field and Exempt/Nonexempt is critical. Finally, a moderator should be selected for this exercise. The individual should be chosen carefully and possess advanced facilitation skills. Care should also be taken to select someone with no predisposition toward the existing system. For these reasons, it is advisable to use an external resource when possible.

Most focus groups can do a pretty reasonable job of developing a set of measurement criteria and completing a preliminary assessment in approximately four hours. While some pre-work and additional post-meeting work are normally required, with aggressive facilitation the team need only assemble for half a day to work through most of the model and begin answering most major questions about system health and well-being.

Collecting data using survey methods requires considerably less time on the part of most individuals. Input time may vary depending on the exact structure of the survey instrument but most questionnaires focused exclusively on the performance management system can be completed in less than 30 minutes per person. Like any survey conducted via mail, however, the full data collection process normally requires a couple of weeks to complete. Moreover, surveying people only gets you to Step four on the model. Analysis, decision making and follow-up processes must be handled separately using some other method. For these reasons, we will work through the model assuming the more comprehensive focus team format. Those who wish to do something more indirect will need to make the appropriate adjustments.

STEP ONE: CALCULATE OPERATING COSTS

Regardless of the method of data collection, the first type of information needed pertains to operating costs. To participate in a discussion as a strategic business partner, it is necessary to be able to talk about money. What does the existing system cost to operate? How much money is spent each year just to implement the status quo?

The answer to this question is surprisingly easy to approximate. It also provides an excellent perspective from which to commence an inquiry. It helps get across the point that no system is free and normally demonstrates that making no changes to a system has a cost assigned to it.

Appendix G provides a series of questions that can be used to collect data for approximating system operating costs. The emphasis is on the time people must invest in completing the forms, reviewing them up-line for edification and approval, sharing the information with employees and then following up with employees during stewardship.

An Example Case

Here is a typical example based on a composite of organizations I have worked with. Appendix H contains a completed cost assessment form for a 1,000-person organization that tracks this discussion.

XYZ Corporation supervisors were required to complete a seven-page performance evaluation form for review with employees. Two additional pages needed to be completed on each manager to feed the succession planning system, assemble a corporate training plan and protect against lawsuits (or so they thought). It took an average, conscientious manager three hours to complete all the preparatory paperwork.

After completing each individual review, supervisors were required to present summary information to a review board including their direct manager, their peers, an HR representative (normally a manager) and the Executive in Charge. When the individual being reviewed worked for a cross-section of the organization, senior management would expand the review panel to include input from other line managers familiar with the work of the employee being evaluated.

In order to insure a fair and equitable distribution of grades, department-wide rankings were determined in these sessions. Occasionally adjustments were made to individual ratings following these reviews. The number of management/supervisory/executive participants in each session ranged from four to twelve, with an average of perhaps eight.

To prepare for each review, XYZ Company required an employee to complete a four-page input sheet. In addition, many supervisors requested that their employees complete the evaluation on themselves. Employees were not normally required to evaluate themselves, but pressure was placed on them to look critically at their own behavior. The average, conscientious employee spent approximately 3.5 hours in preparation for her annual review.

At this company the formal discussion between employee and manager normally took about 90 minutes. Many lasted a full two hours, while others were completed in only one.

Stewardship of the evaluation process at XYZ Company was supposed to be more elaborate than it actually was in practice. The process called for three quarterly follow-up meetings of approximately an hour each. These were intended to make sure that the desired changes were actually taking place. In reality, people seldom conducted these follow-up sessions. There was never enough time to get meaningful work done and the system imposed no obvious negative consequences for skipping them. Actual time spent on formal stewardship was probably closer to an hour per employee per year. When analyzing the data, we used a figure of two hours as a compromise between what was intended and what was actually taking place.

Appendix H shows an example of the completed cost chart, including algorithms that estimate that the existing system at XYZ Company takes an average of 19,000 hours and costs approximately $710,000 in direct labor. Because our example was made in round numbers, it is easy to compute that the annual investment in the performance management process was approximately half a week in time (19 hours). Likewise, it represents approximately half a week's pay ($710) per employee.

Please note that our cost algorithm has attempted to assess direct labor costs only. Other figures could also be interesting to estimate, including the cost of printing and copying this information. One must also consider systems support and/or printing fees if special forms are used. Finally, one must consider the potentially significant cost to store and maintain ready access to all of this highly protected data. All told, these additional costs could easily add up to an additional 10 to 15% of the total.

To discover why these figures are important, one needs only to compare them with others of note. For example, the annual training budget. For many companies, an investment of this magnitude would represent the single largest consistent developmental expense in an average year. For almost all companies, it represents a significant fraction of all developmental investment.

To be sure, not all companies employ PM systems that involve quite as much bureaucracy as XYZ Company. From a business perspective, that is good. When it comes down to return on investment, the lower the investment, the less pressure there is on the return. The more time and money that is being spent on the performance management system, the more bottom line impact one should expect to receive from its operation. In the end, we must decide whether we are satisfied with the value equation.

STEP TWO: DETERMINE KEY BUSINESS PURPOSES

With most organizations I've led through the assessment process, completing the cost algorithms is a sobering experience. Unfortunately, it is not usually as sobering as what occurs in step two when we attempt to determine the top five key business outcomes that the performance management system should be designed to create.

As we saw earlier, when someone with an HR background asks a group of line managers what they are trying to accomplish by conducting annual performance evaluations, the normal response is one of frustration. "I do them because *you* make me do them," confesses one supervisor. "My only true desired outcome is not to get in trouble with HR and Legal for failing to do my duty as a supervisor," says another.

When conversations start this way, they need to be redirected toward the hypothetical. Here are two useful questions: "Why do you think we *should* do performance counseling? Can you think of any positive outcome that could come from the act of formally sitting down and talking with people about their performance each year?"

Normally in response to these questions people start giving the answers they assume the questioner wants to hear. "Performance reviews are supposed to give feedback on performance," is a common answer. "They let people know when they're failing or when they're doing a really good job," is another. "They defend the company against lawsuits," is a third routine response. And finally, in systems directly linking compensation to performance measures you hear, "They justify salary treatment."

Having aired these widely accepted beliefs, the group becomes quiet—content that they have given the correct and obvious answers. Most assume that they are maybe 80–90% on target. They assume that the facilitator will soon fill in the missing 10 to 20% of the answer. They seldom expect it when they are told they are completely and totally off base. They are quite shocked to hear that only one of the reasons mentioned above is considered to be business-related.

Think about it from a true business perspective for a moment. How much is "frank and open feedback regarding employee performance" worth? Why should the business owner or shareholder pay anything for that? How much are you willing to pay for the satisfaction of knowing meaningful feedback has been exchanged?

"Justify salary treatment?" Again, who cares? How does justifying a salary increase impact profitability?

"Let people know where they stand?" How on earth does that make the company a dime's more profit?

"Reduce lawsuits?" Bingo. Now you're talking in business terms. Lawsuits cost money. Preventing the likelihood of lawsuits or reducing exposure from inevitable lawsuits is worth something to any business. Defending yourself, even when you've done nothing wrong, can cost tens, if not hundreds of thousands of dollars.

In the terminology of Fitz-enz, who describes measurement of the HR value chain, reducing lawsuits is an *outcome*. The others represent *processes* which perhaps have outcomes attached to them. It is the outcome that produces impact that leads to value-added contributions. His model is outlined below:

$$\text{Process} \Rightarrow \text{Outcome} \Rightarrow \text{Impact} \Rightarrow \text{Value-Added}[7]$$

A group needs to be taken through the exercise of translating processes into outcomes. For example, "giving people frank and open feedback" is a process. One outcome of this process might be for people to *change their behavior* as a result of what they hear. In fact, this is almost always the highest rated output when a group has to rank a short list for priority.

"Telling people where they stand" normally also leads to the desired outcome of *changed behavior*. Telling people they are failing probably also feeds the outcome of *protecting the company against lawsuits*. Telling high performers they're doing great probably feeds another outcome having to do with *motivating employees to work harder*. While it may be difficult to measure motivational level, clearly employees who give greater effort are likely to contribute more than an equivalent group who don't. The connection to the business is not hard to discern.

Motivated employees may not directly make a company successful. There are too many other factors to consider about the nature of the business: its products, markets, conditions, etc. On the other hand, few would argue that an organization will perform better when employees are motivated than when they are not. Motivation may well affect other key outcomes like attraction (recruiting) and turnover rates.

The same logic applies to all issues raised in this section of the assessment. "Justifying a salary increase" is a *process* that normally aspires to affect *outcomes* of minimizing lawsuits and maximizing employee motivation. Based on what you've read already in previous chapters, it seldom does this. Nonetheless, these are outcomes that affect the business, which the system was *intended* to create.

How to Tell If You've Got It Right

The simplest test for determining if you've got an outcome or a process is to consider yourself the sole proprietor of a large business. Then ask yourself a money question. Would you be willing to pay for "frank and open feedback?" Probably, but only if it results in positive behavioral change that affects the business or in employees who, as a result, work harder and smarter for you. Doing it because lawyers and HR people say you should only begs the question of "Why?" Better yet, ask *"Why is this worth paying for?"* Eventually you will discover the short list of business-related desired outcomes.

Consensus on Priorities

Once a focus group has learned to differentiate between outcomes and processes, prioritizing a short list of achievements that the system *should* promote is relatively easy. A good facilitator can normally help a group of up to twelve achieve consensus on such a topic in less than two hours.

In addition to ranking the top four to five desired outcomes, the group should be instructed to weigh them for impact. To do this they need to distribute ten points among the total number of outcomes based on their perceived relative importance. In some instances this can give significant additional insight that is very useful in decision making stage of the assessment model.

STEP THREE: CLARIFY CUSTOMERS

The next step is to determine who the PM system should be designed to serve. Given the new insight into desired outcomes, exactly whom is this system trying to please?

This question comes from the Quality Management principle that stipulates that all work is done by process. Each process has inputs and outputs. And each process has customers. In a service function, such as HR, most often customers are internal to the organization. By definition, the focus of most HR systems is on the humans that reside within the organization. Seldom do HR processes have commercial consumers or shareholders as direct customers.

Going through this discussion is another exercise in clarification. I have yet to lead a group through an assessment that did not list employees as the first and primary customer of the performance management system. After all, it is their behavior we are trying to change and their careers we are having the most impact on. Interestingly enough, not a single company has ever challenged that assumption.

Immediate supervisors and managers are almost always cited as the second customer group. Legal and Human Resources normally come in third and fourth, although the sequence sometimes switches. In some cases it makes just as much sense to consider them together in a virtual tie. Legal/HR are followed, typically, by senior management. Some insist on including the shareholder as a final customer of the process.

The facilitator should ask a group to achieve consensus on a ranking list of no more than five customers. After that, they should be requested to prioritize the importance of each of these groups (again by distributing ten points among all customers chosen). This exercise is normally quite quick and painless. It's what happens next that represents the surprise.

STEP FOUR: GATHER DATA

Step Four is where the pieces start fitting together. Having determined what the system should be accomplishing and who it should be serving, the next step is relatively obvious. It's time to do what any other service organization would do in the outside world. Go to your customers and ask them how you're doing. Specifically, how is the system performing in each of the five areas just ranked as priorities?

For example, ask employees if the review process causes them to change their behavior in a positive way. Ask them if they leave their annual reviews with a strong motivation to work harder. Also ask their supervisors. Ask Human Resources and Legal customers whether the PM system is helping eliminate and minimize lawsuits. Are the review forms currently in use being used for or against the company during litigation?

Ask executives whether they think the system is contributing effectively to internal promotions. Are they happy with the slate of available candidates when a senior level opening occurs? Also ask employees if they feel like they're getting ahead and being well prepared for advancement. In short, ask each group of customers how effectively the PM system is achieving the business objectives that have been carefully prioritized in Step Two.

Given that most systems were not designed to directly accomplish business objectives, most fare rather poorly. To use Fitz-enz's terminology which we discussed earlier, most PM systems were designed for what they do (process) rather than what they produce (outcomes).

As a result, they are more effective at demonstrating compliance with the task of talking about past comments and how well contributing in any measurable way to the business. Over the years, the process orientation has made these systems more and more complex, time-consuming and costly. Oftentimes, this complexity has made the focus on business outcomes even more indirect.

The PM System Assessment Matrix

Appendix I is a matrix designed to help structure data gathering for this stage of the process. Once business outcomes and customers have been defined, the matrix can be used to collect and present information. Detailed instructions for form completion are included on page two of the form.

The matrix can be used to present data in two different ways. It can either be displayed in raw form or weighted for impact. Weighting helps place greater emphasis on customers and business outcomes that have greater strategic importance. For example, in some systems the business outcome of changing behavior might be construed as three times more important than preventing lawsuits. Weighting would allow the table to be impacted by this strategic decision.

While weighting makes analysis more complicated, in certain situations it can provide substantially greater insight into system performance. Examples of using both weighted and non-weighted methods of analysis will be presented below. Before we discuss data analysis, however, let's review some other key data points that might be assembled to give the analytical process more material to work with.

Other Key Data Points

In addition to collecting responses to questions based directly on the matrix, numerous other data points can be assembled that also give insight into the effectiveness and efficiency of an existing PM system. We will explore four other types of information that should also be assembled as input to the data analysis phase of the inquiry. These are exit interviews, turnover rates, legal activity and recruiting statistics.

Exit Interviews

An excellent source of information about people development systems can be gained during exit interviews. Depending on the process used, one can frequently find comments made about existing performance management systems. Exiting employees are normally very frank in discussing their likes and dislikes with various HR systems.

Many organizations use exit interview formats that include queries into perceived advancement and developmental opportunities. In fact, some even ask specific questions about the level of satisfaction with the performance management system itself.

Not every exiting employee will provide feedback that is relevant to this kind of inquiry. Quickly combing through a stack of recent exit interviews, however, will frequently produce fertile ground to explore further. They may either explicitly or implicitly cite problems with the PM process. The time investment is small for such a rich potential payback.

Turnover Rate: Percent, Ratios and Trends

Another potentially important source of feedback on a company's development system is employee turnover. While there are many potential causes for turnover that have nothing to do with the existing PM system, a clear business purpose for many systems is to minimize turnover. Knowing how a company is doing relative to others in the area and industry helps determine a potential strength versus area for improvement.

Examining turnover more closely can yield deeper insight. Breaking data down by "regretted" versus "non-regretted" and exempt versus nonexempt can prove very insightful. Looking at turnover rate over time with critical business issues highlighted by date of occurrence can also prove meaningful. It is equally important to compare turnover rates with other companies in your industry and region. The Saratoga Institute is an excellent resource for such benchmarking data.

Lawsuits: Volume and Direct Cost

Most groups I have worked with have cited the goal of reducing legal exposure as a business outcome that can be impacted by a good performance management system. Summary data concerning each labor-related lawsuit or discrimination charge defense would be useful in determining the cost and impact of any existing or future system. In addition to tracking the number and severity of discrimination charges, tracking total dollars spent defending the company against all (even spurious) charges can help establish some form of baseline measure.

Damage to company image resulting from public awareness of overt contentiousness is harder to calculate. For some companies, however, bad press gained from public airing of employee disputes can be very costly. If this situation applies and damage estimates can be approximated, these should also be included in the mix.

Recruiting: Volume, Percentage of Outside Fills, Total Cost

Information about hiring is another fruitful area of inquiry for those interested in calibrating the effectiveness and efficiency of their performance management systems. For higher-level jobs, the percent of promotions from within versus external hire is an excellent barometer of PM system health. Theoretically, the higher the percentage of outside fills, the lower the regard for the internal systems of selection and development. This could, of course, vary greatly by organization. Some make no attempt to grow talent from within. For other companies, however, it is considered a failing to have to go outside to hire for other than entry-level employees.

In addition to gathering data regarding the rate of placement, assembling information on cost of placement can also prove very informative. Hiring a high-level manager or executive can easily cost well into six figures when you add headhunter fees, signing concessions and relocation costs. Missed opportunities that go along with prolonged downtime are hard to quantify but should also be noted in the assembled information, when possible. The cost to retrain and bring a newcomer up to speed can also be substantial.

STEP FIVE: ANALYZE THE DATA

The next step is to take all of the assembled data and do something with it. While it is not the purpose of this book to teach basic data analysis, I will briefly describe mechanisms one can use to analyze both quantitative and qualitative data. We will start with a discussion of what to do with data captured on the PM Assessment Matrix.

Matrix Analysis: An Unweighted Example

Appendix J is an example of a completed assessment matrix. In this example, ABC Company has a system in place for ten years maturity that is most highly regarded for its contribution to career potential enhancement. All four customer groups that appraised this system see it as having a minor positive impact. The system is judged least effective at motivating employees to work harder. Three of the four groups rate the system as having a minor negative impact on motivation.

At ABC, executive management is the most satisfied customer, although they only rate the system at a 70% effectiveness level. This means that they regard the existing PM system as having a minor positive impact on increasing employee promotability.

HR/Legal are the least satisfied customers with a total effectiveness rating of only 55%. This would indicate that overall they assess the system as having between a neutral and minor negative impact. They are least satisfied with the system's role in preventing lawsuits and enhancing motivation. It is regarded as having a minor negative impact in each area.

Example #2: Weighting for Impact

Appendix K displays a matrix completed on the XYZ Corporation. At the time of the assessment, XYZ had been practicing their existing form of performance management for a little over six years.

XYZ had slightly different business objectives for their system than ABC Company. Some might argue that their objectives also seemed less directly tied to business outcomes than those of ABC. Nonetheless, their customer base for the PM process was the same.

In order to get a more detailed determination of system performance, XYZ Corporation weighted the importance of both customers and business outcomes. Weighting makes the table slightly more crowded and complicated than the one performed on ABC Corporation, yet it also reveals additional insight.

During the weighting process, XYZ representatives determined that the system should be heavily skewed toward the importance of inducing *positive behavioral change*. They assigned 50% of the value of the system to that outcome. They viewed *rewarding for performance* and *planning for succession* as worthy of 20% emphasis each with the remaining 10% assigned to *feeding the training system* for the company.

While all business outcomes for this system were rated quite poorly, rewarding for performance was seen as the worst. Only executives were under the impression that the system was neutral in impacting this business outcome. All other customers felt the system had a minor negative impact on rewarding for performance. Positively changing behavior was regarded as slightly above neutral in value in terms of accomplishing business objectives. Providing appropriate input for the company's training plan was rated slightly below neutral in value.

With respect to customers, XYZ also felt strongly that employees were the primary customer base. They gave 50% emphasis to employees as customers, followed by 30% assigned to managers and supervisors. The remaining 20% was divided evenly between executives and HR/Legal. This weighting helped doom the system in terms of its perceived effectiveness on positively changing behavior. The minor negative rating given by employees more than offset the minor positive impressions held by executive, and HR/Legal customers. Even with a neutral grade given by managers and supervisors the employee vote pulled the total for this dimension down below the neutral mark for the category as a whole.

Given the weightings applied to its customers and business outcomes, the system is perceived as having a slightly negative overall impact. It is literally working against the very business objectives it intended to obtain. Couple these findings with what we learned from the table in Appendix H about costs. XYZ is spending an estimated 19,000 hours a year, or $710,000 in direct labor, to produce these negative results. Clearly this analysis would appear to have generated a compelling business case for change.

Qualitative Feedback

We will not attempt here to explore the infinite possible revelations that could be uncovered by examining the qualitative data we collected in Step Four. Suffice to say that it would only be worthwhile to analyze data of this manner. Simply reviewing the information for red flags and signal flares aimed at the performance management system may uncover great insights.

Looking at what competitors are doing as a means of benchmarking is a useful tool. Comparative data is normally available through industry groups, trade publications, or specialty consultants. Again, the Saratoga Institute is an excellent place to start.

Looking for trends in exit interviews can often produce dividends. Performing content analysis of this information according to reason for termination and regretted versus non-regretted losses can help yield valuable insight.

One thing to keep in mind when you analyze regretted losses is that truly talented people are seldom restricted to a particular market niche. Benchmarking positions within a company only to other companies in your industry may, indeed, backfire on you. A good automobile insurance salesman might also be able to sell computer software. An accountant can quite easily transfer skills across industries. So can HR people and many engineers. Unless your industry sets the pace for the market, when in doubt, think big. It may help you keep a firmer grip on your most desirable talent.

Here are just a few examples of what I mean. A specialty chemicals company lost its highest potential systems manager to a major soft drink manufacturer. A financial institution lost a controller to a bread company. An engineering consulting firm lost a project engineer to a government salt dome contractor. An oil and gas company lost a highly regarded female geology manager who left to open a jewelry store.

In the same way that people are not necessarily tied to an industry, many are not tied to geography. They can move from the city to the country or country to the city or city to another city. They can even move to other countries. Look carefully at your work force to determine the appropriate geographic base of comparison both in setting up expectations and in analyzing trends.

In a market where people have choices, unemployment is low and "Help Wanted" signs abound, competition for talent can be fierce. Your customers may be even just as likely to compete for your best people as your competitors. The only affordable way to truly protect the tremendous investment you have in this talent base is to create a work culture that makes people want to stay. At a minimum, you must achieve par with the broader market.

STEP SIX: MAKE A BUSINESS DECISION

Gathering data and displaying it on a table presents a picture of current reality. Like it or not, that is how the system is perceived to be working by those who have been sampled. The issue becomes what to do about it.

There are two major questions that must be answered to help make a business-based decision for any change. First, "How bad does it hurt?" Second, "What does it cost to fix?" When the pain is high and the price is low, change is an easy sell. When pain is marginal and cost is high, forget it. It is easier to leave things alone. For most of us there are ample candidates for change that have greater payout.

How Bad Does It Hurt?

Most conventional evaluation-based performance management systems rate on average in the middle of the spectrum. They generate about as much good impact as bad. Their contribution is roughly neutral.

Pain in this circumstance can come from a couple of different avenues. First, it can come from a value equation that has to do with cost. If one is investing substantial time and effort into a system and getting literally no net benefit, most companies consider this a source of anxiety.

A major airline recently estimated they spent 46,000 hours of employee time per year (equating to an estimated $1.56 million in salaries) to operate their evaluation system for 4,000 employees. Despite the fact that they had just redesigned the system two years earlier, an ad hoc team concluded that the impact of the system in achieving the four most critical business objectives was completely neutral.

While one could argue that they were doing no net damage and only "wasting" $390 per employee per year, that gave the ad hoc team little solace. With tight control of budgets they viewed it as almost unconscionable to knowingly spend resources this way.

Another source of pain comes from the realization that a good system could provide some key benefits that are currently not being provided. Very few companies I have encountered have clear business-related goals for their performance evaluation system before performing a benchmarking exercise. As described earlier, they do what they are doing out of force of habit.

When challenged, the goals they articulate are bureaucratic and uninspiring. Justifying salary increases, giving people feedback, and documenting the files are not activities that light many emotional bonfires. The exercise that defines true business-based reasons for having a formal exchange about performance issues, however, serves as inspiration for many.

Once a company determines that it is possible to have a system that creates behavioral change, motivates employees to work hard, reduces turnover, increases internal placements, and reduces legal exposure, it can be disconcerting to have hard evidence demonstrating that their current system fails to deliver these outcomes.

A car rental company once upgraded me to a Lexus. I drove the car for a week. When I returned from my trip, my Saturn was waiting at the airport. The little car that I had previously driven with no complaints now seemed sluggish, uncomfortable and perhaps even unsafe. I felt what psychologists call "relative deprivation" now that I had concrete evidence that something better, in this case much better, existed in the marketplace.

How Much Does It Cost to Fix?

If a system has been determined to be ineffective, another factor in making a business decision to change has to do with the cost of repair or replacement. In the above-example, obtaining evaluative data on a Lexus caused me to reevaluate my expectations for a car. In addition to reliability, I had introduced outcomes like comfort, responsiveness and accident avoidance. Awareness of these issues made me less happy with my current situation. However, the cost to correct it was substantial. Trading a Saturn for a Lexus would triple start-up and double ongoing operating costs. For me, in this case, the value equation was close to balanced.

In the same way, one must look at costs associated with changing performance management systems. It is important to consider the time and energy that must be invested in training, as well as consulting or other expenses, when contemplating system modification or conversion. These costs will normally be a one-time expense. In addition, one must consider ongoing expenses.

Based on the nature of the changes made to the system, ongoing expenses can be either increased or reduced. Normally when converting a conventional evaluation-based system to Catalytic Coaching, there is a net reduction of time spent by managers and supervisors. In some cases, depending on the prior system, there may be a slight increase in time required on the part of the employee. New ongoing costs can be quickly estimated using the cost assessment algorithm in Appendix G.

An increase in ongoing costs is a different issue for companies implementing a performance management system for the first time. Since they were making no prior investment at all, 100% of the time needed to complete the new system is a new burden to the organization. Catalytic Coaching, as we will see later, is particularly good for companies facing this dilemma because of its lean structure. The last thing a company needs to do is to go from total laissez-faire to heavy bureaucracy and control. It is better to start off lighter and add more value-added paperwork carefully over time.

Once the costs have been determined to implement changes and operate the new system, it is simply a question of weighing the value of the gains versus the cost. The heavier the gains and the lighter the cost, the easier the decision to make a change. The decision can then be integrated with the overall people development strategy for the business.

STEP SEVEN: MONITOR FOR CONTINUOUS IMPROVEMENT

Whether a new performance management system is implemented, an existing system is adjusted, or no changes are made, a PM system should be monitored periodically over time. A typical solution would be for companies to survey a cross sample of their population at least once a year.

Follow-up assessments can be conducted in a variety of ways. Assembling a vertical slice group to answer questions in a team setting is the method I prefer. A well-chosen group of seven to twelve individuals who resemble the customer base is best. Be sure to include a blend of line and staff, managers, supervisors and employees, exempt and nonexempt. Be also sensitive to location and culture, if you have employees in more than one work site. A well-facilitated two-hour session is normally all it takes to gather the critical data to recalibrate a system whose customer base and business objectives have already been clearly defined.

To properly gauge progress, it is important to use the same assessment criteria (customers and business outcomes) developed in the original benchmarking exercise. If the task is a routine check of an ongoing system, a questionnaire given to a random sample of each population of customers will suffice. If the task is to demonstrate the impact of a major change in systems, combining this with data obtained from a newly formed vertical slice ad hoc group is recommended. Data obtained from this method will be richer and more likely to provide information useful to make early adjustments to the new system.

Fine-Tuning for Optimal Performance

When examining data on a PM system's performance, look for evidence of slippage and sloppiness in system administration. Supervisors systematically missing due dates or employees consistently submitting incomplete paperwork are sometimes signs of reluctant participation.

If the problems are widespread, you might need to modify some procedure or design feature. If, however, the problem symptoms are isolated to one area of the company or a select few supervisors, you may need to look closer at what is going on in those areas or with those individuals.

One thing almost everyone notices after converting to Catalytic Coaching is what appears to be a more obvious disparity between good and bad people managers. Stated succinctly, it is harder to hide incompetence using this system. This phenomenon will be described in more detail in Part III.

If you can develop a method to identify those struggling with the new system, it normally makes sense to provide some form of additional (remedial) training. As the number struggling with the process grows smaller and smaller, you are eventually left with those that cannot function effectively without constant redirection. In these cases it often makes sense to contemplate "Plan B." This might involve reassigning managerial or supervisory duties.

"Holding the Gains"

Ongoing process measurement is the only way to insure that the benefits gained through systemic change will be retained. Practitioners of Quality Management describe this practice of ongoing measurement "capturing" or "holding the gains" that come about through continuous improvement or process redesign efforts.

One group spent several weeks determining how to measure the cycle time in a complicated salary administration process. After documenting the process in tremendous detail and determining baseline performance over hundreds of transactions and several weeks, they were able to streamline the process from 37 distinct steps with cycle time averaging nine days to one of 18 steps averaging less than four days.

Six months after celebrating victory over bureaucracy, the group measured the process again to determine that it had crept back up to an average of seven days. They made the necessary corrections to get the system back down to a four-day cycle again. Six months later it was back to seven. Only after they began monitoring the performance of the system on a weekly basis were they able to keep the average at its most efficient level.

This is not to imply that an organization should conduct assessments of its performance management system monthly or even quarterly. In most cases, a yearly check up involving a random sample of the population will do fine. Assessment intervals greater than a year, however, may expose the organization to deterioration in system performance. Periodic checkups play a crucial role in preventing relapses.

FINAL TALLY

In summary, this chapter has attempted to make the case that measurement of performance management systems is critical at all stages of development. It can be used to determine an existing system's health and provide data to make an informed business decision on when change makes sense. It can be used to estimate the best option for change. It can be used to make sure that process changes actually result in better performance. And it can help make sure that gains in performance do not get locked in for posterity.

We discussed in this chapter a seven step model for performing analysis on PM systems. We also reviewed several examples of using this process to learn about PM system performance. Every attempt was made to make the assessment of assessment as streamlined and informative as possible.

Our goal in Part II was to inform you as consumers. The purpose was to educate you on what makes a good system and how you will know one when you see it. Deming was fond of calling this kind of systemic insight "profound knowledge." Only by having this kind of learning breakthrough can you expect to make changes that truly add lasting value. Without profound knowledge we often end up wandering aimlessly through the fog. Profound knowledge of systems and measurement is like having a map and a compass. The fog may not have lifted, but at least we can rest easier knowing that our best efforts to improve will actually result in true progress.

Part III

Catalytic Coaching

If you want truly to understand something, try to change it.

—Kurt Lewin

If the argument in Part I is correct, most performance management systems currently in use are both ineffective and inefficient. Because of inescapable liabilities built into the very paradigm that defines the prevailing practice, poor performance of most performance management systems is almost virtually assured.

The history of change outlined in Part II underscores the critical importance of coming to grips with the prevailing paradigm. With all the energy that has been devoted to improving performance management systems, few changes have resulted in meaningful sustained improvements. Our analysis here taught us that only by developing a deep understanding of the principles that undermine the traditional system can we break the mold and change for the better.

Up to this point we have concentrated primarily on raising awareness of a problem and discrediting most conventional attempts to resolve it. In other words, our energies have been focused primarily on *what we should not do*. By use of logic and example we have tried to prove that Dr. Deming was right. The performance evaluation process is inherently flawed and cannot be fixed. Rather than just discard it, however, we argue that it should be replaced.

Part III shifts concentration to *what we should do*. It introduces Catalytic Coaching as a viable replacement system. In the next six chapters we will discuss a performance management system that has as its primary focus the task of assisting individuals to develop and grow within the context of an organization. Central to this discussion will be introduction of a very simple but powerful four-step model.

Catalytic Coaching was defined earlier as a comprehensive, integrated performance management system built on a paradigm of development. It is designed to enable individuals to improve their production capabilities and rise to their potential, ultimately causing organizations to generate better business results. Catalytic Coaching helps each employee determine her true potential and take effective action toward realizing it. It features clearly defined infrastructure, methodology and skill sets. It assigns responsibility for career development to employees and establishes the boss as developmental coach.

As discussed previously, the term "catalytic" is used to describe the emphasis this system places on producing meaningful business results. Unlike most systems that follow the prevailing paradigm, it is action-oriented. Instead of focusing on the process of giving feedback or completion of forms for a file, Catalytic Coaching is focused on producing five business outcomes:

- positive behavioral change
- motivation to work hard
- retention of key contributors
- internal promotions and succession
- prevention of and protection against lawsuits

By concentrating so intently on desired outcomes, it simplifies and clarifies the way we approach people development in organizations.

Catalytic Coaching is designed specifically to overcome the logical flaws of the prevailing paradigm, which render it ineffective. It utilizes a strategy four approach to change by substituting a model based on development for one based on evaluation.

THE ROAD AHEAD

Chapter 8 begins with a more detailed explanation of Catalytic Coaching and an overview of the model. We will get a bird's eye view of the whole process, from beginning to end. The rest of this section will describe the steps of this process in more detail.

Chapter 9 outlines Step One, the activity of obtaining employee input to the coaching process. It makes little sense to try to coach someone without knowing first what they hope ultimately to achieve in their work lives. Step One makes sure a supervisor has the information needed to be a useful and effective coach. It makes systemic Covey's recommendation to "first seek to understand and then to be understood."

Chapters 10 deals with Step Two, the act of providing coaching guidance from management to the employee. In this chapter we discuss in detail the process of giving feedback to an employee and the manner in which a coach helps an employee take ownership of the responsibility to continue on a path of improvement.

Chapter 11 also covers activities that occur in Step Two for some employees. The topic is follow-up coaching and the extra measures that are taken when an employee is given a message that demands significant behavioral change. We discuss the critical contribution of a second coach (Coach²) who helps make sure the message is received properly and the employee has every opportunity to come to a positive resolution of the perceived problem.

Chapter 12 describes in detail Step Three, wherein the employee creates a Personal Development Plan to help achieve the desired performance improvements. It sets forth a method of creation, review and approval of developmental activities.

Chapter 13 outlines the fourth step of the model. Step Four has to do with the joint stewardship of the Personal Development Plan. All the work to this point of the process makes no real difference if the ideas and suggestions for behavior change are not acted upon. Step Four insures that this is done and that the proper balance of responsibility is allocated between the joint partners in the improvement process.

Chapter 8

Catalytic Coaching:
A Process Overview

I despise appraisals. I detest judging others or having them judge me. It strikes one as so unfair and arbitrary. Shouldn't a manager be a coach not a judge?

—William Latzko and David Saunders[1]

They shall beat their swords into plowshares, and their spears into pruninghooks; nation shall not lift up sword against nation, neither shall they learn war any more.

—Isaiah 2:4

This chapter will introduce Catalytic Coaching as a healthy alternative to many of the systems that are being used today to promote performance improvement in corporations. This chapter will set forth its philosophical foundation and distinguish it from traditional systems.

We will begin with a discussion about the need to reduce the number of objectives we're trying to achieve with this new methodology. Then we'll compare traditional evaluation-based systems with one based on a coaching model. Next we'll review five fundamental ways the two approaches are clearly differentiated. Finally, we will conclude with a brief overview of the Catalytic Coaching model in its entirety.

REDUCING OBJECTIVES

Peter Scholtes was one of the first to begin actively writing and speaking about the urgent need to find alternatives to traditional performance evaluation systems. In 1993 I attended one of his very first public seminars on the subject. In it, he offered three pieces of advice for someone trying to generate a viable replacement system.[2]

1. Think Differently
2. Just Say "No"
3. Debundle

The first two suggestions he took right from Deming. "Thinking differently" meant seeking what Deming referred to as "Profound Knowledge" about how systems really worked. Without this, most proposed new methodologies would be just a minor variation of the ones they are trying to replace (or what we have called "tweaks").

"Just say 'No' " was the notion that we have already discussed that implied that having no process was better than having a defective one. Scholtes was quite accurate in his observation that corporate lawyers, HR leaders and other business executives are normally the least comfortable with this strategy. Their rationale seems to be that doing something poorly at least demonstrates an attempt to address a difficult issue. Doing nothing would appear to be shirking their responsibility.

The third idea, "debundling" was worth the price of the seminar to me. Quoting from one of his handouts, here is what he said:

Take all the perceived benefits of performance appraisal . . . and devise a separate process especially designed for each. The best way to give employees feedback is much different than the best way to determine pay increases.[3]

Scholtes argument was that companies typically tried to accomplish too many things with one process. Like one of those old home stereos that featured an AM/FM radio, eight-track tape deck, turntable and speakers all in one giant wood box, these systems were designed to accomplish a lot while producing very marginal output. Most tried to please far too many customers with far too many expectations for deliverables. Because so much is attempted with these systems, very little is normally accomplished.

The key then is to separate, focus and simplify. Extending the audio system analogy, we need to go from an old fashioned integrated system to one featuring modern separate components. We need to think carefully about features for value and utility and then assemble a series of systems each designed to produce that functionality. This might mean abandoning the eight-track player in favor of a cassette deck or the turntable in favor of a CD player. The cost and sophistication of each component can be selected based on perceived business need.

For example, many indicate that one of the most important objectives of a performance system is to help people develop and grow. Others indicate that the system needs to be able to justify annual salary increases. Separating features designed to distribute monetary rewards from those promoting development allows each to be simplified and focused for impact. While each is important and would seem to have natural ties, they do not necessarily have to be driven from the same base system. Trying to do them simultaneously with the same system may, in fact, reduce the probability of satisfactory achievement of either goal.

The process described in this section of the book provides key components of a system simplified and focused on people development. It is designed to help individuals take ownership of their own transformation process. It focuses on work and improvements that should be made in the current assignment while also engaging the mechanisms needed to assist those with the capability and drive to transform themselves into competitive candidates for advancement.

Others, through the Catalytic Coaching process, will come to realize they do not have the skills or capacity to excel or prosper in the organization's current or future incarnations. These people will either naturally evolve out of the organization or be encouraged to find a better match elsewhere. The Catalytic Coaching process will make cases of inadequate performance short-lived.

Catalytic Coaching is built on a firm foundation of frank and open communication. It involves a focused and facilitated dialogue between a manager and her direct report. Few managers have been given in-depth training on how to discuss sensitive issues about performance and potential with their employees. Even fewer employees have been trained to understand their critical role in the process. Therefore, Catalytic Coaching depends heavily on communication training.

Despite the fact that the process is designed to employ common sense and appears deceptively easy, training sessions for coaches are essential to get things off to a good start. Orientation sessions for employees are also required.

DISTINGUISHING BETWEEN COACHING AND EVALUATING

The primary purpose of a performance coaching system is to help people improve the way they do their work. Any other goals or objectives are ancillary. We have already spoken about the many objectives of a classic performance evaluation system. It is also supposed to help people improve their work, but its primary objective quite often becomes to justify salary treatment. In addition to this basic distinction, a coaching system differs from an evaluation system in four other ways: perspective on time, connection to pay, primary customer, and approach to inquiry.

Perspective on Time

Perhaps the biggest difference between coaching and evaluation-based systems is their perspective on time. The performance *review*, almost by definition, is focused on the past. For most, it is the twelve-month period immediately preceding the current review. In some companies the review period is longer or shorter. Bottom line, however, is the fact that the discussion will normally focus on judgments about behaviors in a previous, fixed time period.

A performance coaching system, by contrast, is focused on the *future*. Since the primary purpose is to help someone grow and improve, *activities that occurred in the past are important only to the extent that they tell you something about challenges and opportunities for the future*. If someone made a high-profile error in the past reviewing period, but that is not likely to ever happen again, it will probably not be documented or take up much discussion time in a true coaching exercise.

Evaluations are about grading work completed yesterday. Coaching is about focusing energies to improve work to be done tomorrow.

This difference in focus between the two systems is particularly noticeable when someone changes jobs during a review period. If the employee worked for the previous supervisor for nine of the last twelve months, a debate normally ensues about who should conduct the evaluation. Various compromises are struck, but there always seems to be confusion and debate. Those void of confusion have typically established rules slanted in favor of the manager who spent most time with the employee during the evaluation period.

It is particularly interesting when someone changes her area of work completely. Say, for instance, that an accountant leaves the Payroll Department to become a buyer in Purchasing. She does this after finishing five years in Payroll, including the first ten months of the review period. In most evaluation-based systems, the manager in the Payroll Department would wind up conducting the formal review. After all, it would not be fair to rate the transferred accountant against her new peers in Purchasing yet. It would seem most equitable for her to get one more review based on her old role and assignment, then to convert over the following year.

When examined from a coaching perspective, this solution makes no sense. If the individual is now a buyer, why would we want to talk with her about her contribution as an accountant? That has no relevance to influencing her future behavior in purchasing. Who cares what the old boss thinks? It's more beneficial to hear what her new boss thinks of the work he's observed so far.

If the employee was a great accountant but has gotten off to a slow start in purchasing, that should lead to a difficult, but productive discussion. If she struggled before, but gives every appearance of being a superstar in her new position, why then it can the past? Her new boss, no doubt, will help her focus on things she needs to improve to get up to competitive speed within her new department. Her former boss should be solicited for input in determining equitable salary treatment, but would not normally provide the focus of the coaching discussion.

Connection to Pay

The implication for a performance evaluation is that there is a direct correlation between the evaluation of performance and this year's pay increase. If I did well during the past review period and you recognize that with a good performance write-up and rating, I expect to get good salary treatment. If I am told that I have done an outstanding job this last year, I expect even more. We have already discussed the inevitable difficulties with this implied commitment; however, in a performance evaluation–based system it is always there.

The link between pay and commentary in the Catalytic Coaching process is more indirect. To be sure, there must be a logical correlation between the type of information that is conveyed to an individual and her salary treatment. Nonetheless, the coaching process is not designed to justify the amount of an increase. That is a separate and distinct discussion. Some companies elect to hold coaching sessions and salary discussions at different times of the year to reinforce this separation. While it sometimes helps to do this, it is not critical to do so. Timing of these discussions can be adjusted to fit the needs and preferences of the business.

The purpose of the Catalytic Coaching process is to help someone improve her performance such that she can either retain her position, improve the contribution in her current job and/or increase her ability to compete for a promotion. The theory is that by maximizing her performance and potential, in the long run it will maximize her earning power.

Breaking the direct connection between pay and performance evaluation liberates the coach to be more open about areas where improvement is needed. In facing these issues and making the necessary changes, an individual increases her chance of earning advancement. As we have discussed, too often systems that link the two more directly promote softer treatment of imperfections and provide less motivation to make critical change.

Primary Customer

We have already discussed the confusion over the multitude of customers that are involved in the typical performance evaluation process. When attempting to determine who is served first or best by the system, however, one has only to examine to whom they appear to be written. On most forms, the primary audience is clearly not the employee being evaluated. Otherwise, why would he or she be referred to in the third person, as in the examples below?

> George tries very hard to stay organized, but seems to struggle with juggling multiple priorities.

> Sally is an outstanding manger of people. She inspires others to follow her lead.

> Tom needs to improve his public speaking skills. He really struggles at the
> podium.

Clearly, the primary customer of a document that speaks of individuals like
this is not the employee. One can argue as to whether the writer is addressing
his own superior, the HR department or perhaps the "official personnel file."
Whichever it is, this style of writing is a dead giveaway that the employee is a
mere auditor of the evaluative process.

In the coaching process the primary customer should always be the employee
being reviewed. This is made clear by the way that issues are communicated on
the page. As part of a coaching process, George would be given the challenge
to improve:

> Managing multiple priorities: Develop ability to coordinate three or more
> major assignments simultaneously.

Similarly, Sally might be told directly that she has the following strength:

> Outstanding Manager of People: You inspire others to follow your lead.

This difference is more than subtle. It clearly communicates that *the primary
customer of this process is the person being reviewed.* The words on the page
are intended for George or Sally to improve themselves and their contribution
to the company. Others who read or review the form are merely auditors.

Approach to Inquiry

One foundation principle underlying the entire Catalytic Coaching process is
a deep-seated passion for simplicity and directness. Most systems I have examined appear to be created as if the designer were paid on commission for
each hour he can obligate managers and employees to spend engaged in the
evaluation process. This is seen in the length and complexity of forms and the
convoluted process steps. It is also seen in the inability of the people being
appraised to recall or explain what was said to them immediately following their
performance discussion.

Most performance appraisal/review forms are several pages long. I have seen
some that are twelve pages, with a minimum of about an two. Even the longest
forms are crowded with words; some having print so small it can barely be read.
Some include complete, comprehensive reviews of all personal goals for the
year.

Most force the supervisor to evaluate the individual against a long list of ideal
attributes. Some attributes are engineered based on a long and complicated organizational assessment of the behaviors that are deemed as critical to success
in that specific organization. Some use "competencies" specific to each and

every job. These are also defined by a complicated process involving hundreds of hours of work by both employees and consultants. Nonetheless, as discussed earlier, most of these very expensively tailored attributes and characteristics end up looking quite generic.

Core competencies painstakingly prepared by a mining company that would fit any oil and gas, high-tech, or manufacturing company I have ever seen. When you get down to basics we have a lot of things in common across very different industries.

More importantly, rating an individual's performance against two dozen attributes can be both tedious and shallow. It can also be confusing. Glancing over three pages of data to determine which areas are really in need of focus is time-consuming and distracting.

Occasionally, I have spoken to an employee who reports that she received insight from reviewing a long and comprehensive list of attributes—*very* occasionally. Having reviewed thousands of these completed forms, I normally feel a compulsion to put the paper on the table and just ask the supervisor to tell me directly what performance issues the person needs to improve. Remarkably, they can almost immediately do so.

The requirement to answer a litany of prepared questions or points of inquiry is an indirect approach at getting to issues of importance. The perceived advantage is that this method is comprehensive. By forcing a supervisor to respond to an exhaustive series of direct questions we can be assured he did not forget to consider something important.

One section of a comprehensive evaluation form I used to have to require supervisors to complete asked them to choose three characteristics from a list of eleven that most applied to the employee being evaluated. Instructions to this task informed them that "both experience and research have demonstrated that the 11 characteristics listed below are relevant to success at QRS company."

The characteristics listed included the following:

- Team player
- Energetic
- Shows initiative
- Dependable and stable
- Intellectually effective
- Gets job done/follows through
- Makes effective personal impact
- Relates well with peers and direct reports
- Relates well with superiors
- Thorough in planning and analysis
- Creative

To this day, I have no idea what difference it makes which of these attributes is checked off. Is being labeled "Creative" better or worse than "Intellectually effective"? How do you feel about telling a 55-year-old man that he "Shows initiative"? What if your direct report feels she should have been described as a "Team player" instead of "Dependable and stable"? What kind of discussion can this possibly lead to?

This is just one example of what might be called the "Follow the Yellow Brick Road" (FYBR) approach to performance management. The FYBR approach says essentially that it is not your responsibility to reason out what we are trying to do here. Just answer the questions laid in front of you one after another until you get to Oz. The Wizard designed this process so that you don't have to think.

When you examine the really long forms that are used in performance evaluations, they are normally riddled with FYBR questions. The Catalytic Coaching model is built on the premise that with a little training and practice, most supervisors do not have to be forced to take such a long and winding path to comment insightfully on performance issues.

If you take a more direct approach and ask supervisors more focused questions, they just might come up with more comprehensible answers. And . . . they would feel more intelligent and involved in the process of helping their employees improve and grow. The Catalytic Coaching process features a short series of direct questions. They are logical questions that make sense to the person asked to respond to them. The Wizard of Oz has left the building.

The supervisor is not the only one confused by the Yellow Brick Road Approach to performance management. Anyone presented with eleven pages of data is going to have an interesting time remembering what they were told. The most eloquent spokesman in the world would have a hard time listening to her subjects recap the results of her two-hour counseling sessions. Given all that material, who knows what an employee will be able to recall?

A short, direct approach provides focus. Why discuss performance versus nineteen attributes that are worthy of neither special praise nor condemnation? That just makes it harder to sort out the four on either end that are worth concentrated discussion. Every participant in the process (supervisor, employee, senior management, etc.) should be able to understand the logic and value of each question posed. Completed properly, the answers should be easy to understand and remember. Eliminating extraneous questions and reducing the volume of paper that must be completed assists the employee and supervisor in focusing their time and attention on meaningful discussion points. By taking less time and being more meaningful, it also encourages more frequent performance discussions.

CATALYTIC COACHING: A PROCESS OVERVIEW

As depicted on the model in Figure 8-1, the Catalytic Coaching process involves four major steps. Those steps will be reviewed very briefly here. The

Figure 8-1
Catalytic Coaching Process

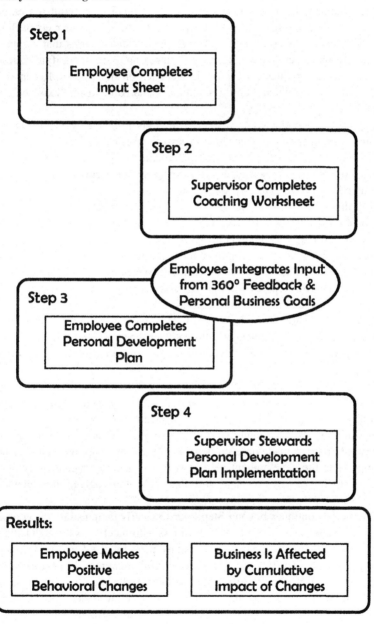

Step 1
Employee Completes
Input Sheet

Step 2
Supervisor Completes
Coaching Worksheet

Employee Integrates Input
from 360° Feedback &
Personal Business Goals

Step 3
Employee Completes
Personal Development
Plan

Step 4
Supervisor Stewards
Personal Development
Plan Implementation

Results:
Employee Makes
Positive
Behavioral Changes

Business Is Affected
by Cumulative
Impact of Changes

remaining chapters of this section of the book will explain these steps in more detail.

Step One of the Catalytic Coaching model involves upward feedback from an employee to the boss. This step makes sure that the manager listens first before speaking. It insures that she receives critical data about the employee before ever attempting to give performance feedback or career counseling advice. The session is conducted by the employee and requires that a supervisor merely engage in active listening along with asking relevant clarifying questions. The employee is requested to provide feedback on three items. Recent accomplishments, new skills and abilities acquired, and career aspirations and considerations.

Step Two is conducted at a later date. It is initiated by the manager and involves giving the employee three types of information: Strengths, Areas for Improvement and Development Recommendations. Specific procedures are used for the conveyance of each type of information. Comments are synthesized and prioritized. They are carefully worded to be positive in tone. The form used to convey this information is one side of one piece of paper. In these sessions, the manager normally does most of the talking, but the employee asks clarifying questions and makes comments as appropriate.

Step Three is where the employee takes the feedback gained from Step Two, combines it with other information (gained from 360° Feedback or other available sources), and prepares a one-page Personal Development Plan. It may contain courses to be attended, work activities to be prioritized, assignments to be undertaken or a variety of other options. The plan is reviewed in a brief meeting between employee and manager. Ultimately, when they come to agreement on this document the employee is empowered to begin implementing the activities it contains.

Step Four of the model involves stewardship of the action plan. A requirement is made for the employee to report on progress in implementing the development plan at least quarterly. This can involve a face-to-face meeting or as little as a submission of a development plan to the manager with tick marks and notations indicating progress made on each item. While it is the employee's responsibility to implement the development plan, it is the manager's responsibility, through the stewardship process, to make sure that those items agreed upon actually do get done.

The model continues in good Step Four to clearly demonstrate the connection between Catalytic Coaching and the business. Ultimately it is through behavioral change that the effort spent on this activity pays for itself and produces value for the company. To the extent that meaningful behavioral change comes from this process that positively affects the company's business performance, it is a good system. To the extent that it merely provides feedback or fills files with completed paperwork, it is of no more value than the traditional performance evaluation system it was designed to replace.

IN SUMMARY

This chapter began the discussion of Catalytic Coaching. It laid the foundation for the model and showed how it is different in design and intent from most traditional systems. To begin with it is more streamlined and focused. It attempts to accomplish less, but it concentrates on items of the most importance to the business.

Catalytic Coaching was described as a system devoted to improving the contribution people make at work. It has a future orientation and is direct in approach to dealing with performance feedback. It breaks the traditional tie between perceptions of performance and pay and it defines the employee as the primary customer of the development process.

Having reviewed each step of the Catalytic Coaching model from on high, it is now time to explore each step in more detail. The next chapter will review Step One, in which the employee provides her boss with data needed to function as an effective coach.

Chapter 9

Step One: Employee Input

A good listener is not only popular everywhere, but after a while he knows
something.

—Wilson Mizner (1876–1933)[1]

If you would judge, understand.

—Seneca, Medea (ca. A.D. 60)

This chapter will explain the critical first step of the Catalytic Coaching methodology. Step One, as highlighted on Figure 9-1, involves the employee providing input to the supervisor for use in the coaching process. We will first
explore the rationale for such a step. Then we will cover the way in which the
coach should approach the encounter. Finally, we will discuss the actual forms
themselves and review some cases that serve as examples of the power and
value of Step One.

WHY BOTHER?

When I first began working on an alternative method to try to help employees
change their work behavior, we utilized a one-dimensional approach. We directed all energy in the system toward downward feedback. We concentrated
on the material that now forms Step Two of this process and helped the manager
clearly articulate his perspective on the need for change. We used this process
with excellent results for years before it dawned on us that something essential
was missing.

Perhaps our first clue that something was missing came from reading Stephen

Figure 9-1
Step One

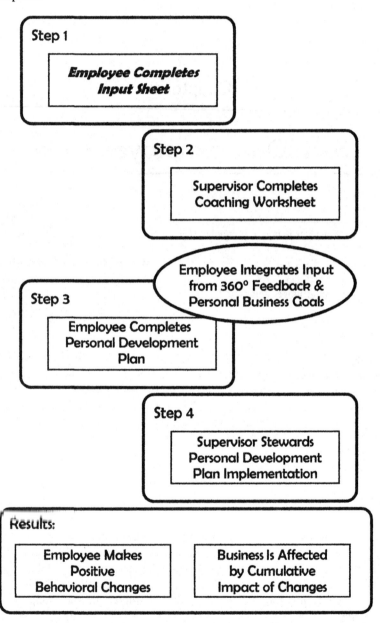

Step 1
Employee Completes
Input Sheet

Step 2
Supervisor Completes
Coaching Worksheet

Employee Integrates Input
from 360° Feedback &
Personal Business Goals

Step 3
Employee Completes
Personal Development
Plan

Step 4
Supervisor Stewards
Personal Development
Plan Implementation

Results:
Employee Makes
Positive
Behavioral Changes

Business Is Affected
by Cumulative
Impact of Changes

Covey's *Seven Habits of Highly Effective People*. With the fifth habit Covey conveys the importance of listening before talking. Here is how he expressed it in his own words:

If I were to summarize in one sentence the single most important principle I have learned in the field of interpersonal relations, it would be this: Seek first to understand, then to be understood. This principle is the key to effective interpersonal communication.[2]

Uncomfortable Questions

Covey's principle raised several interesting questions. How can one be an effective coach without truly understanding the desires and aspirations of the person being coached?

Should we assume that just because a young professional is bright and ambitious, that he ultimately aspires to be a supervisor or manager?

Why are we surprised when a forty-something headquarters professional asks to be considered for a job that would require her to move her husband and kids from their big city home town to accept a developmental assignment in the country? Does this mean she wants on the fast track? Perhaps she just wants out of the city. Does she realize most people who start down this development path do so at least ten years earlier? Do we have the same things in mind for her future? When did this change in career interest first take place?

How could we ever know about an engineer who has aspirations to lead the public relations function? Or the accountant who dreams of moving to sales? What gives with the electrician attending law school at night? Do these people know they're not anywhere on our succession plan? Should they?

Perhaps the biggest question is this: Might knowing the answers to this kind of personal question alter the role of the coach? If so, we'd better gather the answers to these questions *before* we sit down and start talking.

Getting to Know You

The only way to get answers to the personal questions raised above is to ask each individual to speak to you of their aspirations. While a select few may do some of this probing on an informal basis, if it is not institutionalized it will done inconsistently and in an undisciplined manner. Most managers and supervisors never discuss such lofty questions with their people. In fact, many are scared to do such things for fear that they could be accused of discriminating or somehow being biased. And in this modern litigious world, that fear is not without foundation. To build an effective coaching-based performance management system, we must obtain input from the employee at the beginning of the process. We must *know*, not guess, what individuals that entrust their careers to us want and need out of our system before we give them guidance. In short, a

comprehensive method to promote positive behavioral change must commence
with the formal gathering of data from the employees we are trying to coach.

THE PROCESS

The process for gathering information in Step One is very straightforward. It
normally begins with the employee completing a Coaching Input Sheet (see
Appendix A for an example). It concludes with a review session where the
employee presents the information to his manager/coach. In so doing, there are
only a few simple rules that must be followed.

Roles and Responsibilities

First and foremost, it is critical to recognize who has ownership of this part
of the process. *For this activity to be successful, the employee must take responsibility for Step One.* After all, it is his career that is at stake. Most employees, almost by definition, have more than a passing interest in stating their
case and clarifying their needs and desires.

Having ownership means that the employee needs to invest the time to answer
the questions posed in this forum thoughtfully and completely. For most, this
will involve approximately an hour of actual work. For many it is less, with a
few a bit more. Ownership also means taking responsibility to schedule a meeting to present the material orally that he attempted to capture on paper. This is
the employee's meeting and opportunity to speak. For Step One, the employee
is the *presenter*.

The primary role of the coach in Step One is that of *listener*. Beyond providing time on her calendar to meet with the employee, the coach's role is to
come to the session prepared to obtain and digest important information. The
biggest challenge is to resist the urge to take control of the meeting. *This is not
the proper setting for giving downward feedback and instruction. It's time to
listen, ask good questions and learn.*

What to Do

During the session, it is important for the coach to display effective skills in
active listening. This is best facilitated by looking directly at the employee
(instead of reading from the input sheet). It also helps to ask clarifying questions.
Sample questions might be:

> You describe your building project as a disappointment. Are you aware that
> most others see this project as very successful? What about it for you was
> disappointing?

> When you say that you're not interested in leaving the Chicago area for

other opportunities, do you mean this as a permanent restriction or can you imagine some time in the future when this might change?

Questions like these not only show interest, they help obtain critical information that will allow the manager to better help coach the individual entrusted to you. By the simple task of asking good clarifying questions, the manager may actually help the employee come to new realizations about his wants and needs.

What Not to Do

For the sake of clarification, let's review a pair of examples on the kind of questions not to ask. We'll use the same two issues that were cited above.

> I see you have the building project listed in the wrong column. Any kind of disappointment it may have caused was far overshadowed by the fact that it was labeled a success by senior management.

While intended to be supportive, this way of addressing the issue will likely be perceived as judgmental. Instead of boosting the employee's esteem, it might serve as another blow—implying that he cannot assess situations with proper accuracy.

Let's try the second one.

> What's this about not wanting to leave Chicago? If you put that in writing, you may as well kiss any chance of promotion goodbye. We need to change that statement so that it doesn't kill your career.

This response makes some pretty big assumptions. First, it assumes that the individual has a primary focus on upward mobility. Second, it assumes he hasn't thought through the logical consequences of what he put down on paper.

While it is possible that both of these assumptions are correct, it is also possible they are not. Only by engaging the employee in a non-threatening, non-judgmental dialogue is the coach likely to find out the real story. If she moves too aggressively and starts giving advice too quickly, the employee will likely bow to implied pressure. The coach may thus miss an opportunity to find out what this employee really values and aspires to in her career. An important avenue for influence will be lost.

It is obvious that these two contrasting approaches are likely to produce significantly different impact on the quality of dialogue between manager and employee. In the role of boss we frequently speak very freely and directly with employees. When functioning as coach and talking formally about career issues, we need to slow down, take a deep breath and think through the implications of these ideas thoroughly before we share them with the employee.

In Step One, the best coaches are normally perceived to be those who ask the most clarifying questions. See Chapter 16 on skills training for more concrete advice on acquiring requisite coaching competencies.

Risk-Taking Behavior

Step One of the coaching process requires an emotional investment on the part of the employee. She is being requested to share sensitive and ego-baring information with the boss. Done conscientiously, this involves risk-taking and trust.

To be an effective facilitator of this activity, the coach must be on his best behavior. Too frequently with our direct reports (and perhaps spouses and children as well), we operate using baser instincts. We say what comes to mind without a great deal of thought about the manner in which our comments might be perceived.

To be worthy of the trust extend to him by this process, the coach should have in the forefront of his mind that he is speaking to someone important about something that is important to her. He should treat the employee as a valued client and consider her words and questions as if future business depended on the professionalism, grace and charm demonstrated during the interview.

If a manager begins acting like a caring, nurturing coach in this meeting, it will do much to set the tone for the entire coaching process. If the coach proves to be a positively oriented, active listener during this part of the process, he will be modeling the behavior he hopes the employee will follow when she enters Step Two and the responsibility is reversed.

THREE BIG QUESTIONS

So far we've talked a lot about *how* to interact with employees during Step One, but we have yet to cover *what* specifically to interact with them about. We will do that now.

I have always admired simplicity in a system. I am a big fan of Dale Carnegie and the elegant way his teachings boil down a process to its bare essence. Keeping procedures simple and logical greatly aids people in developing competency as they stretch themselves and try new behaviors. Following his principle, we have attempted to consolidate the first step of the Catalytic Coaching model into three concise questions. Obtaining the answer to these three questions should put a manager of supervisor in position to do an effective coach.

While some might argue the utility of a slightly different series of five questions or nine or thirteen, we are content with the breadth and depth of what can be obtained from asking only three. Following the philosophy of keeping procedures simple and logical, we have elected to go with as few core questions as possible. Additional questions can be added as specific business needs call for them.

In Step One, the core issues and correlating questions the employee needs to address for his coach are highlighted below. Each will be explained in detail later in this chapter.

- *Contribution*: What have you (the employee) done for us (the organization) lately?
- *Improved Capacity*: What have you done for yourself lately?
- *Development Needs*: What do you want to be when you grow up?

We offer no apologies for the deceptively simple appearance of these questions. To begin with, they are a lot more sophisticated than they look. In addition, people are able to remember them. Having them easy to remember makes this process more spontaneous and intuitive to those involved. And all involved will understand the purpose behind asking each question. The discussion can go more smoothly when both parties understand the goal here is to share information that is relevant to the coaching partnership.

A telltale conversation took place in a car on the way to an airport one day. The Vice President of Sales had missed an overview of the new coaching process and needed clarification on Step One, which was new to him. Before the HR expert was able to utter a word, the VP of Global Manufacturing stepped in to explain. He had never received formal training on the process but had just completed his first experience with Step One earlier that week. He replied: "It's easy, Hank. You just have to answer three basic questions." And he proceeded to recite them from memory. As the person in charge of spreading this new technology around the company, that was the most positive feedback the HR expert could have ever received.

This is not rocket science, but used properly it can be very powerful. We'll talk about the manner in which the information is used shortly. First, however, let's examine in more detail the root issue behind each question.

Q1: "WHAT HAVE YOU DONE FOR US LATELY?"[3]

This general question is a rather straightforward way of asking someone to account for his major contributions in the previous period. It reminds the person being coached that they are a producing asset of the company and are assumed to be making an ongoing and valuable contribution. It's a simple way of saying that it is time to remind the organization of your achievements for the past year.

Rest assured, it is not necessary to give someone a formal document to complete that has this exact question written on top of it. Some might interpret the wording as threatening or cavalier. Indeed, it may be translated on paper into simple *Accomplishments* and *Disappointments* for the year. The question as stated above is useful in conveying the essence of this step in the process, however. It deals with the issue of *why* Accomplishments and Disappointments are important. This is where the employee brags about his contribution or struggles to explain what he has done that is value-added. The simple wording helps make overt the business nature of the employment contract that has always been present.

Appendix A is a generic format that has served well for this step of the coaching process. It strives to achieve the essence of this question by asking an individual to list his accomplishments and disappointments for the year. This makes the form look a bit more sophisticated and professional. Regardless of exact wording, everyone involved should be aware that this is the opportunity for the individual being coached to "show his stuff." It implies both account-ability and pride of workmanship.

More Problems from the Past

Too often with a traditional evaluation process it is the boss's responsibility to cite the achievements and disappointments of her direct reports. This is both time-consuming and dangerous. It is far too easy for a supervisor to forget a key contribution that occurred months earlier. Doing this can cause serious prob-lems.

When the employee notices the absence of a key citation on her annual re-view, she may question the validity of the entire process. "Were you really even paying attention?" the frustrated secretary might think. The cynical senior ac-countant may respond by quipping, "I guess you left out that achievement in order to have an easier time justifying giving me a 'Meets Expectations' per-formance rating." Whether they say something to the manager about an omis-sion or not, they will be thinking about it. And they will tell friends and family if they think it hurt them.

In addition to preventing omissions, having to prepare an answer to this ques-tion can be rather instructive for the person being coached. The high achievers will quite frequently be surprised by the volume and breadth of accomplishments they've managed to amass over the course of one short year. It can be rather invigorating for the employee to do a recap of her annual accomplishments.

"My gosh. Look at all that I accomplished in the last year," a Director of Engineering said after answering these questions in Step One of the coaching process. "I spend so much time worrying about what I have yet to do, that I hardly ever take time to recognize how far I've come. I really accomplished a lot in the past twelve months." Preparing this part of the document helped her almost look forward to her pending annual coaching session. She was excited to share her impressive list of accomplishments with her boss. Having her boss merely acknowledge that she had accomplished so much made her feel good about herself.

On the other hand, imagine the opposite situation where an individual has very little to show for herself in the way of significant accomplishments. She came up short on almost all of her objectives and hasn't got much she can legitimately use to demonstrate her contribution. Here's a conjecture. I'll bet she won't want to have this kind of conversation a second time next year. At least not if she values her job. And interestingly enough, at this point, all the pressure is coming from the employee. Her boss has yet to utter a word.

Scary Disappointments

Just a quick word about Disappointments. Some people find it intimidating to have to write down their shortcomings. As the children's saying goes, "That's for me to know and you to find out." Perhaps if the employee doesn't say anything, the boss won't notice. Nonetheless, this form of critical self-analysis begins the important process of examining his performance honestly and objectively. In an evaluation setting, this reluctance has a very logical foundation. Since we are not using the coaching process to determine a label or grade, however, and since it is not linked directly to salary treatment, the focus on personal improvement is easier to sell.

Those with a strong balance sheet (strong accomplishments offsetting minor disappointments) are likely to be more up front and honest. Those with potential deficit situations may still need a reality check. Either way, this provides the coach with some valuable information about how clearly the individual being coached sees herself. Regardless of perceived accuracy in self-description, remember that this is only input. It is not necessary to debate achievements or disappointments with a direct report during this step. The coach will have a chance to respond with downward feedback on relevant issues in Step Two.

Q2: "WHAT HAVE YOU DONE FOR YOURSELF LATELY?"

This is an interesting question that speaks to the issue of professional growth. On paper this may translate to asking the individual to highlight new skills and competencies he has acquired over the last year. What important new experience has he gained that will allow him to make a better contribution in the time ahead? What new relationships has he created that do the same?

With this question we are moving out of the realm of production and into what Stephen Covey calls "production capability."[4] In explaining the difference, he reminds us of the story of the goose and the golden egg. In this case, the achievements listed in response the first question are eggs. Now we're talking about the goose. What has been done to help the goose retain or improve her capability to produce eggs in the future?

This is another question that calls for introspection. When first asked the question, an individual might begin making a list of the training courses she has taken recently. Unfortunately, however, this is missing the point. Attending a seminar does not increase production capability. This state may be achieved by putting into practice something learned in a classroom, but merely absorbing new information in a seminar or workshop does not count.

Likewise, certificates do nothing to increase production capability, unless they allow someone to provide new services. CPA or Notary Public certification, for example, would allow someone to perform new functions. Hence, these might qualify. So would achieving instructor status in a train-the-trainer course. An engineer obtaining a law degree by going to school at night is an admirable achievement, but the connection to production capability still must be logically explained. How is obtaining this degree useful in improving her contribution to the company?

Whether an individual has a long list or a short list of new capabilities, asking the question sends a very important signal to the person being coached. It conveys the value the company places on continuous learning and personal growth. In so doing, it helps reinforce the importance of the ideas espoused by Peter Senge in *The Fifth Discipline* as he describes the nature of a constantly improving "learning organization."[5]

Senge describes the learning organization as creating a critical competitive component for businesses of the future. "The organizations that will truly excel in the future will be the organizations that discover how to tap people's commitment and capacity to learn at all levels in an organization."[6] The future of an organization may in large part be dictated by the capacity of its people to continuously learn and grown. Question two reminds each and every employee of their critical role in that process.

Q3: "WHAT DO YOU WANT TO BE WHEN YOU GROW UP?"

This question is the killer. It's the one that never seems to come up in most evaluation-based systems. It seems to be considered taboo. As a coach, however, if you could ask only one question to unlock the motivational riddle that is an employee, this is the one you'd want to ask. Why? Because everything hinges on the response.

As you'll see on the example in Appendix A, this question can easily be translated into two more formal queries. One asks directly for career aspirations for the short, mid and long term. The next asks for relevant background data that might help clarify willingness to invest in this desired future and shed additional light on the subject of things like pay and mobility issues.

At this point it may be instructive to review two relevant cases that help illustrate the incredible value of this question. The first one turned out successfully; the second did not.

The Hidden HR Executive

Being in the HR department provides one with lots of information about people. You know who are on the high potential list and who are inches from the door. It's a privilege to have this kind of information, but also a burden.

Mary was an HR VP for an international manufacturing company who was charged with strengthening the management talent within her department and ultimately grooming a viable candidate to one day succeed her. In examining the list of possible candidates she spotted a young manager named Murphy in operations. Murphy had some interaction with Human Resources, as he coordinated the safety and labor relations part of the business. He was highly regarded throughout the organization and could probably be promoted into Mary's open position. Nonetheless, when she approached the Vice President of Global Operations, to whom Murphy reported, she was asked not to consider him.

It seemed that Murphy was currently being groomed as a possible candidate to one day run one of the field operations. He had a very general kind of management talent and it was conceivable that this could work out. The only problem was, this was not what Murphy wanted to do.

When his boss asked Murphy Question Three one day, he was not given the answer that he expected. The young man did not have aspirations to run a plant or to rise further in the operations organization. Quite the contrary. He aspired to some day lead the HR function. Despite the fact that he only had relevant experience in two or three of the key HR areas, he knew enough about the function to have this as his clear goal. In fact, he'd pretty much felt that way for years. It's just that no one ever asked him until the evaluation process was converted to a coaching process and Step One questions were asked.

To make a long story short, within 60 days of making this formal declaration Murphy's reporting relationship was changed. He kept the same responsibilities but reported through Human Resources. Six months later his duties were changed to expose him to parts of the HR function where he had the least background. The organization sent him to the appropriate classes and continued to expose him to needed information. Murphy worked hard and quickly demonstrated aptitude for all knew areas he was given responsibility. Over the course of the next year, he became recognized as the strongest generalist in the department. When Mary left the organization eighteen months later, Murphy was promoted to Vice President of Human Resources.

Had the organization not made the switch and begun rounding out Murphy's resume, he would have almost certainly been overlooked for the position of HR Vice President. In all likelihood it would have been considered too much of a stretch for someone lacking key experiences within the department. Years earlier they had gone outside the organization to find Mary and could well have done so again.

Filling the job internally saved the company an estimated $100,000 in search firm and relocation fees. It also saved an excellent employee. I have no doubt Murphy would have left the company eventually had his aspirations continued to be stifled. Another important part of this win-win scenario is the signal it sent to the organization. An insider had filled a top job. Even those having no aspiration to Human Resources must have been encouraged to see that internal people can be developed to fill the top slots. Everyone came out a winner.

Losing Frieda

The flip side of this story is not as satisfying. It involved an industrial hygienist named Frieda. Frieda was new to her organization but got off to a great start. Her job required her to operate from headquarters, but interact heavily with the field organizations.

Frieda was an instant hit. The feedback was both quick and positive from primary customers, the managers running their field operations. Frieda blended in well and made a solid contribution from almost the first day. When her boss talked with the HR Director about Frieda's potential to advance within the company, both became excited. They felt it was quite possible that one day Frieda could actually run one of the field operations. She was that good. To get there, however, she would have to prove herself on many different fronts and broaden herself well beyond the normal scope of an industrial hygienist.

To accomplish this task of demonstrating potential, they started loading Frieda up with opportunities. They sent her across America and Canada and on special assignments to Europe and South America. There was even talk of Asia. Frieda had almost as busy a schedule and as many frequent flier miles piling as her boss and top executive did. They put her on special high profile teams and projects, well outside the normal scope of the industrial hygiene profession. For a bright, hard-working, professional this was it. Frieda had made it to the fast track. Or so her management team thought.

During her exit interview, Frieda let her bosses know how much she appreciated their confidence in her and the potential for advancement they saw and were trying to help her realize. Unfortunately, however, Frieda did not aspire to be a general manager. Limiting or not, Frieda thoroughly loved the field of industrial hygiene. Doing that work extremely well was really what she aspired to. She also wanted more of a home life. The constant travel was not for her. Because of their tremendous enthusiasm to help her grow, Frieda felt uncomfortable confronting her managers about her true needs and desires. The company had no formal mechanism to solicit this kind of information at the time. She made comments in passing, but they were too subtle to alter the master plan of her zealous growth-focused managers. By the time they had the discussion about needs and desires, Frieda had already accepted another job. There was nothing they could do to get her to stay. By not knowing *her* answer to the personal question, her managers had projected their own feelings on the situation and guessed wrong. In so doing, they lost a heck of a good employee, perhaps the best industrial hygienist either had ever seen.

In practical terms what this meant is that they had to commission another headhunter to track down another hygienist. Frieda had cost the company approximately $60,000 in fees and relocation costs and had taken six months to locate and recruit. The odds of them finding someone they liked as much as Frieda were slim, indeed. The price of ignorance in this case was very high.

THE BIG LESSON

The central theme to these two stories is the same. You can't do an effective job as coach unless you first take the time to gather some basic data about the individual you are coaching. The three big questions discussed in detail in this chapter provide a good starting place for making this determination.

Also keep in mind that these aspirations and conditions can change over time. In fact, a good coach will frequently help shape them with the employee. By making collection and discussion of these data points a mandatory part of the annual review process, you will gather and stay on top of this critical information.

Chapter 10

Step Two: Management Guidance

The great French Marshal Lyautey once asked his gardener to plant a tree. The gardener objected that the tree was slow growing and would not reach maturity for over 100 years. The Marshall replied, "In that case, there is no time to lose; plant it this afternoon!"

—John F. Kennedy[1]

This chapter will discuss in detail Step Two of the Catalytic Coaching model, as illustrated in Figure 10-1. This is where the manager functioning as coach provides guidance to the employee. We will begin this chapter by defining the roles and responsibilities of the participants for Step Two. We will then discuss the three critical components of the process and review how forms are completed and discussed with employees. Follow-up coaching, which also occurs at the end of Step Two in some cases, will be discussed in the next chapter.

ROLES AND RESPONSIBILITIES

In Step Two, roles are reversed from Step One. Here, the manager is responsible for calling the meeting and leading the conversation. It is her turn to talk. The employee now becomes the listener and the one who seeks clarification.

Prior to the meeting, a coach must complete a Catalytic Coaching Worksheet (see Appendix B). This will form the structure for the meeting and record of the issues that were presented and discussed. The form itself will be described in detail below, along with a thorough explanation of its logic and flow.

Before we get into specifics on the content of the message, however, it is important to note that during the interview the manager is encouraged not to

Figure 10-1
Step Two

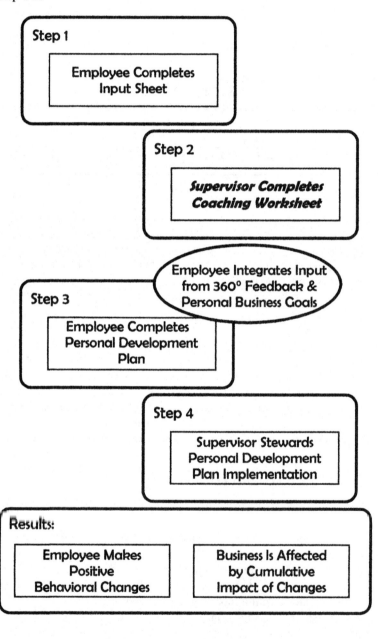

Step 1

Employee Completes
Input Sheet

Step 2

*Supervisor Completes
Coaching Worksheet*

Employee Integrates Input
from 360° Feedback &
Personal Business Goals

Step 3

Employee Completes
Personal Development
Plan

Step 4

Supervisor Stewards
Personal Development
Plan Implementation

Results:

Employee Makes
Positive
Behavioral Changes

Business Is Affected
by Cumulative
Impact of Changes

provide a copy of the completed worksheet to the employee. With paper in hand the employee may read ahead of the coach and not truly be concentrating on what is being said. Experience has demonstrated that it is much more effective to notify the individual that he will receive the original copy of the form following the discussion.

For his part in this discussion, the employee needs to mirror the role of the manager in Step One. He should ask clarifying questions and seek examples of issues that are unclear. He should try to be non-defensive and open to feedback. He should remember that the coach is providing only an opinion on his work performance, not objective reality. Nonetheless, this is a very important subjective reality to try to understand.

The coach's goal and entire focus of the interview should be to help the employee improve his performance. It is not about judging or labeling. You will notice on the form that there is no letter or number to convey relative rating or ranking of this person's performance compared to anyone else. There is nothing on this form to convey anything about salary treatment. The subject is 100% focused on, as Stephen Covey calls it, production capability.

THE PROCESS

The core of Step Two is represented by the *Catalytic Coaching Worksheet*. The worksheet is built around three basic topics.

- Strengths
- Areas for Improvement
- Development Recommendations

As was true of Step One, this step of the process is very focused and concise. The most promising employee can be written up on one side of one piece of paper. So can the person you'd like to fire today, if only Human Resources and corporate counsel would let you.

Sometimes one must resort to the use of legal paper when the message compels it, but never should you be forced to go beyond one side of an 8½ × 14 inch paper. If a 25-year work history can be summed up in one page on a resume, so can one year's performance guidance. Like a good resume, it sometimes takes more energy and insight to write less. Again like the resume, the end product is normally more effective in performing its task in the more consolidated form.

Make Messages Memorable

The main reason for the brevity, of course, is to make the information conveyed on the document more likely to be understood and remembered. Very few, if any, will carry around their nine-page annual evaluation around in their purse or back pocket. On the other hand, some actually do find ways to keep handy the simpler, more meaningful one-page form.

Realistically, we should not expect the average employee to carry their forms around with them following the review, no matter how compact or meaningful we make them. For employees to make true changes based on what we give them, therefore, it helps if they can just remember it. When completed properly, key components from a Catalytic Coaching Worksheet can easily be committed to memory. In fact, some can be very hard to forget.

Gauging Success

The ultimate test of the Catalytic Coaching interview can be conducted a day following the Step Two discussion. Just ask the employee, "What did you learn?" and you will find out how well the message was transmitted. A key follow up question would be, "What are you going to do differently to improve your performance in the future?"

Imagine asking these questions with a traditional performance evaluation system. If you do, odds are very high that they will talk about one of two things. They will comment about their grade:

> I learned that I am a "Two" again this year. I have no idea what I could do to get to be a "One."

Or they speak about their salary increase amount.

> I learned that my increase will be three percent again. You know, I really need more than that to put my two kids through college.

When you query them about behavioral changes that might help improve their performance in the coming year, a typical response you will get is, "I guess I'll just have to work harder." Others will mumble something about a course they are signed up to take. In order to see why Catalytic Coaching produces different results, we need to examine the contents of the worksheet in more detail.

THE MESSAGE

There are three critical discussion areas that must be covered in Step Two of the Catalytic Coaching model. Like the questions asked in Step One, these are very logical and straightforward subjects to talk about. They are also very powerful. They include three fundamental components:

1. Strengths

2. Areas for Improvement

3. Development Recommendations

Strengths

A conversation aimed at improving someone's performance should always start on a positive note. It is more than simple courtesy; it has to do with credibility and effectiveness. Convincing someone to change his behavior is a difficult thing to do. If the individual wanted to do things a different way, he would already being doing it. The fact is, most of us do what we do because it is easy or comfortable or familiar. We are creatures of habit, and our habits comfort us. Change is painful. Changing habits is seldom fun. With few exceptions, most of us would like to be left alone. If we wanted to change, we'd already be doing things differently.

Oddly enough, these principles apply to even the most obvious choices in our lives. We know that eating less fattening foods and dieting would help us lose weight, but the vast majority keep on doing it the old way. We know that we should be developing a family budget that includes savings for our children's college, but most of us delay doing it. We know that staying up late and watching movies on TV will make us tired in the morning, but some of us watch them anyway. We know that we should be paying more attention to our children and spouse, but many find it easier to put off doing those activities. There's always tomorrow to get started.

Avoiding Pain

If someone points out to us one of these obvious challenges, what do we normally do? For many of us the response is automatic. Our first reaction is to critique her right back, if not out loud, then at least silently to ourselves. "If you know so much about diet and exercise, how come you're still twenty pounds overweight?" goes the internal dialogue. "You'd stay up to watch TV, too, if you had to work as hard as me. I have no other time to relax. At least I'm not like you, sedating myself with alcohol at night," continues the change demon inside.

You get the picture. Our defense mechanisms are pretty good. Most of us are zealous advocates for the status quo when confronted about the need for change. And our number one method of defense is to discredit the messenger. When the messenger is your boss, this is only too easy.

"She never really liked me. I know she prefers Steve because he caters to her every whim," the voice of lethargy speaks. "Who is she to give me career advice, anyway. I haven't exactly seen her racing up the organization lately," it continues.

Because I'm Different

Perhaps the easiest excuses to justify staying the same are the "Because I'm
————" rationales. She doesn't like me and she's saying these things about me
because I'm:

1. Black/Hispanic/Asian/Indian/White
2. Not Black/Hispanic/Asian/Indian/White
3. Female/Male
4. Older/Younger
5. Taller/Shorter
6. Overweight/Underweight/Perfectly Proportioned
7. Lacking a College Degree/Have Too Many Degrees/Have the Perfect Degree

You get the picture. Anything can be used as an excuse to not have to change.
Since most human beings have a basic instinct to remain comfortable, we each
keep our favorite "Because I'm different" excuses always ready and available
for use.

Disarming Defense Mechanisms

Let's return again to the task at hand. We are trying to formulate a discussion
that is consciously designed to prompt someone to change what he or she is
doing. We have already said that this is the most important purpose of the
exercise. Giving feedback is not the end of the process. Obtaining positive behavioral change is our desired end state.

Starting things off on a positive note does several important things. First and
foremost, however, it is "disarming." Try using the "Because I'm ————"
defense on a supervisor who just told you that you are the most productive
worker in the organization. Further, you are one of the most knowledgeable
people she's ever worked with on a subject you are very proud of. How biased
does that sound? If it's true, and you'll know if it's true or not, the internal
voices are temporarily silenced.

Building Credibility

Citing strengths builds the credibility of the coach. Oddly enough, credibility
in this instance can't be assumed. No matter the rank of the person doing the
coaching, no matter how high in the organization he or she might be, that does
not insure them credibility as a coach or counselor. They must earn credibility.
It cannot be mandated. The employee must grant a manager coaching credibility,
she cannot command it.

This truth about coaching is worth highlighting: *No matter how piercingly accurate a coach is in determining an employee's areas for improvement, her credibility is shaped first and foremost by the perceived accuracy and fairness of the strengths she recognizes and articulates.*

A superficial "newspaper horoscope" style profile of strengths will yield minimal credibility. The coach will be seen as skimming the surface in a generic and shallow fashion. "If you can't recognize my strengths, why am I to assume you can recognize my weaknesses?" the employee might wonder.

Tough but Fair with Alfred

Alfred was an underachieving account executive with a large manufacturing company. His boss, a Sales and Marketing executive, called on an HR professional trained in Catalytic Coaching (Helen) for assistance in conducting an intense performance discussion. Alfred either had to improve his sales production or they were going to have to remove him from his position.

Despite the tremendous urge to immediately confront Alfred with a list of behaviors that were threatening his employment, Helen convinced the executive to start the coaching session with a discussion of Alfred's strengths.

Alfred was on the verge of losing his position because of a recent series of very serious errors in judgment. Nonetheless, he was more than flattered to hear that his boss recognized his superior knowledge and working relationship with a key account.

Alfred's reaction to the feedback on strengths was very typical of how people respond in less threatening sessions. "Thank you for noticing that. I am very proud of the relationship I've built with that client. It's taken me many years to get where I am today. I appreciate the fact that you would put that down on paper about me," he said. He had a similar response to the three other legitimate strengths that Alfred's boss reviewed with him.

Being honest with Alfred about the fact that he was doing great with in some important areas did not prevent the executive from telling Alfred that his job was at risk for other critical mistakes. It did, however, demonstrate to Alfred that the boss was being fair and could see the good as well as the bad in his behavior. It built credibility in the relationship that allowed the executive and Helen to work together with Alfred to ultimately resolve his performance problem and salvage his career. Without the credibility built by citing Alfred's well deserved strengths, Helen predicted that Alfred would have used a "Because I'm different" defense to construct an alternate explanation for the job pressure.

Since Alfred was 62 years old, and the highest paid account executive in the firm, he might have seized upon those data points when interpreting the cause for his dilemma. After all, if it were age or pay level that was at the root of his problem, how could Alfred change either factor? Given this interpretation, Alfred could disregard the other counsel as just an excuse to "run him off." Not only would he not put any energy into changing his behavior, he might start

seeking legal counsel of his own and preparing for an inevitable court battle.
And if his behavior had not changed, he probably would have got it.

Giving Positive Recognition

The final reason for citing strengths first is perhaps the most obvious. Putting
strengths down on paper is a way of reinforcing behavior that is highly desirable.
The field of psychology teaches us that behavior that is not reinforced can
sometimes be "extinguished" due to lack of perceived interest. Clearly, here is
a chance to tell someone things that you both probably know, but it sure feels
good to get out in the open and down on paper.

Companies that have adopted this strategy of beginning Step Two with a
review of Strengths have had very positive experiences with the approach. It is
extremely gratifying to tell someone that he is good at something or has distinguished himself in some way. It feels right to do this. It gives nothing away in
the event of a prolonged confrontation, and it clearly helps encourage a contin-
uation of the behaviors that are most valuable to the institution.

AREAS FOR IMPROVEMENT (AFI)

Very few individuals would claim to have achieved a level of performance
that is void of improvement. Even world renown athletes like Michael Jordan
or Wayne Gretzky, who have dominated their sports for sustained periods of
time, are not likely to report that they ever ran out of things to work on. In fact,
the best are perhaps even more conscious of their many Areas for Improvement
than the rest with far fewer blessings.

Most companies who have participated in the Quality process endorse the
basic principle of "continuous improvement." This principle states that we are
always on a quest to get better. Perfection may not be achievable or sustainable,
but we will look for anything and everything we can to make improvements in
the way we do our work. Even relatively minor improvements in the way we
work can add up to make large differences in performance over time.

The Areas for Improvement (AFI) section of the Catalytic Coaching Worksheet is designed to highlight three to five behaviors that, if improved, could
help optimize an individual's contribution to the company. There are several
rules and procedures for completing this portion of the form.

Positively Stated Themes

The issues listed for improvement should be stated positively. In other words,
instead of stating that a Tax Manager "fails to delegate properly," we might
list an Area for Improvement that reads as follows:

Delegation—Learn to use a more effective and empowering approach to
assigning and stewarding work.

This form of telegraphic labeling (citing a term and then providing an explanation) can be very effective. When quizzed a day or two following the interview, the employee will often remember the one or two words that form the
title of the AFI. Specifically, the Tax Manager will repeat, "I have to work on
delegating work to my direct reports. I guess I need to make them feel better
about what I ask them to do." If this is what he repeats, the message got through.
This critical part of the mission has been accomplished.

As we've already discussed, being able to recite improvement areas from
memory should increase the likelihood that the employee will remain focused
on this short list of behaviors to modify. Since the first major goal of the Catalytic Coaching system is to create behavior change, this would seem a very
worthwhile achievement.

Brevity and Priority

Looking very quickly at the form, one will notice that there are only four
spaces provided for Improvement Areas. The same is true for Strengths, but
most managers seldom challenge the issue of having enough space to cite positive attributes. When it comes to ideas on what their direct reports can do
differently, however, some enthusiastic managers could write a phone book (or
at least a healthy dozen entries).

Ambitious agents of change should learn to exercise restraint. Nothing is more
intimidating than an exhaustive laundry list of things to do. Especially when the
items on the list are behaviorally based, meaning we're asking them to improve
how they get things done. Changing routine behavior is frequently painstaking.
Relearning requires hard work and focused attention.

Remember again two things about the way humans behave: (1) We're probably already doing the best we know how; (2) Ineffective or not, this is what
seems to be comfortable (otherwise we'd already have changed the way we
operate).

An economist from the last turn-of-the-century by the name of Vilfredo Pareto
provided valuable insight on the subject of focusing energies of change. The
"Pareto's Principle," or "80–20 Rule" as it is sometimes called, states that
80% of all problems are normally caused by 20% of the associated activities.
Logic would conclude, therefore, that it would be wise to concentrate on the
20% first to get maximum benefit from the time you have to invest in performance improvement initiatives.

I had a friend once who retired to his home. "Great!" said his wife, "Now
you can finally get busy working on that 'Honey Do List' that you've put off
for years." You can imagine his excitement as his dreams of non-stop golfing
and fishing trips were dashed to the ground. Fortunately, his wife was pretty

clever. She never let him actually see the whole list. Instead, she gave him five items at a time, rank ordered. When he finished with those she gave him more. He never did learn how long the big list actually was. But at least he kept his sanity. He could handle a list of five.

When it comes to changing behavior, it is always best to keep the list of improvement initiatives short. Four major improvement projects is all that can be reasonably expected for most of us in a given calendar year. If you pick your areas wisely, four is plenty. The challenge is to pick the improvement areas that will make the most difference and place them at the top of the list. They should be positioned such that if only one new skill or behavior were adopted in the coming year, the most valuable one to master would be listed number one.

The Long and Winding Road

For many, the improvements noted on a Coaching Worksheet will not be perfected at the end of the first year, no matter how much the individual works at it. That is particularly true when the behavior to be changed is deep-seated or complex in nature. It is okay and expected, therefore, for some issues to come up for a second or even third time. Likewise, over a series of years, certain key issues may rise or fall in priority based on the relative evolution and progress that is made.

One final word about the number of improvement areas you choose to note. Please bear in mind that these things you are asking someone to change deal with production capability and not with production itself. As such, they are layered on top of goals and objectives that are already in place for the business. And, it is important to note that by asking someone to perform their work in a new or different way you may be forcing them to slow down and/or modify results-getting practices they have used successfully in the past.

Telling a Vice President that she needs to "Improve Working Relationship with Direct Reports" is a common request. If this change includes reducing "command and control" tendencies it may be viewed as being in the long-term best interest of both the individual and her corporation. However, learning new behaviors may slow her down a bit at first, and this must be factored into business goals that are set. The point is, important changes take time. There is also real work to be accomplished with deadlines and timetables and critical milestones. We must pace ourselves when it comes to expecting large-scale change.

Most people want to do a good job. When you point out flaws and ask them to improve their performance, and you do it in a constructive way, most will want to make the changes. When you give them too much to accomplish such that they cannot fairly expect to address these areas, it can be disheartening. By focusing and prioritizing you stand the best chance to form an effective partnership for change.

CHARACTERIZING FOR IMPACT

The Catalytic Coaching model is built on the premise that some form of impact characterization increases the value of an improvement message. This has nothing to do with grading or rating. It has to do with describing the impact of an issue that is being established as an Area for Improvement. More specifically, we need to inform the employee as to the primary value of each improvement theme that is being conveyed.

The Catalytic Coaching methodology uses three basic characterizations:

• Performance Impacting

• Potential Enhancing

• Job Threatening

We will describe each of these characterizations below and then give a few examples of messages they might be used with.

Performance Impacting

We use the terminology "Performance Impacting" to describe a message that is the most basic or common. It implies that improvement in this area will help the individual make a bigger or better contribution in their current assignment. It does not necessarily imply deficiency. It represents an opportunity to enhance personal impact and productivity. Almost everyone, even your most outstanding performers, should have key areas for improvement that can be characterized in this manner.

Examples of Areas for Improvement that might be characterized as Performance Impacting might be "Time Management" or "Written Communication Skills." It would be hard to argue that improvement in either of these two areas would not yield a greater contribution in a current assignment.

More specialized examples might be "Familiarity with Key Accounts" for a new sales representative or "Knowledge of Field Operations" for a corporate controller. Increased knowledge and familiarity in each of these areas would likely assist each in performing their current assignments.

Potential Enhancing

An Area for Improvement described as "Potential Enhancing" is one that deals more with issues affecting promotability than with performance in the current job. Potential Enhancing AFIs are generally reserved for people that are on the advancement trail. They form sign posts to lead toward a desired new position. Describing an improvement theme in this manner tells the employee where she is currently perceived as below ideal expectations for a coveted position. It gives her a goal to shoot for to help improve her chances for advancement.

Examples might include "Formal Presentation Skills" for a high-performing systems engineering manager who has no current requirements to give presentations. However, because he has expressed interest in being considered for the position of Information Services Director, the AFI is relevant. The IS Director position provides many opportunities to give presentations to the senior management team. To be more competitive as a possible IS Director candidate, demonstrated improvement in this area would be beneficial.

Another example might be "Team Leadership Skills" for the senior secretary who has aspirations to one day cross over into the professional ranks. While she may not be required to serve as a team leader in her current capacity, showing skills and capabilities to do such may make her more competitive with others who will compete for the entry-level exempt position she is seeking.

Job Threatening

The third descriptor we call "Job Threatening." Labeling an Area for Improvement as Job Threatening sends a clear signal to someone that his job is on the line due to a specific behavior or skill set. If he does not demonstrate significant and sustained improvement in an area labeled Job Threatening, this employee will not remain in his current position. Transfer, demotion or termination of employment are all options that could result from failure to resolve this performance deficiency.

Notifying someone that they have a Job Threatening AFI is normally not a pleasant experience. Nor is it an experience that is engaged in lightly or without a great deal of thought and preparation. A very strict set of guidelines should be used for conveying these messages. It will be outlined below. First, however, let's review a couple of examples of Areas for Improvement that might be labeled Job Threatening.

I Guess You Just Have to Be There

"Attendance and Punctuality" is a theme that seems to come up over and over again with low-level employees who are struggling to balance out their lives. Sometimes we may have suspicions of off-the-job alcohol or drug abuse. Bottom line, however, is that employees must show up to work in a predictable fashion. After several attempts at oral counseling and/or previous reviews listing this as a Performance Impacting issue, it may become necessary to formally "send a shot over the bow" with the clear message that employment is at risk over these fundamental issues.[2]

Another Job Threatening issue might be "Meeting Time and Budget Commitments" for a Project Engineering Manager who consistently runs over time and budget deadlines on major projects. At some point her job is in danger if the practice continues. Describing the AFI as Job Threatening clearly and une-quivocally sends the message that fulfilling these commitments is a fundamental part of her job that must be performed much more accurately. The company cannot afford, and will not continue to have, overruns and time delays on major projects. The manager is being given fair warning that continued problems in this area will lead to a movement out of this key position. Depending on per-formance in other areas, availability of open positions, etc. this could mean demotion, transfer or dismissal.

A Serious Message Demands a Careful Process

It is always good practice for a Catalytic Coaching Worksheet to be reviewed and approved through the individual's chain of command. However, the Cata-lytic Coaching methodology normally *requires* that any worksheet that has even one Job Threatening Area for Improvement be approved by at least two other key people. Normally, this is the Head of Human Resources and the Corporate Attorney.

The Head of Human Resources should examine the case to make sure that the steps that are being taken are fair and free from bias. She should also insure that the form is completed in a manner that gives the best chance at producing the desired behavioral change. Finally, she should double check to make sure that all critical parties are in the boat and of one mind. When the individual receiving the coaching is at a high enough level, she needs to make sure the appropriate company officers are aware of what is about to take place. In many instances, the Executive in Charge will request an opportunity to personally review all worksheets completed on members of her organization that are given a Job Threatening message.

The Company Attorney should examine the case for equity and fairness as well, but his slant should be to ensure that the company's interests are being protected from a legal standpoint. He must feel comfortable that the message is consistent with those given in similar cases in the past. He must carefully con-sider potential exposure from the perspective of Equal Employment Opportunity, Affirmative Action, and the Americans with Disabilities Act among others.

The goal of each of these two reviews is not to censor a manager or restrict her from being straightforward in talking with an employee. Rather, it is a process of checks and balances designed to assist her in being straightforward and constructive and to protect her and the organization from time and resource-intensive responses to claims of inequity and unfairness.

The next chapter will discuss the activity of insuring fairness in more detail. More specifically, it will cover the subject of follow-up coaching, a formal procedure taken to insure that those being given strong performance messages receive extra assistance to help prompt change. It will also define and clarify the critical role of someone called a "Coach^2," a kind of coach's coach who provides extra assistance to the employee and manager for this kind of interaction. Rather than belabor the subject any more at this point, let's finish discussion of Step Two by reviewing the use of "Development Recommendations."

DEVELOPMENT RECOMMENDATIONS

The third section of the Catalytic Coaching Worksheet covers things the coach is prepared to do for the employee to assist her in attempting to improve the aforementioned Areas for Improvement. This can include recommendations for training, mentoring or exposure to different work experiences. It can also include regularly scheduled skills-based instruction, counseling and feedback sessions. Whenever possible, it should include suggestions for performing currently assigned work using the new desired behaviors.

Before we go over each basic type of recommendation, however, please be reminded of the importance of semantics here. These are things the coach and the organization is *recommending* for the employee to take advantage of. Whenever possible, they should not be mandates. This is important in keeping with the clear objective of leaving responsibility for personal development on the shoulders of the employee.

The coach gives advice and counsel. The coach provides resources. The employee must elect to take advantage of these recommendations, if she wants to improve. The task here is to guide, influence and sell. It is the employee's future that is at stake. The coach and the organization will make decisions based on how well she performs.

Training

Perhaps the first thing that most of us think about when we begin brainstorming development recommendations is some form of training. Usually, we think of formal classroom training that is provided by the company, offered at colleges and universities, or marketed by a professional training organization. Depending on the size and sophistication of your company, you may have either limited or extensive internal offerings. Smaller organizations seldom have extensive internal capacity to provide such services.

The training you recommend to your employee should be selected based on several obvious criteria. The nature of the improvement needed, level of the person being coached, budget for training expenses, quality of offerings from various sources, experience with those sources, etc. Whenever possible, it is helpful to consult with a specialist from your Human Resources or Training Department for suggestions on the best type of training to recommend. A well-organized HR function will normally provide a list of training options sorted by typical improvement areas.

It is important to note that classroom instruction is not the only way for individuals to obtain training services. Other very viable options can include videotapes, audiotapes, or CD ROM–based interactive sessions. Insight can also be achieved through the reading of books. It helps to know something about the learning style of the individual being coached. Most of us have a preferred method of absorbing new information. While the common denominator may be classroom instruction, variables such as budget, time and preferred learning styles may render another type of training equally or even more effective.

Mentoring

Is there anyone in your organization who already has the skill set that you are asking your employee to acquire? If not, what about a sister organization? Sometimes the coach himself has the desired set of behaviors. Often, however, you can find a peer who is willing to allow the employee to learn from her. When approached properly most employees are willing to help a colleague who really wants to learn.

Successful mentoring depends on a clearly defined relationship. Expectations need to be laid out clearly in advance. How much time will be required? How frequently should they expect to get together to do the mentoring?How will they know when they're done?

Since the supervisor is attempting to gather data in advance of reviewing it with the employee, and it is ultimately the employee's decision on whether to accept a mentoring relationship, the supervisor should not make any formal commitments to the activity of mentoring. She should scope out the possibility that services could be offered along with gaining permission from any appropriate managers for the time to be allocated for the mentoring work. Most commonly, therefore, mentoring must be offered subject to formal agreement by all interested parties. The coach merely lays the groundwork to see that coaching is possible with one or more mentor candidates.

Work Assignments

Perhaps the most neglected development recommendation is the most powerful. It is extremely empowering to take work already assigned to someone as an opportunity to experiment with new behaviors or skills. Here is a relevant example.

The Manager of the Physics Lab has been given an AFI that has to do with Delegation. He is perceived as too controlling and not able to let things go. On his current list of things to do is an assignment to research a new product. After taking a short course and doing some additional reading on more effective methods of delegation, he has agreed to use this as a "test case" to practice the new skills. He will attempt to work with his direct reports in a new way that is more empowering and less controlling.

Here's another example. The Manager of Employee Relations is new to the organization and has been given an AFI to Increase Familiarity with Operations.

One of her first assignments has been to create a new Policies and Procedures manual for use at locations throughout the company. While she could just mail this document to each of her twelve plant sites, she agrees to personally visit each field site. In fact, she schedules an extra day at each site to tour the facility and spend some time with each local management team. This activity will take considerably longer than just sending them the manuals through the mail, but it will probably be worth it in the long run if she, by so doing, increases her familiarity with operations.

An important similarity exists across these two examples. In neither case are we asking the employee to do additional work. We are asking them to do work already assigned to them differently.

How about one more? The Administrative Partner has been asked to learn Microsoft PowerPoint so that she can assist others in the department in generating presentations. Her boss has a presentation that is already prepared on Word. He gives her seven days to see if she can convert it to the PowerPoint format. She's already started reviewing the training manual but has not attended class. She has a peer next door who is an expert and would be willing to give her advice when she gets stuck. If she is not able to figure out the program, the boss is covered with his current version of the presentation. She proceeds to work on the project during her spare time and at night, finishing it in six days. While she has not mastered the art of PowerPoint, she is well on her way. She also feels very excited about her contribution to the presentation and future contributions she'll be able to make once she further masters the program.

Let's close this discussion about work assignments with a quote from one of my former bosses. He'd been around the block a few times, and he knew something very important about the way people generate development plans. In short, he felt training was often used as a panacea for all deficiencies. He was quick to point out that attending classes did not mean new skills were being learned or utilized. From his vantage point: "People grow more from what they learn in job assignments than from fancy training courses. Sending people to classes is an overrated development tool."[3]

Those of you who have made much of your living connected with training and educational processes might find this sentiment initially discomforting. On further examination and reflection, however, you may come full circle. What is suggests in essence is to invest more creative energy in selecting job assignments while tempering the instinct to prescribe coursework for key development needs. It is definitely healthy food for thought.

Coaching and Counseling

Many times what employees need to continue their development is additional coaching. Once a year is not sufficient. They need feedback on a much more frequent basis when they are trying to change behavior that is deeply ingrained or when trying to adopt new behaviors that seem so elusive.

When this type of assistance comes from the supervisor or manager, it might easily be thought of as coaching. One could call it mentoring, and it is, but it is a special kind of mentoring when it is coming from one's boss.

Performance Problems

We talked earlier and we'll talk again next chapter about the special needs for feedback that occur whenever an individual is given a Job Threatening Area for Improvement. In addition to being careful in constructing and delivering a message of this sort, however, additional communication is often a critical component of the employee's development plan. For their own peace of mind, those whose jobs have been threatened need and deserve frequent updates on their progress. By providing a regular day and time to discuss progress on the critical issue(s), the coach is assisting in the development process. She is helping the employee make continuous improvement in his efforts to change.

In meetings held each week every other work or once a month, she gives feedback pertaining to any AFI that is Job Threatening. She gives positive feedback when improvements are noted and negative when things have not improved or continue to deteriorate. She gives as many examples as possible to illustrate these points.

When things go well over an extended period of time, the interval between meetings can be lengthened. Eventually, after periods of significant and sustained improvements, a new worksheet should be written that takes the individual off probationary status. The critical issue may have been resolved completely or may continue to be of concern, but at a lesser level of importance (i.e., it has become Performance Impacting).

When things don't go well and no progress is noted or expected, a different kind of decision must be made. If someone cannot or will not change to meet minimum requirements for a given position, they must either be moved or removed. If the coaching process is performed properly, they will almost welcome the change. No one likes to fail to meet expectations over a long period of time.

Up-and-Comers

Sometimes it seems like we spend all our time on the problem cases with little left over for the high performing individuals who both need and deserve our attention. This is an undesirable state of affairs. One of the greatest investments we can make in our people involves our time. Offering to spend formal time each week, month or quarter giving feedback and guidance to an employee is, therefore, a legitimate and valuable development recommendation. For the neophyte with lots of questions and strong ambition, it is particularly valuable.

Based on the AFIs for each individual, we should consider offering time to perform additional coaching over and above what is done annually in the formal review. Setting up a standing appointment for lunch on the first Tuesday of each month might be a way to make sure you find time to give attention to a new and aspiring member of your work team. Care should be given, of course, to not overlook the needs of others who also deserve attention. The key concept is balance.

Words of Caution

Before we conclude this discussion, it is important to review a very common misunderstanding about this section of the Catalytic Coaching Worksheet. No matter how clearly we try to explain the intent of the Development Recommendations activity, a certain percentage of those completing the form always seem to get it wrong.

It is a mistake to use this section to slip in a fourth and fifth Area for Improvement, although this often occurs. In other words, a supervisor will indicate an action item in this section that does not connect in any way with the Areas for Improvement noted above.

Let me give an example to illustrate. Let's say we have a member of the support staff who has been given the following four Areas for Improvement that are all listed as Performance Impacting:

• Increase typing speed

• Increase familiarity with our key clients

• Improve time management

• Learn responsibilities of Fire Warden for the floor

Including the following under Development Recommendations would not be in the spirit of the process:

• Cover for VP administrative partner position

• Take PowerPoint course

• Represent department on annual picnic committee

Each of the activities recommended above might represent a legitimate development activity, but they are not connected to any of the top four priorities that were listed above. Hence, they represent additional things to do rather than ideas for how to deal with the challenges already set forth. This serves to dilute the carefully crafted message above and leaves the employee with less assurance that the manager is prepared to help out with the top four priorities that were mentioned previously.

Piling It On

Some organizations seem to be obsessed with the need to create endless "To Do Lists." This can lead to frightening cases of "initiative overload." One company we worked with seemed to have no ability to restrain themselves to a reasonable set of expectations. Each year they required executives and managers to create personal productivity goals, team goals, department goals, company goals, 360° Feedback development goals and personal improvement goals. They literally had goals about making goals. It was maddening. It was frustrating. It was ineffective.

This inability to see the forest for the trees resulted in people just shutting down. Since it was impossible to meet all of the objectives, and since no one seemed to be interested in paring them down, people were forced to choose whatever goals made sense to them. The only problem was that no matter which goals someone accomplished, there were always many more to feel guilty about neglecting. In the end, it left even the highest achievers feeling unsatisfied and frustrated. It was a frequent discussion topic of exit interviews.

We are reminded of this story at this time because the members of this organization were particularly prone to sneaking extra goals in the Development Recommendations section. It was instinctive. They had been conditioned to believe that a good manager was a good goal creator. The more things you could think of for your employees to improve, the better the manager you were. If that were true, this organization had bred managers without peer.

A few words come to mind for those who live through this kind of experience: overwhelming, exhausting, intimidating and demotivating. Sometimes it is good to benchmark organizational practices that serve as a model of what *not* to do.

A WORD ABOUT TIMING

The Catalytic Coaching methodology requires that Step Two be completed at least once a year. It can, however, be used more frequently if a manager feels it would be useful. Discussions based on the Step Two worksheet that occur at intervals other than the one scheduled each year are called "off-cycle" discussions and can also be used with great impact.

Off-cycle sessions can and should be held any time a manager feels the employee could benefit from carefully crafted feedback. The mere fact that they are being conducted at times other than the routine date can be used to the coach's advantage. If the message contains strongly worded feedback, the employee can be encouraged to make progress on deficient AFIs before the "formal" cycle commences.

The manager (with HR counsel whenever possible) may elect to hold the off-cycle worksheet out of the official personnel file if progress is noted. Employees sometimes find this tactic highly motivational and work hard to quickly change the AFIs on which they are counseled. Those who fail to make progress find their time in the troubled assignment to be shortened substantially. The point here is that the form and process are to be used when trouble or opportunity is first noticed, not just once a year at a prescribed date.

The Story of Shirley

We will end this chapter with another "tale from the front." This intervention took place in an organization that had adopted the practice of Catalytic Coaching and involved the use of an off-cycle discussion. It provides an excellent example of the power of this process to help bring about positive behavioral change.

The situation in question involved a woman named Shirley, a senior administrative assistant in a marketing organization. Shirley appeared to have a Dr. Jeckyl and Ms. Hyde aspect to her personality. She was, on the one hand, a stellar performer and, on the other, a totally disruptive work influence. Over time the second aspect of her personality threatened to negate all the good performed by the first.

Despite the pleasant outward demeanor Mike, the HR Manager, witnessed whenever he walked past Shirley in the hall, she was, according to multiple reports, mean as a snake. Mike found this particularly challenging to grasp because Shirley was a very religious person with a large family. She spoke frequently of church activities and children and seemed to be the model citizen. She had also been with the company for more than 25 years.

Regardless of Mike's impression, reports began flooding in that Shirley was extremely hard to work with. She supported a Vice President and two senior managers. She apparently gave the Vice President excellent service while snubbing the others. In fact, she could be quite abrupt in dismissing her managers' requests for assistance. In addition, there were complaints from peers who found Shirley cold and demanding. When she wanted something, she wanted it NOW! She frequently used her Vice President's name to bludgeon her way into getting what she desired.

What really got Shirley in trouble, however, were the complaints from external customers. Every once in a while someone would call in and let a company representative know how rude Shirley was to them over the phone. She literally told customers that she didn't have time for them or their problems. Those who witnessed the problem thought it to be a real liability for the whole company. People Shirley was rude to made some substantial buying decisions.

Following a series of bad incidents, Mike helped Shirley's Vice President complete a Catalytic Coaching Worksheet on her. Correctly reflecting Shirley's performance, it was full of both high highs and low lows. Two areas were listed as Job Threatening. Despite her great strengths and extensive service, Shirley was warned that her job was in jeopardy.

Perhaps the best thing that the Vice President did in this process was to build in some very positive development plans. Among other things, he offered to pay for Shirley to attend the Dale Carnegie Course in Effective Human Relations. She was the first nonexempt person the company had ever offered to send to the course, having only sent three professionals previously.

When Shirley had a follow-up meeting with Mike, she reported that her first impression of the confrontation was disconcerting. She wanted to write the whole exercise off as a veiled attempt to "run her off." Her best guess was that it was because she was a powerful female, and her bosses didn't like that kind of strength in a woman. This did not jibe well, however, with the fact that they were offering to send her to a relatively expensive course that had heretofore only been offered to some of our top professionals. She also observed that the course was fourteen weeks, so this didn't suggest they were trying to run her off quickly.

To make a long story short, Shirley agreed to go to the course. In fact, she went with the specific quest to learn how to "win friends and influence people" without having to resort to her traditional "power tactics," as she liked to think of them.

Not only did Shirley attend the course, she won awards in it. She was later asked to serve as a Graduate Assistant to help teach others what she had learned. More importantly, she began applying these new skills and behaviors on the job. In so doing, she saved her job and career. In fact, she was later transferred to a new group and placed in a position of greater independence and accountability. If she continues this pattern of growth she may one day cross over to exempt ranks.

This story appears to have a happy ending. Eventually, over time Shirley kept her greatest strengths and got rid of her biggest deficiencies. She, like all of us, still struggles with certain aspects of her job and business relationships. But her challenges are much more acceptable and appropriate for the position she holds in the company. What a great loss for all concerned had they not found an effective way to help Shirley change.

IN A NUTSHELL

In the Catalytic Coaching model, Step Two is where the rubber meets the road. This is where the manager gives downward feedback to the employee with a focus on bringing about meaningful behavioral change. Because of the knowledge about desires and needs gained in Step One, the interaction can be tailored to meet the individual needs of each employee. The specific mechanics of Step Two help maximize chances that the interaction is successful.

Conducted properly, Step Two should result in an exchange of information that is extremely valuable to an employee. Being freed from the necessity to justify a label or grade allows a manager to be much more honest and direct. It encourages the boss to say diplomatically to the employee what those who control the employee's career are saying about the employee behind his back.

Because of this level of honesty, a Step Two discussion can be unlike any ever experienced previously by an employee or her manager. Responding sincerely to the realism of dreams and desires the employee supplies in Step One puts the coach in heartfelt and value-laden territory. It is not uncommon for an employee to express sincere appreciation following one of these interviews. This can happen in the same session that causes that same individual to cry. Those who approach this process with any degree of integrity will find it impossible to consider the activity an inefficient, bureaucratic waste of time. This is the end of the performance review as we have come to know it.

The next chapter will provide additional information on how to deal effectively in Step Two with problem performers. More in depth advice on how to deal with specific types of challenges will be covered in Chapter 17, where we will review what we call "special case coaching."

Chapter 11

Follow-Up Coaching:
The Role of the Coach²

If you have built castles in the air,
your work need not be lost:
that is where they should be.
Now put the foundations under them.

—Henry David Thoreau[1]

When the message to an employee in Step Two is confrontational or formally notifies someone that his job is at risk, another player becomes critical to the effective implementation of the Catalytic Coaching methodology. This person serves as a coach's coach and a process facilitator. We will refer to him as a Follow-Up Coach, or more simply as a "Coach²."

This chapter will describe the critical role of the Coach² as it pertains to Step Two of the model. We will describe who should normally serve in this capacity and give three examples of approaches they might take in effectively executing their responsibilities. While there are perhaps several other approaches that might be adopted, the three chosen should give you a feel for the powerful manner with which Catalytic Coaching can be used to speed significant behavioral change.

FOLLOW-UP COACHING

In the previous chapter we discussed the importance of the organization working in concert to send important performance messages to employees. We discussed how a message that contains even one Area for Improvement described as Job Threatening needs to be reviewed and approved by senior management,

Human Resources and/or Legal. Having gone through this process and received endorsement to confront an employee in this manner, a manager moves forward in the process with assistance from the organization. A formal mechanism involving follow-up is triggered.

The day after a coach gives an employee a Job Threatening performance message the employee is paid a visit by a Coach[2]. The Coach[2] should be a neutral outsider—someone not in the same chain of command with the employee undergoing coaching. She should also be someone with special training to do the job.

Who Should Do It?

In many organizations, the most likely place to find someone to do routine follow-up coaching is in the Employee Relations section of the HR department. Depending on the size of the organization and the level of the person being coached, this could range from a relatively new professional to the Director of Human Resources. Sometimes there is someone in a Training function or in Organization Development that might be trusted to perform this activity. In an organization where no logical person of this capacity exists, it is worth the cost to obtain an outside contractor.

Ideally, all parties should recognize the Follow-Up Coach as being involved with the coaching process from the start. Typically, this is accomplished by using someone who helped introduce the technology to the organization. As such, it is known that she has the skills as a coaching instructor as well as formal responsibility to perform this kind of task.

Above all, the person or persons selected to serve in this capacity must have credibility in the eyes of the organization. Managers must trust them to provide insight and guidance. Legal must trust them not to expose the company to unnecessary risks. Employees must trust them to be honest and fair. They must not be perceived as either an employee advocate or company stooge. And they must be very good at carrying on difficult, painful, and sometimes heated, conversations.

What They Should Do

The work of the Coach[2] normally starts in the preparation stages for the Step Two discussion session between the manager and his direct report. The challenge here is to truly understand what the critical deficiencies are to make sure the form is completed in the most powerful and balanced way. The Coach[2] should become very familiar with the case by virtue of assisting in this preparation.

The Coach[2] must also serve to counsel an inexperienced or nervous manager on how best to conduct herself in the Step Two interview. For inexperienced managers, the necessity to confront someone directly about poor performance is an emotion-laden task. Even those with experience in such matters can often benefit from the assistance of an experienced Coach[2] who can provide objective outside perspective by virtue of being more removed from the relationship.

Once the manager is prepared for the interview with the employee, the next action for the Coach[2] is to debrief the manager following the discussion. She should find out how the manager thinks the conversation went. Key here is to get a feel for how the employee accepted the feedback and request to change. Was he defensive? Did he argue about the legitimacy of the Job Threatening Area(s) for Improvement? How did he respond to the discussion on Strengths? Did he perceive the items listed here to be accurate and fair? How did he respond to the Development Recommendations? Did he object to taking the class or accepting the developmental assignment that we recommended? What did he say at the conclusion of the meeting?

The goal with this interview is to get a feel for where an employee's head is at immediately following the interview. Unless there is a dramatic problem of some sort, the Coach[2] will not act on this information for another day. An employee should normally be allowed at least an evening to soak in the information he has been given. This time may, in fact, change the perspective he has on his counsel. In some cases for the better, in others for the worse.

The real work of the Coach[2] begins when she meets face-to-face with the employee. As stated earlier, this interaction should normally occur on the day after a discussion with the manager. Two days is acceptable in some cases, but it should not extend beyond that under normal circumstances. The goal of the follow-up session is to insure that the employee received the message as intended and is in a healthy mindset on how to deal with it. Because there are many possible ways for the message to be misconstrued in transmission, and because the subject matter can be deeply emotional for an individual, the time frame for follow-up should be tightly controlled.

The mechanics for setting up a follow-up session depend largely on the specifics of an employee's situation. In some cases it is appropriate to call someone and ask them to come to the office of the Coach[2]. If the Coach[2] is a high-ranking HR official who is associated in people's minds with sudden disappearances (layoffs and firings), this is probably not a good idea. The employee might die a thousand deaths on the elevator riding to their meeting with the hatchet man.

It might be better in this case to stage the discussion in the employee's office, on turf that is more comfortable to him. On the other hand, not all employees have offices and if the Coach[2] is unfamiliar in the area, her mere presence might send the rumor mill into overdrive and unnecessarily burden the already self-conscious employee.

If all else fails, the Coach[2] can invite the employee to lunch. Most companies do not dine their employees immediately before firing them, so the fear factor might be lessened. And as long as the Follow-Up Coach takes the employee somewhere out of the normal dining pattern for office employees, the gossip mongers will have little to go on.

Wherever the follow-up session takes place, the next challenge becomes getting the employee to open up about the coaching session. Most often it works for a Coach² to just lay the cards on the table face up. She might try something like this: "I understand you had a coaching session yesterday with Susan. Would you mind if I ask you a few questions about it?" Assuming a positive response, the next question needs to be more open-ended. Often all it takes to get things going is one good question, like: "What did she say?" After that it is off to the races. Using a series of clarifying questions is all it takes to gather all the data you need on the situation.

Some cases are more challenging, to be sure. An employee who perceives the Coach² to be a biased agent of management might mutter a few phrases before they clam up and get stone faced. Each situation is different, and that's why it takes someone with training, and preferably counseling experience, to serve in this role.

Perhaps the best way to teach both the value and technique of follow-up coaching is to go through a few examples. Below are three types of situations that are very common. The first involves an employee who is a hard sell. She tries to discredit her message or messenger so she won't have to change. In this case it is the job of the Coach² to get her attention and help her embrace the message for change.

The second example involves and employee who has taken the message to heart, but perhaps too much so. He is petrified of doing anything wrong and is reacting like a deer frozen in the headlights of an oncoming car. The task of the Coach² here is to help him realize that he can avoid a problem if he takes appropriate action.

The third example represents the logical extreme in coaching: someone who denies the feedback and wants nothing to do with it. He argues with both his boss and Coach² about the importance of change. It is the job of the Coach² to force him to come to grips with the real-life consequences that he is about to experience if he does not accept the message to change.

All three of these examples are based on real incidents and contain dialogue that is as close to what actually happened as possible. As always, the identities of the individuals involved have been somewhat disguised to insure anonymity. We will simply refer to those involved as "COACH²" and "EMPLOYEE."

Example 1: The Hard Sell

COACH²: How did it go yesterday?

EMPLOYEE: All right, I guess. Kind of like facing a firing squad.

COACH²: How do you mean?

EMPLOYEE: He just had it in for me. Looks like he's trying to run me off.

COACH²: I see. Did he say anything specific as to why?

EMPLOYEE: Sure. He said something about showing up to work on time and not taking days off without telling him in advance.

COACH[2]: Have you been doing these things?

EMPLOYEE: Well, yeah, I guess so. But so has everyone else. I think it's just because I'm ——— that he's out to get me.

COACH[2]: I see. Did he give you any numbers to substantiate his feeling that you have had an attendance and punctuality problem? [I already know he did and have the figures that document the employee being absent more than three times the rate of the next member of the work group.]

EMPLOYEE: Uh, well, yeah, I guess. Something about twelve days in the last six months.

COACH[2]: Did he say anything about how that compared to others in the work group?

EMPLOYEE: [Quizzical glance, beginning to realize I must have data.] Yeah. Lots more, I guess.

COACH[2]: Did he tell you anything else that threatens your job?

EMPLOYEE: No, not really. Most of the other stuff was just things for me to work on to improve.

COACH[2]: I see. Like what?

EMPLOYEE: [Employee proceeds to explain two of the three remaining Performance Impacting Areas for Improvement. When quizzed, he recalls most of the third.]

COACH[2]: Did your supervisor tell you what he likes about your work performance?

EMPLOYEE: [Another glance. This one confirming the realization that I must have a copy of the coaching worksheet and am in on the whole conspiracy.] Yeah, he said something about my typing skills and how quick I turn around work projects.

COACH[2]: Interesting. Is that true?

EMPLOYEE: Absolutely! I type 92 words a minute with zero errors and I know what format these guys want. I'm the fastest in the department.

COACH[2]: Wow. That's impressive. Any other strengths that he listed?

EMPLOYEE: [Dialogue continues as the Coach[2] prompts the employee to recall things said about other positive feedback.] I really hadn't recalled all that. I knew the conversation was gonna change over to something negative soon, so I guess I really wasn't listening all that well in the first part.

COACH[2]: I see. Now that we have reviewed the material again, how does it seem to you? Are these positive things he's saying pretty accurate? Are they fair?

EMPLOYEE: Yeah, I guess so.

COACH[2]: Would they be equally true of Mary or Jane who work in jobs similar to yours?

EMPLOYEE: No way. At least not most of them.

COACH[2]: Interesting. Doesn't sound like somebody who ''just wants to run you off'' to me. Perhaps what your boss was trying to say is that you're great when you're here. He just can't depend on you right now. Maybe the real message here is not so general, but rather very specific.

EMPLOYEE: So I guess that means I've got to start showing up each day on time without any more excuses.

COACH[2]: I think you've got the message very clearly now. Aside from what he's already listed that he'll do to try to help you, is there anything else you need from the company to make this happen.

EMPLOYEE: No. I don't think so. From here on out, it's up to me.

After a bit of rehashing, the first example turned out okay. Despite the best efforts of the supervisor, the employee was trying to shift responsibility for the problem to someone else in an effort not to have to change. The Follow-Up Coach was able to help the employee see the illogic of her position. In the end, he helped her accept responsibility and confront the real issue that faced her. Let's try another one where the employee had a different initial reaction to his coach's message.

Example 2: Deer in the Headlights

COACH[2]: How did it go yesterday?

EMPLOYEE: It was pretty intense.

COACH[2]: How do you mean?

EMPLOYEE: She told me my job was on the line. I can be demoted, transferred out of the department or terminated if I don't start getting my work turned in on time.

COACH[2]: I see. Did she tell you anything else you need to improve?

EMPLOYEE: Yes. She gave me three other things to work on, but none of the others is job threatening. The next most important is improving my familiarity with PowerPoint and Excel. She also thinks I should speak up more at meetings and share more in the leadership roles on projects. The final point was something about making better presentations.

COACH[2]: I see. It sounds like you were listening quite attentively during your review. Did she say anything about things you currently do well?

EMPLOYEE: She said I am really good with numbers. She said I work hard and put in lots of hours. She said I know a lot about my specialty area of tax accounting.

COACH[2]: How do you feel about what you were told yesterday?

EMPLOYEE: I'm scared. I didn't get a lot of sleep last night. I can't lose my job. I've got two kids in college and one still in high school.

COACH[2]: Did she have any suggestions for you on how to improve or give you any ideas on the things you can do to keep this from happening?

EMPLOYEE: She said she'd send me to Time Management School and help to teach me to use a planner. She said I could work with Ed to see how he breaks down his projects and uses a more systematic approach to attack his problems. I think Ed uses a software program that she said she'd buy me, too, if I want it.

COACH[2]: Sounds like you received the message loud and clear. Anything else your boss or I can do to help you?

EMPLOYEE: Maybe you can tell her that I got her message and really want to do better.

This is something I've needed to get a handle on for years. I'm not going to rest until I figure it out.

COACH[2]: I'll give her that feedback.

In this instance the message from the coach was received loud and clear. Perhaps too much so. The Follow-Up Coach helped the employee make sure that the boss understood the message was received. This allowed her to immediately devote her energies to helping the employee change and abandon any temptation to continue to sell the need for change. It also allowed her to send a message of encouragement back to the employee reemphasizing her commitment to help meet the employee half way.

When a manager/coach receives a message from a Follow-Up Coach like this, it is like a patient getting a healthy report from a physical following surgery. While not confirming success, it is valuable information that the operation went well. Prognosis for a full recovery should be very positive.

Because things do not always go as planned, we must examine at least one other example involving follow-up on Job Threatening messages. In this case, the employee provides the Follow-Up Coach with a skills challenge.

Example 3: The Double Barrel Approach

COACH[2]: How did it go yesterday?

EMPLOYEE: Fine.

COACH[2]: What did you learn?

EMPLOYEE: Not much. Typical review.

COACH[2]: [Puzzled.] Weren't you given a rather straightforward message about needing to make some changes?

EMPLOYEE: Oh, you mean about needing to comply with the company dress policy and follow my supervisor's orders.

COACH[2]: Exactly.

EMPLOYEE: Well, I've been thinking about it.

COACH[2]: [After a brief pause.] I take it by the fact that you're wearing blue jeans, sneakers and no tie that you have elected thus far not to accept this counseling.

EMPLOYEE: Like I say, I'm still thinking about it.

COACH[2]: [Leaning forward in her chair.] I see. Do you mind if I ask you a question?

EMPLOYEE: No. Fire away.

COACH[2]: Are you independently wealthy?

EMPLOYEE: [Sitting up in chair for the first time.] Say what?

COACH[2]: [Calmly] Are you independently wealthy? Do you need the income from the company to pay the rent or make car payments?

EMPLOYEE: [Incredulous] You're kidding, right? Man, I have two kids at home plus three others that I have to pay child support for.

COACH²: [After a brief pause.] Do you like working here?

EMPLOYEE: Uh . . . It's okay. I've been here for ten years. I don't know any place better.

COACH²: Then this really puzzles me . . . [As she pulls out copy of Coaching Worksheet from her coat pocket and begins unfolding it.]

EMPLOYEE: [Sitting upright and leaning forward with eyes wide open.] What do you mean?

COACH²: As I understand it, you were just told yesterday that if you did not start coming to work with slacks, dress shirt and a tie, that you faced the likelihood of dismissal. Despite the fact that you may be the best draftsman we've got.

EMPLOYEE: [With voice slightly breaking.] I guess I didn't understand it that way. I think it's stupid for draftsmen to have to wear ties.

COACH²: That's interesting, but it's a company policy. And you were requested repeatedly to comply. You can't just pick and choose which rules to comply with, at least not at this company.

EMPLOYEE: I guess I hadn't really thought of it that way.

COACH²: There's also some other things on this form that you probably need to pay attention to if you want to stay employed here. Nothing you couldn't change in a week, if you wanted to, but you're going to have to at least make the effort.

EMPLOYEE: [Leaning forward and reaching for the worksheet.] Do you think I could have another copy of that form? I threw my other one away.

This example, like the others, is taken almost verbatim from a real situation. The next day the employee showed up to work dressed according to company guidelines. Most remarkable, however, was the change in his demeanor overall. Soon the employee, who for years had been regarded as the resident cynic, began taking voluntary leadership roles on teams. What a remarkable change in attitude and performance! What a tremendous relief to his supervisor!

IN SUMMARY

This chapter covered in detail the extra activity that occurs in the Catalytic Coaching model when an individual is given a strong performance message. In those cases where Job Threatening message is communicated it becomes a formal part of Step Two. Part B, if you will. In some cases, it can amount to an insurance step simply confirming that a message was received as intended and will be acted upon. In other cases it gives a critical second opportunity to convey a serious message meant to drive home the need for change. When executed properly it can salvage a relationship or save a career.

We covered the critical role of the Follow-Up Coach, or Coach² and what kind of person it takes to do this kind of work. Those trained in this skills set and given the opportunity to practice follow-up coaching will receive a tremendous education in how people think and what it takes to convince them to change. Some organizations may wish to consider putting high potential line managers in the position on a temporary basis so that they can build new skills and capacities. If you elect to do this, however, just remember to provide them with requisite training and make sure that they have a more experienced coach to turn to for advice in solving the most difficult problems. In a large organization this might mean identifying a Coach[3] (the Coach's Coach's Coach) who makes sure all the Coach[2]s are given any support that they need. We'll talk more about this in Part IV when we discuss the challenges of acquiring coaching competencies and building infrastructure to make the process work.

Because follow-up coaching can be so powerful, some might wonder why we do not recommend using it for all employees who go through the coaching process. The answer, of course, is simple economics. Follow-up activities can double the amount of time invested in the coaching process. Thinking back to our measurement discussion in Chapter 7, it makes sense to spend the money to add the practice whenever the incremental results it provides sufficiently outweigh the expense. As fewer misunderstandings and communication breakdowns normally occur in passing along less threatening messages, most organizations adopting this system have elected not to use it unless they anticipate a possible problem.

While in most organizations the number of people receiving Job Threatening messages will be small, providing those who do receive such messages follow-up support is critical. Follow-up coaching is a critical sub-routine to the Catalytic Coaching methodology.

Chapter 12

Step Three:
Personal Development Plan

The method of the enterprising is to plan with audacity, and execute with vigor; to sketch out a map of possibilities; and then treat them as probabilities.

—Bovee[1]

Our doubts are like traitors and make us lose the good we oft might win by fearing to attempt.

—William Shakespeare, *Measure for Measure*, act I, scene IV

Success is not the result of spontaneous combustion. You must set yourself on fire.

—Reggie Leach[2]

As depicted in Figure 12-1, the Third Step of the Catalytic Coaching model involves creation of a *Personal Development Plan* (PDP). This chapter will describe the process that is used to complete the PDP. We will also discuss in detail the proper roles for employee and supervisor in Step Three. Finally, we will review several examples of both effective and ineffective PDPs.

In keeping with the spirit of our program, the Personal Development Plan should be centered around a very concise and highly focused document. In almost every case, the PDP should be no more than one page in length. An example of a blank PDP form is included as Appendix D. While this form can be customized to meet the needs of any specific situation, care should be taken not to expand it considerably beyond its ideal state. This is where the organizations prone to "piling it on," that we spoke of in the previous chapter, need to exercise some restraint.

Figure 12-1
Step Three

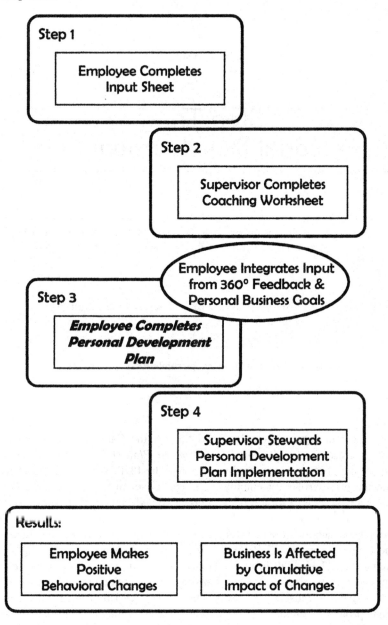

Step 1
Employee Completes
Input Sheet

Step 2
Supervisor Completes
Coaching Worksheet

Employee Integrates Input
from 360° Feedback &
Personal Business Goals

Step 3
Employee Completes
Personal Development
Plan

Step 4
Supervisor Stewards
Personal Development
Plan Implementation

Results:
Employee Makes
Positive
Behavioral Changes

Business Is Affected
by Cumulative
Impact of Changes

PROCESS OWNERSHIP

One of the most important design issues inherent in the Catalytic Coaching methodology has to do with ownership. While the supervisor or manager may feel great ownership in the business and an obligation to make things better, individual performance improvements must ultimately be accomplished by the employee, not her boss.

A football coach may see potential in a young running back. Because of his greater experience, he may know exactly how to tap into it. He must not forget, however, that it is the young running back that must perform the requisite wind sprints to get faster. It is the running back that must do the sit ups and push ups to get stronger. The coach can only give advice and encouragement.

Using this logic, the Personal Development Plan must be owned by the employee. To be sure, the supervisor/coach should have some say in the matter. But in the end, the employee must take ownership and responsibility for the areas she elects to improve and the actions designed to facilitate the improvement.

With this in mind, the obvious person to take first shot at drafting the Personal Development Plan is the employee. To complete this form, the employee should consult the material put forth by her coach in Step Two of the process. She should consult the Development Recommendations section on the Catalytic Coaching Worksheet for specific suggestions made by her coach.

WHEN SIX IS BETTER THAN SIXTY-THREE

As clearly indicated on the process map, the employee should also make use of information received from 360° Feedback sessions or other forms of personal development work, if those types of assessment tools have also been utilized. The goal here is to have one development plan that integrates all production capability improvement issues. Having separate development plans for each type of feedback will usually prove ineffective.

As we have already discussed, individuals have only so much time to budget for improving the manner in which they do their work. Three different lists of overlapping goals and objectives each stated in slightly different terms, at best, serves to dilute energy. At worst, it can leave even the most conscientious employee feeling totally overwhelmed.

One clearly focused list of six to nine top desired action items has a lot higher probability of being completed than three different lists and a total of 63. Even if the individual were able to complete sixteen of the items from the larger list, the items completed may not be the ones of greatest impact. Frequently they will be either the items of most interest and least threat to the employee or the quickest and easiest to accomplish.

The Catalytic Coaching methodology encourages the employee to work diligently on a smaller number of improvement actions, but it concentrates on the items few that will likely produce the greatest amount of meaningful behavioral change. One of the primary contributions of the coach to this process is providing assistance with focus. It is her job to see to it that employees hone in on action items likely to have the greatest impact.

COMPLETING THE PDP FORM

The task at hand, then, is to come up with a short list of activities to try to concentrate energy on. The employee must develop action items centered on at least two, but no more than four of the Areas for Improvement noted by the coach. In most cases, she will include specific action items obtained directly from the Development Recommendations provided by the coach. She is not compelled to do exactly as the coach recommends but should start with these ideas as input. If she elects to put forward an alternative action, she should be aware of how it differs from what the coach originally suggested and be prepared to explain the logic of her choice and its benefits.

In rank order, the employee should repeat the themes she wishes to address. Appendix E shows an example of a completed form. In this instance, Sally, a manager for a restaurant, has proposed to work on three basic Areas for Improvement and one Strength (we will discuss the inclusion of a Strength later in the chapter). Under each of these headings she has chosen two to three activities, giving her a total of nine action items to complete for the coming year.

When completing the first draft of the PDP, the employee may want to suggest modification of some of the specific development recommendations put forth on the Catalytic Coaching Worksheet. For example, if the coach suggested attending a seminar on Time Management sponsored by a local university, the employee might request that this be modified to a Franklin/Covey school on Time Management that is being taught locally in the coming month. If the costs are similar and the coach has no particular bias about either of the courses, this may be perfectly fine.

A manager should be pleased when an employee makes a modification to one of her development recommendations and, if at all possible, should grant the request. By making the change, the employee has taken ownership of the means of improvement. As a consequence he will normally work harder to integrate the new ideas into practice. It is now *his* idea. The manager has truly assumed the role of coach and advisor.

Getting the Picture

Looking again at the example of the restaurant manager above, consider that the original recommendation by Sally's boss was for Sally to improve knowledge of key customers by greeting each customer group at their table each night. Sally enhanced this by suggesting that she be allowed to take a photograph of the most frequent customers to aid her memory and speed her learning process.

She made this exciting for the customers by offering them a free copy of a souvenir photo before they left the restaurant that evening. Meanwhile she was able to use a second copy of the picture for flash cards and include it in a computer file with information about key customer preferences. Total cost for this project was estimated to be $800 for a six-month pilot.

Sally's boss was delighted to approve this expenditure. Not only did he think it was a good business idea, he saw this as a wonderful sign that Sally understood the importance of his counsel. It was clear she both understood the AFI and wanted to take action to address it. Furthermore, if this effort proved successful, Sally's idea might be utilized throughout the entire restaurant chain. Both Sally and her coach were excited to "see what developed" from this interesting and creative approach to performance improvement. Each felt ownership and pride for being associated with this novel idea.

Seeking Support for Change

Sometimes an employee may need additional time to complete a normal task because he is experimenting with a new type of behavior. For example, a senior professional may initially be slower using e-mail than he was giving stacks of letters to an administrative assistant to type. If an AFI is for him to learn to better utilize technology, however, this may be a worthwhile short-term slow down. Likewise, if he feels that participation on a cross-functional task force would aid some aspect of his development, he might appeal for sponsorship when completing the PDP. Under any circumstances, if the employee feels that extra time or resources are needed to fulfill a development recommendation, now is the time to negotiate those terms.

Most meaningful change requires either time or money; sometimes both. This is the primary reason we must limit the number of initiatives undertaken in a given year. We must remember the dilemma of production versus production capability that we spoke of earlier. While it is in our best interest to work on production capability (the ability to produce golden eggs), we should not forget that the overall objective remains maximizing golden egg production. To be successful in the long run and create a culture built on continuous learning, we must adopt a pace of concentrated personal change that is sustainable over time.

Instant Payback

If you examine the PDP form carefully, you will notice that it does not concentrate exclusively on Areas for Improvement. As we noted with our example of the restaurant manager above, there is a space intended to include one Strength as well.

The principle here is that one should look for methods of giving instant payback to the organization. By requesting that each person discuss ways of sharing at least one Strength, we help build a culture that reinforces sharing information and skills. Including it on a formal review sheet like the PDP recognizes the importance of mentoring and helping others. And since successful Catalytic Coaching frequently utilizes the technique of mentoring, this allows people to literally get credit for doing the right thing and helping others improve.

This is a chance to encourage your most gifted marketing manger to spend time with a green but promising newcomer. It's a chance to encourage your one master payroll clerk to share the secrets she has gathered over 30 years of work history. It's a chance to have your newly hired CPA teach her more senior colleagues in the department how to use the Internet.

Most people feel proud to be noted as a subject-matter expert and are willing to share information, if approached properly. Some do naturally. Others don't. Institutionalizing the sharing of best practices by asking individuals to share and teach as part of their development plan is a big idea with far-ranging consequences.

THE INTERVIEW

Because he owns this part of the process, the employee should lead the discussion on the Personal Development Plan. The coach must provide a time and place for the meeting, but it is the employee who brings the completed form and talks through his development plan as drafted.

The goal of this meeting should be to emerge with a plan that is endorsed by both parties. Even though the employee "owns" the plan, the manager controls access to the resources normally needed to put it into operation. For the purposes of this exercise, it clearly "takes two to tango." The length and intensity of the meeting will normally vary depending on how many of the coach's ideas have been integrated into the development plan and how many new initiatives have been added. An average of a half an hour per employee will typically suffice.

Clarification of Expectations

If an employee appears to have completely disregarded a strong message from the coach and built a plan around easier and less critical improvement areas, the discussion can be rather interesting. Here the coach's task is to challenge the individual to take on the most significant changes first, even if they are more difficult. Improvement initiatives of lesser importance should be moved down the list or moved until a time in the future when the bigger performance gaps have started to close.

Under no circumstances should the coach feel reluctant to challenge an employee who seems to have gone off on a tangent. This step of the process helps demonstrate whether an accurate and complete understanding of the coach's comments have been heard and understood by the employee. If it is obvious that the message has been improperly interpreted or misconstrued, extra care should be taken to insure that that situation is corrected. When a serious gap is detected or there is resistance in accepting a modified message, the coach should enlist the assistance of the HR coordinator or a Coach[2].

Making sure that a Personal Development Plan is completed properly is important both for the individual and the company as well. A fundamental principle surrounding the creation of a PDP is to follow the logical advice to place "first things first." Stephen Covey and Roger and Rebecca Merrill speak eloquently and elaborately on this topic in a book devoted totally to the subject of time and life management. Their guidance on this subject literally helps clarify the role of the coach and speaks eloquently to a major theme of personal transformation.

Relationships are essentially transactional. But the reality is that most of the greatest achievements and the greatest joys in life come through relationships that are transformational. In the very nature of the interaction, people are altered. They are transformed.[3]

It is the coach's job to work closely with her charges to promote this kind of transformation. It is the responsibility of each individual being coached to define the goal of that transformation in the context of their companies and to actively seek personal metamorphosis.

Back Down to Earth

As stated earlier, it should be clear from the completed PDP how much of the intended message got through and how well the employee took ownership of the challenge. Even in cases where the employee takes the easy road instead of the hard one, a good coach should probably be able to come to a consensus during the meeting with the employee on a revised development plan. Only in cases of extreme disconnect should a coach have to send an employee out of the meeting with the assignment to completely revamp her personal development plan.

If many changes are made to the form as first drafted by the employee, the coach should spend the last segment of the interview making sure that there is really buy-in. A slump-shouldered employee with a resigned disposition is not likely to attack his improvement plan with gusto. The only way to expect meaningful change is for the employee to accept the plan and work diligently to implement the activities it contains.

Until a coach is convinced that the employee owns the plan and views its implementation as a personal necessity, she should not conclude the session. One excellent strategy to rekindle an extinguished flame is to revisit the information in Step One of this process. The Coaching Input Sheet contained at least a preliminary answer to a very important question about this individual's desires and aspirations. The stronger the tie between the action plans in Step Three and the desires and aspirations in Step One, the stronger should be the motivation.

PHIL COMES TO TERMS

Phil was an Engineering Manager with a thirteen-member staff. He was regarded as a brilliant technical mind but was hard on his people. He barked orders at them and did not involve them in any significant decision making. Phil's employees did not like working for him and passed this information up-line whenever it was possible to do so. The grapevine was full of "Phil stories" wherein his indiscretions were recounted.

Phil's style had been tolerated for years, and despite the fact that he was given informal counseling by his supervisor, only recently (with the introduction of Catalytic Coaching Worksheets) were any of these deficiencies ever addressed in writing. Previous to this he had always been graded in the top 30% and even in this year was awarded a handsome bonus.

Phil didn't feel much motivation to change. He knew intuitively that he was not likely to break into the top 10% without a complete overhaul in the way he worked. Even if he could change, he was skeptical it would result in a rating of "Outstanding" due to "politics." He regarded his own boss as "soft" and not very technically astute. He got a lot done, in part, because of his dictatorial management style. He feared loss of productivity if he attempted to become more sensitive and democratic.

Phil listened politely to his annual counsel and kept producing results the way he knew best—by pushing his employees to their limits. Sure, his Personal Development Plan indicated a willingness to attend a workshop on management style. For two years, however, he pushed off the opportunity due to the press of more important business issues. He even used the fact that he missed going to the workshop as representing a personal sacrifice made to maximize production of business results.

Over time, the organization began to change. Teams became more prominent and a participative management style was more and more expected. When news came that the company was going to acquire another organization, Phil was not worried. In fact, he participated on the acquisition team and helped make the decision to purchase it.

During the due diligence exercise, Phil treated members of the other organization as his conquests and talked openly of doubling the size of his engineering group. He made people angry and depressed at the thought of having to work with him.

After a great deal of discussion and soul-searching, the company terminated Phil effective with the acquisition. Phil was given an unwanted severance package. The big new job went to a manager coming with the acquired company. This gentleman was not as technically brilliant as Phil. He had nowhere near the depth of experience. But the people in the acquired firm liked working for him. Those in the acquiring organization gave strong support to the new leader and were greatly relieved to have Phil ushered away. Phil's reluctance to take responsibility for his own development cost him his job. Whether he could have changed or not, is not certain. He never really gave it a try.

TABETHA'S QUEST

Tabetha was a bright, ambitious lab technician who had posted for an opportunity to become a sales representative. Others had made this conversion in the past, but Tabetha did not make a very compelling case to follow suit. Yes, she was bright enough. And she had a sparkling personality. She could talk a starving man out of his last hunk of bread. But . . . it did not appear to Harold, the HR Director, that Tabetha was really looking at the full requirements of the job with objective clarity.

The new position would require Tabetha to move from a small, suburban (town where she had grown up among friends and family) to the city of Detroit. It also involved converting from a ten-minute daily commute to being on the road four out of every five work days. The last incumbent had driven more than 50,000 business miles the previous year.

Tabetha was a single parent of a fourteen-year-old boy. While she had an aunt in the greater Detroit area, the move just didn't make logical sense to Harold.

In the process of helping Tabetha talk herself out of the opportunity, Harold began exploring other options and interests. She had been less than fully challenged in her current position for some time and had used the education reimbursement system to obtain a Masters degree at night. Her major was Public Administration. It seems that her ultimate career goal was to one day run for public office. Her ideal job with the company was somewhere in the Public Relations Department.

Harold did some homework for Tabetha and informed her that they actually had one current opening in the PR department. It required, however, relevant experience in PR. Tabetha applied for the job anyway, and they turned her down. The external market was full of candidates who were significantly more qualified and they could not afford to train someone for a professional position on the job.

There was only one entry-level support staff position in the PR department and it was filled. But Tabetha let it be known that she was interested. The Head of Public Relations let her know that it was at least conceivable that the position could open up at some time in the future. If Tabetha was patient, perhaps something would break. In the mean time, however, if she truly wanted to be competitive for even the entry-level nonexempt position in PR she would need to strengthen her resume.

Despite having a Masters degree, Tabetha had very modest computer skills and no exposure to PR work whatsoever. The last two people who had successfully obtained the entry-level job were experts on the computer with at least some previous PR exposure.

Being the tenacious achiever that she was, Tabetha asked the PR Department Director to give her a list of things she would need to do to be competitive for an PR opening, should it ever come. He helped her generate a Catalytic Coaching Worksheet that reflected her Strengths and Areas for Improvement with respect to an entry-level PR position and together they constructed a Personal Development Plan. She had some very basic ground to cover to become competitive for the job.

Over a series of several months Tabetha began chipping away at the items on the PDP. She was making pretty good headway when the position she so coveted suddenly became vacant. Four other internal candidates expressed interest in the position. Some were better qualified with respect to one dimension of the job or another, but the personal time Tabetha had dedicated to improving her PR skill set was very persuasive. In the end, the entire department decided that Tabetha was the best match for the open position and she was offered the job.

Tabetha is now making rapid progress in demonstrating that she should be promoted to the professional ranks. Those who know her track record of achievement would not want to bet against her.

IN CONCLUSION

Step Three involves transfer of ownership for the improvement process back to the employee. It also involves a concrete determination of what specifically will be done to address opportunities to improve production capability. The secret to making sure that meaningful and significant change is accomplished lies in defining the Personal Development Plan.

Writing the PDP helps give the employee ownership. Reviewing it helps the manager insure that critical performance feedback is accurately received and a reasonable improvement plan has been put in place. The meeting need not take long to have a powerful impact. Like a quick checkup visit to the doctor, most find the experience of Step Three relatively painless. They also value the clean bill of health when they're told that their chosen approach to personal improvement is satisfactory.

Those who are told to stick around and take additional tests also benefit from this checkup. We are dealing with an individual's career health and well-being. If the doctor/coach feels compelled to talk some more, it is in the patient/employee's best interest to listen. Making absolutely sure there is quality in this dialogue is the express purpose of Step Three. Making sure that what is discussed and decided gets acted upon is the purpose of Step Four. This will be the topic of our next chapter.

Chapter 13

Step Four: Stewardship

Opportunity is missed by most people because it is dressed in overalls and looks like work.

—Thomas Edison[1]

One doesn't discover new lands without consenting to lose sight of the shore for a very long time.

—André Gide[2]

As depicted in Figure 13-1, the fourth and final step in the Catalytic Coaching model has to do with stewardship. The best development plans in the world are of little value unless they are acted upon. The stewardship step makes sure that the Personal Development Plans gets implemented. In this chapter we will review the roles and responsibilities of both coach and employee. We will also examine the process of stewardship in its simplest form. We will then conclude the chapter with additional tales from the front that give special insight into the stewardship process.

ROLES AND RESPONSIBILITIES OF THE COACH

Ownership for this part of the process is with the coach. While the employee has primary responsibility for creation and implementation of the development plan, the coach has responsibility to insure that there is follow-through.

We said earlier that a football coach could not run wind sprints nor do sit-ups for his players. For his team to improve, however, he must make sure that the players do these things. Despite the fact that the players know that these

Figure 13-1
Step Four

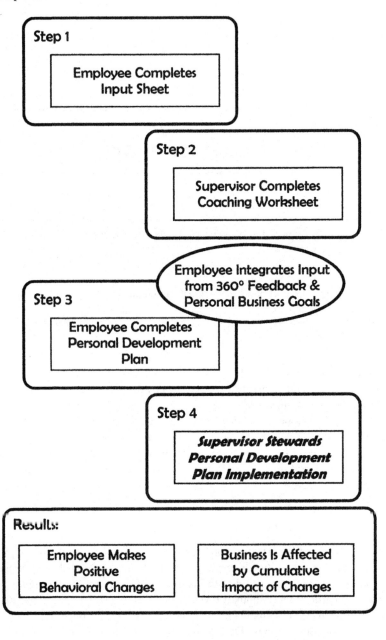

Step 1
Employee Completes
Input Sheet

Step 2
Supervisor Completes
Coaching Worksheet

Employee Integrates Input
from 360° Feedback &
Personal Business Goals

Step 3
Employee Completes
Personal Development
Plan

Step 4
Supervisor Stewards
Personal Development
Plan Implementation

Results:
Employee Makes
Positive
Behavioral Changes

Business Is Affected
by Cumulative
Impact of Changes

exercises are necessary for their growth and improvement, it can be very tempting to skimp or procrastinate. The coach serves as their conscience by holding them accountable.

I learned something very interesting about coaching as I wrote my Masters thesis in college. As a student of communication and the art of persuasion in organizations, I was curious about the techniques used by the varsity football coach to motivate his players to get excited about the big game. I asked our coach if I could sit in the locker room and do analysis of his pep talks.

While my study took more than a year to complete, the coach gave me perhaps the greatest insight in the interview preceding my first observation of an actual speech. He said,

I am willing to give you access to my talks on Saturday (game day) under one condition. You have to agree to also attend meetings on Mondays, Tuesdays, Wednesdays, Thursdays, Fridays and Sundays.

You see, on Saturdays, when there are 70,000 people in the stands, I don't have a problem getting the guys excited about doing their best. Their girlfriends, parents and classmates are motivation enough. Where I really have to be a good motivator is on Sundays and Mondays and Tuesdays. Practicing hard on those days is what's going to make all the difference in the game. But because the reward is so far away and practice is hard, it's easy to slough off. If you want to see real motivation at work, you need to be here on those days.

This was a very wise man and a great football coach. He went on to win the league championship that year and won three bowl games in a row. And he was right about where the work gets done. All the fancy academic tools I used to dissect his motivational tactics merely confirmed that the hard motivational work was done on the off-days, just as the coach said.

Like the football coach, it is the manager's job as employee coach to insure that her trustees do what they need to improve. In our case, this means following up on the Personal Development Plans that the employees themselves helped design and create. It seems putting them into practice is not always as easy as drafting them in the first place.

To extend the analogy all the way, writing the PDP is like playing on game day. Everyone important is watching. Putting the plan into action is like practice. The crowds are no longer present and there are plenty of opportunities to get distracted and lose focus.

Best Intentions Don't Produce Change

Most employees leave the Personal Development Plan interviews with the best of intentions. When reality sets back in and the unrelenting pace of work continues on its normal rampage, however, it is very easy to let painful activities with long-term payoff slip. It is the coach's job to make sure that the employee has every chance to follow through on these commitments.

Changing fundamental behavior can be uncomfortable and difficult. A good coach helps remind his charges that there is a higher purpose behind the painful activities. Over time the cumulative change efforts will reap dividends. Failure to change or inability to make progress does not directly harm the coach. It is the employee whose career is most significantly impacted.

ROLES AND RESPONSIBILITIES OF THE EMPLOYEE

The most important task of the employee in the stewardship process is to "Just do it." He must simply act upon his commitments—even when they involve hard work. He should not wait for others to tell him. He must take ownership and begin implementation of improvement plans immediately. He must follow through even when the improvement activity becomes monotonous or difficult.

In addition to doing the work, the employee must keep his coach informed about his progress. The employee should stay on top of his own PDP and keep his manager/coach apprised of completion status. When roadblocks or delays are encountered, he should take the initiative to speak with his coach about alternatives. He should not wait until a formal review is requested to bring up issues that delay implementation of the plan; it only hurts him by so doing.

THE PROCESS

The stewardship process does not have to be either tedious or taxing. With a goal of minimizing paperwork and bureaucracy, it can be kept very simple and straightforward. It need involve no new forms or elaborate procedures.

As implied above, constant and continuous dialogue between a manager and employee regarding progress with each Personal Development Plan is ideal. It is also a bit unrealistic to think that the majority will follow through in this manner. As a way of insuring minimal compliance, however, it is perhaps best to require formal reviews once a quarter.

Don't be scared by the word "formal" in this context. It is not really so frightening. To effectively steward implementation of a Personal Development Plan, a coach should ask her employees to take a copy of the final/approved PDP form and write with a colored pen on top of it. Each quarter they should change colors of ink.

More specifically, employees should check off action items that have been accomplished, noting dates of completion in the margin. They should jot down notes about action items that have been started with a brief comment about progress. Sample notes might include:

- "On schedule"
- "Delayed start one month due to Peterson project"
- "Anticipated completion date: 5/29"
- "Substituted course in Real Estate Development. Okayed by GKM"

The completed form should be submitted to the coach on specified dates each quarter. The coach should then review the forms and follow up when there are concerns or changes that need to be made. Some choose to mandate their managers and employees meet face-to-face at least once a quarter for stewardship purposes. For our purposes, the practice should be encouraged when it helps speed the change process and makes a net positive contribution to the business goals the system was designed to achieve.

On Leaving a Trail of Paper

As a mechanism to insure compliance, some systems require that a copy of all stewardship documentation be forwarded to an official in Human Resources. When this is done, it is sometimes considered valuable to create a scorecard that tracks the percentage of PDPs that have been stewarded and the percentage of action items complete. Including stewardship as part of a bonus incentive plan is an another way organizations attempt to increase compliance. The task is not difficult, if one is sufficiently motivated to make it a priority.

As with the choice to mandate stewardship meetings, the decision to formalize a paper trail should be based on business need. If a company is trying to institutionalize a new level of accountability and demonstrate a strong commitment to change, this kind of tactic may serve that purpose. Like any business decision, the costs and benefits of enforcing such a practice should be assessed. Whatever is decided, it is important not to lose sight of the fact the process ends with changed behavior, not a stuffed file or colorful scorecard. Excellent documentation is not an end in itself.

Time Commitment

For the employee, this formal stewardship process should normally take no more than ten minutes to update the form each quarter. It should take the coach even less time to read. If it takes a coach more than fifteen minutes to review and react to a form, she probably needs a remedial reading course. For employees new to their position, it often makes sense to reinforce the process with a ten-minute discussion. The coach should look for things that she can do to help insure that the employee follows through on the original commitments. Together they should agree on modifications if circumstances or priorities have changed since creation of the original document.

Most managers are delighted to hear that the total time they need to invest each year in stewardship should be less than an hour per employee. They are also pleased to see that their role is primarily oversight versus being in charge of form completion. Employees are typically less impressed to learn that their burden is merely an hour or less each year. They are usually happy to have the option of just writing on top of an existing form, rather than being responsible for completing something entirely new or facing a mandatory interview.

Because Step Four is so simple and logical, and the burden so light, it is not hard to get people to participate actively in the process. This comes as a great relief to HR coordinators who were used to feeling like an out-of-touch bureau-crat when they had to try to force compliance with a more cumbersome ste-wardship system tied to the traditional evaluation-based paradigm. Step Four of the Catalytic Coaching methodology represents a victory for all concerned.

MORE TALES FROM THE FRONT: JANE CRIES "UNCLE"

Jane was a recently hired insurance claims processor who had serious per-formance problems. Despite her strong academic credentials and what appeared to be related experience with other companies, Jane's new employer encountered numerous serious problems with her accuracy and turnaround time. Almost from the start, she produced an inadequate quantity and quality of work, especially for someone who was supposed to have the correct training and experience.

Jane's supervisor worked with a Coach^2 to create a Catalytic Coaching Work-sheet that was used to confront her with the perceived problems. He held his session and went through the material. She was shocked to get the news that she was failing, but worked together with him to create a Personal Development Plan to improve.

The Coach^2 followed the supervisor with an interview that confirmed the message was received as intended. Indeed, Jane understood the problems and agreed to work diligently to make the required improvements. She valued her job and they seemed to have obtained her complete and undivided attention.

Unfortunately, a month later not much had changed. Turnaround time had improved, but was still unacceptable. And the errors kept coming. The super-visor held a second formal interview in which he reviewed recent, specific ex-amples of the problems cited. Jane reported that she had attended the training specified in her PDP, she had also accepted tutoring that it required, and she was doing her best to increase speed and accuracy. She acknowledged most of the responsibility for the errors and vowed to continue working harder.

Two weeks later more new evidence surfaced over the same basic issues. The coach held another session and reviewed it with Jane. She was now a bit more frustrated, but did not discredit any of the complaints about her work. Jane vowed to continue trying.

Following another month of modest improvement but continued problems, the supervisor requested they quit trying to get Jane to change. She was not making sufficient progress. Despite how hard she had tried, she was not meeting minimum expectations. After clearing the situation with Human Resources and Legal, they set a date for termination.

On a bright Monday morning the manager called Jane once again into the conference room where they had conducted their repeated coaching sessions. She took one look at the Coach[2] and another at her boss and before either of had said a word, she took her office keys and ID tag and placed them on the conference table in front of them. Neither will ever forget what she said next.

Jane said, "I hope you called me in here today to put an end to this mess, because I just can't do what you're asking of me. Lord knows I've tried, but I just can't do it." She continued, "I know there is something out there that I can be good at. Maybe I should teach school or manage a restaurant. I don't know. But it's definitely not more of this."

On the day that they fired her, Jane (who just happened to be minority as well as female) did not make any claims that she was unfairly picked on or singled out because she was different. Instead, she thanked both her boss and the Coach[2] for working so hard to try to help her salvage her job. That says a lot about the character of Jane, but also something important about the integrity of the process they employed to try to help her. Neither had any doubt that Jane would move on to find work she was better suited for. The Coach[2] shared his vision of several hundred students out there somewhere whose lives were greatly enriched because "Miss Jane" turned out to be an ineffective claims processor.

SIR JAMES, THE GOOD

One of the most interesting by-products of introducing a comprehensive Catalytic Coaching system is the discovery of managers who know how to work with people, and others who do not. An HR VP learned something about this when she traveled to Europe to introduce the program to managers of her London office.

Rather than being seen as revolutionary and different, the introduction of new forms and procedures merely expedited the process those in the London office were following already. James, the gentleman in charge of that office, was able to quickly adapt to the new system because he was already coaching his employees despite the nine-page "boat anchor" of an evaluation system he was forced to work with previously. When asked to name the four greatest Strengths and Areas for Improvement on each of his direct reports, he did not even hesitate. These were issues he had already sorted out, despite the fact that the previous set of forms failed to ask for this input directly.

James had been going above and beyond the required forms to provide his managers with guidance. He was very direct with them already about what to concentrate on to improve. He used what he called "Personal Goal Sheets" that closely mirrored the PDP worksheet we are using here. And he had routinely scheduled stewardship meetings to make sure the items listed on the Personal Goal Sheets were being implemented.

It was no longer a surprise to the HR VP as to why James seemed to always get more out of his senior management team than his peers in other offices did from theirs. This also explained why the people who worked for James seemed to be the ones chosen to assume other top leadership positions. Least surprising, perhaps, was the selection of James a few years later as Chief Operating Officer of the company.

The experience with James stood in stark contrast with what the HR VP discovered in other areas of the same company. A year prior, attending the annual review of the completed nine-page Performance Evaluation forms she could see very little that seemed to differentiate the good supervisors from the bad. To be sure, she developed a feel for who people might prefer to work with and which managers looked to be best developing their talent, but the traditional evaluation process did little to clearly separate the good people-developers from the bad. Sitting through sessions where supervisors reviewed completed Catalytic Coaching Worksheets, however, made it much more obvious who were struggling with their roles as people-developers. Some of the superstar managers in the previous year were shown to be very limited in their ability to help their work force improve.

Several seemed to question whether it was even their role to be more than just judge or critic. They projected a very Darwinian attitude about the survival of the fittest employees. They saw their primary jobs as merely identifying the top and bottom of a rank list. After all, to try to help someone improve was a form of tampering with the natural environment of the ranking process. Reporting employee flaws and errors and assigning a label/grade by completing the assigned evaluation form was their job. Improvement was not their responsibility or focus.

This method of viewing the process served a manager well in the old evaluation-based system. When they switched to a coaching-based system, some had big problems in adapting to the new mindset and skill requirements. Many who struggled with the new system already had bad reputations as people managers.

System conversion helped identify why they were ineffective. It helped some supervisors change their ways and become more effective. Those who couldn't coach stuck out like sore thumbs. It was as if the bad bosses sported swastika tattoos on their foreheads.

It forced management to address situations where supervisors could not become effective. After a while, managers had to be an impossibly valuable technical talent to survive without effective coaching skills in an important managerial position with people responsibility. The potential losses in productivity and morale became too obvious.

The story of James illustrates the importance of creating a system that goes beyond mere evaluation. It's intent is to standardize and systematize the techniques that make him effective so they can work for a much larger audience. The idea is to clone James—or at least his abilities to develop people.

STEWARDSHIP IN PERSPECTIVE

Catalytic Coaching is not about having a good conversation. It is not about feedback or documenting files. It is not about putting together a really great plan. It is not about creating pretty graphs showing the percentage of stewardship interviews conducted. It is about making important change happen.

Making change happen requires follow-through. It requires work on the part of the employee and active oversight on the part of the manager. It is not always fun. It requires effort and perseverance. But with no change, any effort spent on performance management is of questionable value. Step Four insures that change actually happens.

Some changes are easy. Others are very difficult. For an individual electing to overcome deeply ingrained patterns or limited natural abilities to have a reasonable chance of transformation, he will need excellent coaching. He will need frank and honest feedback. He will need a well-conceived Personal Development Plan. He will need to take personal ownership of this plan. And he will need to invest significant time and energy for its completion.

If the employee is able to make the required changes and one day successfully compete for a highly coveted position, he will remember forever the person who helped coach him through that process. Following through on a long-term action plan that enables this kind of transformation will be one of the most memorable accomplishments in the careers of both employee and coach.

Part IV

Making It Work

We're all pilgrims on the same journey—but some pilgrims have better road maps.

—Nelson DeMille

The Catalytic Coaching model, as reviewed in Part III, cannot operate in isolation. Because of its strategic connection to all other aspects of people management in a complex business environment, it requires a total systems approach to make it work.

Part IV will review some critical actions and conditions that can serve to make Catalytic Coaching successful. As depicted in Figure IV-1, these can be typed in three ways. We will review issues associated with infrastructure, acquiring coaching competencies, and creating commitment.

Infrastructure issues have to do with supporting systems. Chapter 14 will talk about reward systems. In particular we will discuss implications of abandoning a "pay for performance" strategy as it pertains to salary administration. Many organizations interested in converting to a coaching-based performance management system begin with a problem. If they abandon the ineffective task of trying to link salary increases directly to an evaluation grade, what do they do instead? How do they determine a pay increase amount? Can this be done in a way that is fair and motivates people to work hard? Chapter 14 will seek to answer many of these questions.

Chapter 15 will briefly review several other supporting systems that need to work in concert with the Catalytic Coaching model to have optimum impact in attracting, retaining, enhancing and motivating talent. We will discuss the merits of Training and Development, Job Posting, Educational Reimbursement, Em-

Figure IV-1
Making It Work

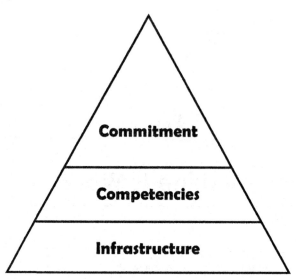

ployee Assistance Programs and even Outplacement. When aligned together these systems can combine to form an integrated catalytic culture.

Chapter 16 will begin our discussion on acquiring coaching competencies. Specifically, it will cover an approach to skills training that includes levels of sophistication required by all employees, those functioning as coaches, and ultimately those chosen to serve as Coach²s or Coach³s.

Chapter 17 will give several examples of these competencies in action with guidance on what we will call "special case coaching." Here we will examine six different classic coaching scenarios with detailed explanation of how the Catalytic Coaching model can be used to facilitate growth and change in each. A model will be introduced that will help coaches determine the root problems in difficult situations and suggest effective strategies. This chapter will outline some excellent content for a coaching skills workshop.

Chapter 18 deals with the topic of creating commitment. That chapter focuses on the pivotal role of organization leaders as role models in the Catalytic Coaching process. It explains actions executives and leaders can take to demonstrate support for the coaching initiative by "walking the talk." It encourages leaders to do more than just feign compliance to prompt cooperation from those below them. It provides advice to leaders on how to use the system to enhance truly their own personal and professional development.

It encourages leaders to approach the subject of self-analysis and personal development courageously by advocating a realistic, truthful and thoughtful approach to personal change. It provides practical information on how to take ownership of personal growth and development challenges and strive for levels of achievement that the less motivated might avoid.

Taken together, these three systemic activities (building infrastructure, acquiring coaching competencies, and creating commitment help insure that Catalytic Coaching works.

Chapter 14

On Money Matters

No one would remember the Good Samaritan if he only had good intentions. He had money as well.

—Margaret Thatcher[1]

My friends, money is not all. It is not money that will mend a broken heart or reassemble the fragments of a dream. Money cannot brighten the hearth nor repair the portals of a shattered home. I refer, of course, to Confederate money.

—Artemus Ward[2]

Follow the money.

—Deep Throat's advice to Woodward and Bernstein during their investigation of Watergate[3]

In Part I we learned that many problems with the prevailing paradigm are in some way linked with base pay. Chapter 4 discussed in detail the mythology of pay for performance and its inherent inability to live up to implied promises. In the Catalytic Coaching model, described in detail in Part III, we broke the direct link between performance and salary administration. Doing this allowed us to better focus on improving production capability. It helped us be more honest with people about improvements that would benefit them and the company. It fundamentally changed the roles and responsibilities for both boss and employee. And it helped drive change that will add meaningful value to the business.

Decoupling performance management from salary administration helped do a lot of good things for us. Most customers of the process (including employees, supervisors, managers, HR representatives and corporate attorneys) should be pleased. Only one customer's satisfaction with the process is likely to have gone down.

A REVERSAL OF FORTUNE

The Compensation Manager used to be happy. As we have seen, he may have been the only customer who was happy with the classic evaluation-based performance management system. As depicted in Figure 14-1, the Compensation Manager had a relatively easy job in the old system. People did whatever they did, filled out all the complicated forms, and gave him a letter or number by a specified date and he was satisfied. With the advent of the coaching process, however, the number/label goes away, leaving him with no data to plug into the computer in Step Two. He now has nothing to "feed the salary system" with. Hence, the drop in approval ratings from the Compensation Manager as an internal customer of the performance management system.

There are ways around this dilemma, however. In fact, they are quite easy to understand and relatively painless to employ. While the focus of this book is on performance management systems, and compensation systems are unique enough to deserve extensive, comprehensive treatment of their own, the least we can do is spend a few minutes patching up the damage to the salary system that conversion to coaching normally implies. This chapter will explore a variety of those practical suggestions.

WHATEVER YOU DO, DON'T DO THIS!

Before we begin a discussion of things that can be done to salvage salary administration, let's make sure that we cover something that is taboo. Whatever you do to keep the 2–5% raises coming, don't continue assigning the traditional letter/grade to each individual coached. And if you fail to heed this stern warning, here's an even stronger one: *NEVER print a performance label on the bottom of a coaching worksheet.*

To do this is to nullify much of the good that was accomplished with the new format. Once an employee discovers that everything on that simple sheet can be summed down to an even simpler word, number or letter, the rest is history. The shorthand is all that will be remembered. From the viewpoint point of the employee, the conversation now boils down to this. "Blah. Blah. Blah. . . . 'Excellent' " Or "Blah. Blah. Blah. . . . '2.5' "

If you don't believe me, here is the acid test. Do a post-interview for a coaching session that has utilized a summary grade. Three days following the discussion session ask the employee what she learned. What she'll tell you is: "I finally made it to 'Outstanding' " or "The jerk gave me a 3 again. I guess I have to start washing his car to get a 2." With one little word/letter/number

Figure 14-1
Traditional Process Used to Tie Performance Ratings to Salary Increases

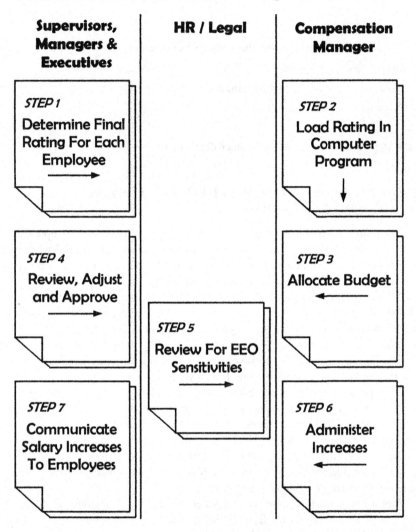

scrawled across the bottom of the page, everything else is wiped clean. Everything.

SIMPLE SOLUTION

While there are scores of different salary systems at work in the market place, many contain very similar features. We cannot possibly address all systems. Instead, what we'll try to do is outline a simple solution that has worked well in multiple situations. It is very straightforward and can be used effectively to build off most systems that were previously in place. The solution involves four steps:

1. Adopt a Common Date for Routine Salary Administration
2. Allocate Budget Assuming Everyone Received a "Very Good" Rating
3. Make Adjustments Based on Performance
4. Check for Consistency and Equity

Each step will be explained in greater detail below.

STEP ONE: ADOPT A COMMON DATE FOR ROUTINE SALARY ADMINISTRATION

For organizations not on a common salary administration date, Step One is to create one. This means that if you have traditionally evaluated employees and passed out raises on their anniversary dates (for hiring or job placement), you will need to move everyone in a given group to the same month.

To do this equitably normally involves pro-rating salaries for all that switch months. Assuming that salary administration dates are spread evenly across the twelve months in a year, this means giving eleven out of every twelve employees some kind of adjustment earlier than the month they normally would have expected. The key point here, however, is to insure that no one perceives that he will lose money because of the one-time switch.

As a quick example, this means that if you elect to go with July as the common date for all the headquarters financial organization, anyone not currently being reviewed in July must move. To accomplish this equitably and with a totally neutral impact, someone due for salary treatment in November would get an 8/12ths of his normal salary treatment come July (four months early). Someone not due for treatment until the following June would get a very small increase, reflecting a 1/12ths adjustment.

From a practical standpoint, you might consider giving someone 1/12th of an adjustment as rather trivial. Symbolically, however, it can be huge. It is of tremendous public relations value for the company to accurately report that "absolutely no one will be disadvantaged by the change in salary administration procedures to support the new performance management system."

When in doubt, err on the side of the employee. The last thing you want is for some cynic to have data she can use to support a contention that the new system is really just a sneaky way for the company to save money on salaries. If the individual spreading this rumor was shorted even $100 a year in the conversion process, the company would be at fault for providing ready ammunition to promote this controversy.

Other Efficiencies

Independent of Catalytic Coaching, many companies opt to convert to common salary administration dates to obtain the administrative efficiencies it can create. In some organizations this has even resulted in the ability to reduce staff dedicated to the compensation administration process.

A part-time activity that was spread out over a year can be consolidated to a full-time job lasting only a few weeks. Surge demands for processing a reduced level of paperwork can be met using trusted contractors. This allows permanent full-time resources to be allocated to more proactive activities.

Perhaps most importantly, the demand on the line organization can sometimes be reduced through conversion to a common date. Business units can select times of the year when they can best allocate time to the practice. They also frequently experience efficiency gains by taking care of their entire business unit in one quick, comprehensive effort.

STEP TWO: ALLOCATE BUDGET ASSUMING EVERYONE RECEIVED A "VERY GOOD" RATING

An experienced compensation administrator can use the system currently in operation to generate an excellent starting point for determining salary treatment. Ask her to generate a report that allocates the entire budget (whether it's 2% or 10%) based on performance scores that are "above average," however that translates in your system.

For example, many systems use numbers or letters as a form of label or grade. In a typical system, a "1" might be used as the best grade, "2" second best, and so on up to "4." These roughly equate to the A, B, C, D and F grades commonly used over the years in most American schools. The numbers or letters are normally used to feed a computer program that generates a recommended salary increase for each individual. Their grade or label interacts typically with their base salary, the budget and salary range to come up with a projected increase amount.[4]

Companies transitioning to Catalytic Coaching will no longer have a grade to plug into the computer. Depending on the system, however, it may be possible to plug in a slightly above average grade for all employees that would generate increases that consume between 90% and 110% of the budget. With minor tweaking, an initial case to distribute all the money (assuming similar performance levels on the part of all employees) with perhaps a little left over to spare.

This step does not imply that everyone gets the same percentage increase. That would not be good for two reasons. First, giving all employees at a given level the same increase amount or percent would fail to make any discrimination in terms of performance. In the next step we will make accommodation for that. Equally important, universal percent or dollar-amount increases would fail to recognize that different employees typically start from different places on the salary scale. Some are very highly paid for their positions and some very low.

Normally the effect of each employee's compa-ratio (position on the salary range as a percent of midpoint), number of months since last salary treatment, and the budget are factored into the computer program that generates proposed increases. Plugging in hypothetical numbers (i.e., giving everyone a "2" or a "B") simply helps it operate to divide up available funds. What remains to be done is the making of adjustments.

STEP THREE: MAKE ADJUSTMENTS BASED ON PERFORMANCE

The next step in this process is to split the company-wide list of salaries down into logical groups. For example, the Financial organization would be issued a list of employees broken down by section (Accounting, Audit, Finance, Tax, etc.) with the computer-generated base salary increases. The same thing would be done for Engineering, Sales, R&D, etc.

The process manager for each group is then given the responsibility to make adjustments for her direct reports. If Linda was a true standout and Paul had a very bad year, the process manager can move funds from Paul to Linda to correspond with that perceived performance difference. To be sure, logical "hog laws" must be created which limit the amount of redistribution that can take place. On the other hand, there should be sufficient latitude to assist the manager in reinforcing a performance message logically with pay.

Stated another way, it is possible to move money within a given structure from one person to another. It is not possible to add more to those you like without getting the money from somewhere else. This remains a zero-sum game. The budget is fixed. It is capped. There is only so much to spend. One can always spend less than the total approved by the corporation. Getting more is a difficult political act. These are, and always have been, the facts of life. This method of allocating limited resources does not change the laws of nature.

Minimizing Bureaucracy

From a procedural standpoint, most systems consider that the initial budgeted increase for each individual is approved, unless the supervisor argues for change. When a change is desired, the supervisor is required to submit a brief statement (normally of one to three sentences) explaining the reason for reallocation of funds.

Examples of justification notes are as follows. Documenting a recommendation to reduce the computer-generated salary increase by $500 a year may be approved with a statement as simple as this: "Failed to accomplish 2 of 5 major objectives set for this year." Or . . . "Increase adjusted to address peer inequity.

Employee at 113% of midpoint while higher performing peers with same length of service are below midpoint."

Similar brief statements can also be used to adjust salaries upward. Documenting an addition of $2,000 to base salary (on top of a budgeted increase of $3,000) may be accomplished by saying something like this: "Consistent top performer. Third year at grade level. Additional increase will move her to 98% of midpoint." Another might be justified by the following: "Employee due for promotion next year. Additional $2,000 puts him at 105% of midpoint."

Interestingly enough, few large changes to the initial computer-generated salaries normally need to be made. In fact, it is quite common for 80 to 90% of the computer-generated zero-based budget to be accepted exactly as drafted. Changes that are made are usually minor. The exceptions, where individual increases are drastically cut, eliminated or significantly enhanced, are normally well known. Documenting these cases takes little time.

DOUBLE-BARRELED COACHING

A typical situation for making a significant adjustment is when someone is being given a Job Threatening performance message.[5] In normal circumstances, the manager will argue that the individual receiving this level of counsel should be denied any base salary increase. Individuals being given a final warning with multiple Job Threatening citations should by definition be "zeroed out." Being informed that they will receive no base salary adjustment usually sends a strong signal to those on the bubble.

Used correctly, reinforcing a performance message with logically consistent base salary treatment can serve as additional motivation for them to pay attention to counseling and make the requested behavioral changes. It also serves to further protect the company's interest in any potential legal contest. Judges, juries and arbitrators clearly understand the message being sent when an individual is informed that they are being deprived an increase they would have otherwise received.

Monies saved here are either diverted to someone with a low compa-ratio (base salary compared to market average) or a standout high performer. Those on the short list for promotion or those newly promoted are common beneficiaries. In certain situations, the money is returned from the department for use in the larger division or other parts of the corporation.

STEP FOUR: CHECK FOR CONSISTENCY AND EQUITY

In Step Four some neutral party (normally from Human Resources or the Legal Department) should check the final results of the base salary budget distribution that come in against knowledge of the people and what is being said about them. Obvious disconnects should be discussed with the appropriate line managers until everyone is satisfied that an equitable situation has been reached.

For those of you squirming in your seats thinking about all the possible Equal
Opportunity exposure, let me remind you of something. Very few people sue
for unfair salary increases. In fact, in my entire career I have yet to see one.
What people sue for is disparity in total compensation. If a person's annual
salary is in line with others of her grade and experience level, the amount of
an increase is incidental.

Likewise, it takes a number of similar people (minorities, females, over-40s,
etc.) being treated consistently different in base salary to give prima facia evidence of discrimination. If you have this type of systemic disparity in base
salaries, you have a problem that has probably been brewing for a while. It
normally takes several years for such anomalies to develop.

Patterns of disparity, when produced by conscious attempts to treat different
kinds of people differently represent a form of bias called "discriminant intent."
Patterns of disparity produced without deliberate attempt to discriminate still
produce legal exposure, however. Authorities call this "discriminant impact."
If clear patterns of disparity exist, whatever the cause, responsible companies
will move quickly to correct them.

If a government agency identifies discriminatory patterns or trends and feels
they need to be addressed, the company may be given detailed instructions on
how to correct the situation. Penalty for failure to comply can be substantial.
Corporations selling products or services to the government can lose all government contracts. It is the responsibility of the Legal and HR staff to monitor
the situation to insure that it never has to come to this.

THE BIG DEAL IS THE BOTTOM LINE

Too many employees get confused by the messages companies send them
about money. They focus on the salary increase amount as the single most
important symbol recognizing their worth to a corporation. They frequently gloss
over a more important issue, which is their total compensation.

As described in Chapter 4 with the story of Harvey, supervisors and managers
get caught up in the excitement of selling an "up-and-comer" on the causal
link between his performance and his salary increase. By so doing, they imply
that performance is the primary driver of the increase amount.

As the story and subsequent discussion pointed out, performance may be the
only variable that the employee has any influence over. Nonetheless, it has not
traditionally been a good predictor of his increase amount. A company's salary
budget and an individual's compa-ratio are much better predictors of individual
base salary increase amounts. While it may not be inspiring to think an individual's annual base salary adjustment is determined mostly by things he has
no control over, this is reality in any market-based pay system.

Teaching employees the way the system really works is only common sense.
Instead of robbing a supervisor of pay as a motivational tool, it demonstrates
the truth about what has really been happening. Most salary administration sys-

tems are created with a good logical foundation and are seen as fair by those who understand the mechanics. When you quit trying to tie annual evaluation of individual performance directly to a salary increase amount, the system will normally appear less exciting but more logical and fair. And a system that is logical and fair is one that you can talk openly about.

OPENING THE BOOKS

Anyone who thinks they can keep employees in the dark about salary anymore has yet to log onto the Internet. Comparative data are everywhere. If you are not paying your employees within a 20% range of the market midpoint for any given position, you are exposed. You run a high risk of losing that individual to someone else who will just pay average.

Because comparative data are so readily available, and because you almost always have to pay market rates, it makes no sense anymore not to be more open with employees about where they stand within the company's pay structure. No, this is not to suggest that you show employees what each of their colleagues makes (although in many cases they already know). Instead, you should consider talking with them about their pay in relationship to the salary grade they are in. To make sense of this information, however, they will need to know something about the grades that could be available to them through promotion or advancement.

As we have described extensively, managers cannot effectively play Santa Claus. They cannot leave big gifts under the tree for employees who do well and coal in the stockings for those whose performance is shoddy. There is a system at work, but it is not really very dramatic. As the latitude for differentiating salary increases based on performance is rather limited, you should be honest with your people and tell them how things work.

Discussions about pay may sometimes be painful, but they are almost always healthy. If the total salary you provide is close to par for the market, you should not lose many people because you have begun speaking about your system. If your system is not on par, you need to make corrections. Talking about these perceived gaps is not bad; it is good. It is treating employees as adults. It is a form of empowerment.

Letting people know their midpoint and salary range for the first time is an interesting activity. Every once in a while someone wants to argue. When they do that with data, the discussion can be uncomfortable for the employer. If they have a point, if you are off by a considerable margin from the market average, you may be given a chance to make it up. If you elect not to up the ante for the pushy incumbent, you may find yourself paying market rate for his replacement when he leaves you to accept a position with your competitor.

A telecommunications company recently paid a retained search firm $45K to find a Corporate Controller. During the first interview with the executive recruiter, the recruiter informed the company that they were not offering a competitive salary package for the local market. The company made a few concessions, but essentially stuck to their guns. They had internal equity issues to consider. If they wanted a lot for a little, they weren't embarrassed about that. That's why they hired the headhunter and paid him a big fee.

Nine months and dozens of recruiting hours later the company had lost four candidates to whom they had offered the position. They ended up raising the salary by more than 20%, paying a signing bonus and doing lots of other things to finally fill the job. The base salary they eventually agreed to pay was still low for the market, however, according to the recruiter. If the recruiter is right, in two years the newly trained Controller will probably leave the company for a job paying true market rates. Then the company will have another opportunity to pay dearly to make the same mistake.

If you're going to lose someone you value, lose him over something other than paying below market for a job. Location, advancement, exposure, broadening. These are all frustrating reasons to lose a valued employee, but they're all more acceptable than market pay.

If your organization must adopt a strategy of paying below the market average for its positions, you'd better have a plan for how you're going to make up the gap—or figure out how to get the most out of second-tier or third-tier personnel. Either way, you should have a strategy that makes sense and holds up over time. It should be a conscious decision.

EATING BUGS

We will conclude this discussion about money with another quick dose of "Dilbert." In fact, the first exposure I ever had to Dilbert was through a cartoon that was sent to me following a seminar on performance management I held in Canada in 1994. Scott Adams, the cartoonist, was still actively employed at a large Canadian telephone company and was not yet in global syndication. I was taken aback by his piercing insight into the formal performance evaluation ritual.

The cartoon depicts a conversation between one of Dilbert's colleagues and his boss. It is annual review time and the boss begins by pronouncing Wally's performance for the year as "fair." He adds, however, that he will raise the appraisal to "excellent" if Wally will eat a bug. In his outstretched right hand the boss holds a giant beetle.

The boss explains his rationale for the proposal as follows: "I didn't have much luck with other management techniques, so I'm kinda winging it right now." After some additional dialogue, Wally leaves the office with a mouthful of bug. "Next!" shouts the boss as Dilbert prepares to go in for his evaluation (and bug tasting).

Of course, this method of evaluating employees is a bit exaggerated. What rings true, however, is the way it characterizes the need people feel to be assigned good grades or labels in a traditional appraisal process. It also depicts well their reluctant willingness to do whatever is required, no matter how meaningless or arbitrary, to be given those grades. The grading system is tied to retention, promotability and, most importantly, to money.

Because of the strong, direct link between performance labels and money, people have been motivated to passively comply with directives for change in order to receive better grades. Their motivation is unfiltered and direct. They do what is required to get a better grade, not to improve their contribution to the company. They do it for someone else and not themselves. They do not really engage their hearts, but only their minds. They do what is required to reap the rewards. After all, the evaluation was sold to them built on a foundation of money.

Catalytic Coaching breaks the direct link between salary administration and the performance discussion. We'd like to think in some small way that by so doing it aids in getting some of the ''bugs'' out of traditional performance discussions. At least that was the aim.

Chapter 15

Building an Integrated
Catalytic Culture

This is not your father's Oldsmobile!

—Popular television commercial

Catalytic Coaching, as outlined in Part III, is a method of performance management that should produce a variety of important business outcomes. As such, however, it is only one component in a larger, more comprehensive people development system. We talked about infrastructure changes needed in salary administration in the last chapter. In this chapter, we will review six other core components of a large-scale, integrated people-development system. Working together, these systems can help create an integrated catalytic culture—one that speeds the pace of meaningful personal and organizational change.

It is not the purpose of this chapter to attempt to give guidance on the creation of a strategic business plan for Human Resources. Rather, we will briefly review the critical need for such a plan and then cover in detail several components that might logically be included. Those components selected for inclusion work closely in concert with a Catalytic Coaching system to form the essential people-development component of an HR strategic plan.

Before we get into detail on the specific elements, let's discuss the business climate that makes a strategic approach to people management essential.

THE LAY OF THE LAND

Ten to fifteen years ago it was quite common for an HR department (or the Personnel function, as some companies called it) to be primarily concerned with some pretty basic stuff. Hiring, firing, pay and benefits were the order of the day. To be sure, many had responsibility for Training and Development and perhaps even a few were involved in the introduction of teaming concepts or Total Quality Management. It was quite uncommon, however, for an HR representative to sit on a senior leadership team and even less common for them to have a strategic role. My, how things have changed.

In the mid-1990's the first of the baby boom generation turned 50. Simultaneously the United States started being recognized as *the* world leader in the push toward global integration of businesses. Automation displaced many low-end, repetitive manufacturing jobs while the service sector of our economy has grown immeasurably. The technology industry, also led by the United States, really took off. As a result of all these forces colliding, unemployment in many parts of the country has hit the lowest levels in modern history. At the time of this writing it hovers barely above 4.5%.

Salary increases for skilled workers frequently exceed the rate of inflation and yet turnover has climbed. The executive and professional search (headhunter) business is thriving. Companies are paying $40K to $50K plus expenses for a search to find a Controller or Information Systems Manager. Then they have to pay moving costs and signing bonuses to the candidates they are trying to lure away with base salaries 20% higher than they were receiving at their previous companies.

In many cities, all levels of the economy are being affected. Recent articles in the *Atlanta Journal & Constitution* reported that more than 43% of the businesses plan to add to their headcount in the coming year, while many are finding it impossible to hire enough people currently just to replace attrition. A reported 20,000 openings for high-tech workers remain unfilled in Georgia alone, with over 75% in Atlanta. Billboards created to advertise daily specials on hamburgers or oil changes now solicit job applicants. Firms are turning away business because they do not have the personnel it takes to do the work that is available for them to do.

On a national scale, the unemployment rate has been hovering at historic lows for the last several years. We have been below 5% since 1997. The Congressional Budget Office projects for this trend to continue, with unemployment remaining below 6% until the year 2008.[1]

What this means to those of us in business is that the best and the brightest have lots of options. They have choices in where they work and what they want to do. They have choices and temptations that their fathers and mothers never had. And many are brave enough to use them to establish individual autonomy.

The illusion of cradle-to-grave employment went out with their father's forced early retirement and their aunt's second "downsizing." Most new entrants in the market today are realists. They are not attracted to a company by fancy retirement benefits. They don't expect any one company to give them a 30-year ride. Based on their experience, they'd have better odds buying lottery tickets.

A shortage of skilled workers has lent ironic meaning to the expression that "People are our most important asset." What was once a hollow PR campaign has now become a brutal reality. In a strong growing economy, attracting, retaining, enhancing and motivating talented people is an essential ingredient in corporate success. And if we project continued economic success just a few more years in to the future, the talent shortage could get much worse.

These are some of the issues that have forced smart business people to recognize the human factor as strategic. It has caused them to shift their thinking about the HR function in their organizations. It has caused them to ask for a different level of contribution from their HR leaders. It has caused them to demand a strategic partnership.[2]

The Rapidly Depleting Asset

In addition to being difficult to obtain and retain, talented employees are important to maintain. Employee skill sets are like cars. They begin to slowly depreciate the moment they are acquired. In this day and age of incredible technological advancement, the rate of depreciation is very rapid. The fanciest degrees and most sophisticated technology are only current for a few years. Imagine, if you will, business life without phone mail, e-mail, portable computers or the Internet. Yet, for many these essential ways of producing work were introduced only as recently as 1995 or 1996.

As we discussed earlier, Peter Senge writes about what he calls "the learning organization." This is a work environment where people continuously learn and grow. In effect, people stave off obsolescence or entropy (winding down) by engaging in a continuous process of renewal or negentropy (winding up). A learning organization requires a culture that supports growth and an infrastructure that helps provide it.

The Origins of "Culture Change Initiatives"

When we first began hearing people talk about the importance of "culture change" a few years ago, many of us didn't get it. If we did, we didn't necessarily buy it. Culture change sounded like some kind of "kinder, gentler, more-caring thing" that sprung from the mind of a senior executive who had just experienced a late-blooming moment of conscience. The story line was seemed nice enough. "We need to change the way we work, empower our people, use teams, etc. etc." But explanations as to *why* this was important normally sounded pretty hollow. Most of the leaders of these large initiatives, when they weren't chanting the mantra of change, seemed reluctant to give up power. They seemed to really like making all the important decisions themselves and often spoke privately about teams being inefficient or ineffective. Why then the charade?

Try this for an answer. Maybe the person who started this whole thing got a glimpse of the future and got scared. Perhaps he saw a business climate where employees were not prisoners. They had choices on where to work. They were no longer content to take orders and follow blindly. They wanted more. Because of the wealth of opportunities in the marketplace, the most talented people were free to pursue preferred working conditions. In this vision, companies unable or unwilling to provide a healthy and productive work environment were left with the dregs of the workforce.

Many companies undoubtedly started large-scale culture change processes out of fear—fear that one day the best employees would have choices and not choose them. For many organizations, this is not a bad bet.

The business motive behind "culture change" has now become clear. This rhetoric did not arise because of a last-minute burst of conscience from a soon-to-retire senior executive. Based on a purely economic perspective, following the sacred law of supply and demand, some of those in the top jobs figured out that people (human resources) had truly become strategic.

MAKING THE HR FUNCTION A STRATEGIC PART OF THE BUSINESS PLAN

The days of classic personnel function are long gone in most businesses. Human Resources can no longer afford to be just a provider of pay and benefits. HR leaders are in need of new skills and new programs. HR must become a strategic partner in the business by helping design and implement systems that support the direction the organization is going.

Companies with aggressive growth plans frequently require additional staff to put them in action. Often they face even greater challenges in splicing together diverse work cultures gained through acquisition and mergers. Those pursuing a strategy of globalization require a globally mobile workforce with vastly different skills and expectations. Companies planning to consolidate or downsize need processes to reduce personnel count while retaining the spirits and enthusiasm of survivors. Changes of this magnitude, to be successful, must be planned for and managed. An effective HR system can play an absolutely pivotal role in this process.

KEY COMPONENTS OF AN INTEGRATED CATALYTIC CULTURE

The next chapter will focus on the task of creating a caring atmosphere. The capability to develop coaching skills and administer a system like the Catalytic Coaching model is absolutely essential. In addition to that, however, there are at least five other HR systems that can play outstanding strategic roles in supporting people development. Each works in harmony with Catalytic Coaching to make the whole greater than the sum of the parts. Clearly, we could list several more initiatives, but these five might be considered some of the most essential sister programs:

- Training and Development System
- Job Posting
- Educational Reimbursement
- Employee Assistance Program
- Outplacement

On the following pages we will explore each of these program features in more depth.

TRAINING AND DEVELOPMENT SYSTEM

An obvious need to support a comprehensive people-development process is an organized Training and Development function. It is inefficient and ineffective to ask every coach completing a Catalytic Coaching Worksheet and every employee completing a Personal Development Plan to fend for themselves when trying to determine training and development options.

Clearly, the size of an organization and its training budget will have an impact on the resources available to develop and administer a training and development system. One only needs to remember the Catalytic Coaching model, however, to find motivation to see this as a prudent investment. The process does not end with a completed worksheet or action plan. It ends with positive behavioral change that results in improved business results. To the extent organized training and development activities contribute to this cycle, they are a worthy investment.

Guidance on how to create an effective Training and Development system is the subject of several excellent books and perhaps an entire industry. One of the more helpful comprehensive resources is *Designing Career Development Systems* by Zandy Leibowitz, Caela Farren and Beverly L. Kaye.[3] These authors take a very systemic approach to the problem. They outline four major steps for building development programs that generate results and help maintain the impact of change.

Also worthy of note is the work by Robert Haskell entitled *Reengineering Corporate Training: Intellectual Capital and Transfer of Learning.*[4] His work is particularly focused on the impact of training on the business. He is riveted on tracing the act of learning all the way to its practical application. This ties in well with the aforementioned model and our notion that the process is not complete until behavioral change creates value for the organization.

Job Posting

One of the most powerful components of a comprehensive people-development system is a Job Posting process. Job Posting will be defined here as any kind of system that informs all potential applicants of open positions before they are filled. Many companies do this by using a bulletin board system;

others have done so electronically on the Internet. Allowing all employees to
see job opportunities before they are filled is a dramatic form of empowerment.
This puts an employee in the position of knowing whether or not she was
considered for a job she coveted.

Too often management has an opening and knows immediately who they want
to put in the job. They have someone in mind that is right next door that they
are familiar with. They tap that person on the shoulder, offer her the job and
the job is filled. Often they are oblivious to anyone else who might have considered that job an ideal opportunity. They make assumptions that are sometimes
untrue.

In companies without Job Posting, rumors frequently float around about
"what you have to do to get ahead." Sometimes people joke about washing the
boss's car, doing her errands or getting her coffee. When a person is disappointed about seeing a job filled without being chosen, she normally won't
confront anyone about it. When someone actually does inquire as to whether
she was considered, she is likely to hear, "Of course you were," whether or
not this is true.

Many delightful surprises can be observed with the introduction of a Job
Posting process. It is sometimes a shock to discover who actually applies for a
job and who doesn't. My record for handicapping job selections in advance
using the Job Posting process is probably no better than 50%. There are just
too many factors you can't see. People post for jobs that you never would have
guessed had relevant background or interest. Even those lacking preferred credentials sometimes make compelling cases.

The one downside of the process is having to notify people who are not
successful in being awarded a job. For a popular position you may be forced to
give eleven people bad news while good news goes to only one.

The positive aspect of this, however, is when unsuccessful applicants learn
what they need to do to become more competitive for a future opening. Working
properly in concert with a Catalytic Coaching system, this disappointment can
help create some critical data to include in the ambitious person's Catalytic
Coaching Worksheet and Personal Development Plan.

Educational Reimbursement

A formal policy to assist individuals in their quest for personal growth is a
key strategic component of an integrated people development system. The ability to work at night toward a basic or advanced degree has helped scores of
individuals elevate their contribution and increase their contributions to their
organizations.

To be sure, there need to be rules about what will be paid for and what will
not. However, generally speaking, the fewer the restrictions the better. Requiring
an immediate payback in the current assignment for college coursework can
often be overly constrictive. The engineer you help get a law degree might

someday run an environmental compliance section, which you didn't even know you were going to need when she started her coursework.

It is not the purpose here to explain in detail what makes an effective Educational Reimbursement policy. There are many good models in the market place to copy. Suffice to say that most organizations will benefit by having some version of this practice included in a comprehensive people-development system. It is an excellent aid for the supervisor attempting to generate Development Recommendations to help his charges overcome key performance hurdles.

Employee Assistance Programs

The skill set of 99.9% of all coaches stops short of counseling individuals for alcohol and drug abuse, marital problems, gambling addictions, financial management, depression or child rearing. And yet, deep-seated personal issues like these often are at the root of an employee's performance decline. How then should they be dealt with?

Most organizations are not equipped to handle these problems with an internal staff. Even if you had a team of psychologists, psychiatrists and general practitioners internally at your disposal, people are often reluctant to truly confide in officials at work. This is the last place they want to talk about addiction or divorce or suicidal tendencies. That is why even the largest companies normally turn outside to an Employee Assistance Program (EAP) for help on these deeply personal, highly technical counseling matters.

A vital EAP is a critical counterpart to a comprehensive people-development process. The basic components of such a program include prepaid services with a firm that is available for all employees (and usually their dependents) in all locations. The plan needs to be well communicated so that potential users understand how to access the services and the terms and conditions that apply (number of visits, hours, etc.). To be effectively utilized, employees must also be absolutely assured of anonymity.

Most companies contract EAP services from a national or international firm. In these cases the company will generally pay a monthly premium for each employee in the covered groups. Rules are established as to the number of visits per individual or "presenting problem." Examples of presenting problems might be depression, dropping grades for a teenager in school, an unexpected pregnancy, etc.

Some plans will be based on a "diagnosis and referral" model. This type of coverage normally provides up to three or four visits to determine the source of a problem. Only very simple cases can be handled all the way to completion. A large percentage of cases are then referred to another source for the actual treatment. The EAP generally can work closely with the employee and her approved medical plans to make the appropriate transfer.

Employee Assistance Programs based on a "diagnosis and limited treatment" model generally allow up to six or eight visits per presenting problem. This allows them to deal with problems completely that are not of a deep-seated or complicated fashion. Naturally, the diagnosis and limited treatment model is more expensive. The cost difference is not generally very large, however. Because it sends fewer people to use medical plan coverage, it can often represent a bargain.

EAPs have become very common in large to mid-size businesses today. They are perceived as a valuable benefit by almost anyone who has used them. Word of mouth is the best way to spread the use and continued growth of an EAP. Even though anonymity is assured, often individuals who have received assistance from an EAP speak openly of their positive experiences and encourage others to take advantage of this valuable free benefit.

Mechanics of the EAP should become familiar to all supervisors and managers. They need to know how it works so that they promote awareness of the program even before problems surface that affect performance. They must also be trained in the proper manner to make a formal referral for employees whose work performance may be affected by issues occurring off the job.

Whenever I introduce an EAP to people, I always let it be known that I have taken advantage of such services myself. I encourage supervisors and other influential members of an organization who have obtained help from the EAP to do the same. Seeking help from qualified outsiders should be seen as a sign of intelligence and strength rather than a lack of critical skills and weakness.

Outplacement

For the purposes of this discussion, I'd like to define Outplacement as a systematic approach to helping employees seek job opportunities outside their current place of business. Usually Outplacement is facilitated by a firm that specializes in this activity. There are a variety of firms that perform such services at a local, regional, national and international level.

Outplacement services are paid for by the organization asking employees to leave. Usually fees are based on the level and/or salary of the individual(s) being displaced. Often they cover assistance for a specified period of time (e.g., three months, six months, or a year).

It may sound silly to talk about Outplacement as an important part of a comprehensive people-development program, but I find two compelling reasons that make it valuable: (1) As an employee's needs change, the company may no longer be a good fit, and (2) As a company's needs change, the employee may no longer be a good fit. What this inevitably means is that there are going to be cases where people must be let go. It is unrealistic and naive to assume that people who start work with you today will be equally well suited to your organization in the year 2020. Everybody knows we'll both be different. No one is sure exactly how.

Having an ongoing relationship with an Outplacement firm is very healthy. Surviving employees see colleagues exit the company following a series of

Catalytic Coaching sessions. Because of the issues of confidentiality, a company cannot justify its position to demonstrate that it was even-handed. That would potentially expose them to legal risks (defamation of character, etc.).

However, if the exiting individuals are given Outplacement assistance, many will make successful transitions to other work. This not only helps to limit legal exposure and limit any potential damage claims, it shows survivors that the company is compassionate and cares about the individuals it has grown apart from.

When questioned about responsibility for "trimming out the deadwood" in an organization, Dr. Deming used to respond with a question himself: "Were they dead when you hired them, or did you kill them?" Translation: Since management controls both selection and utilization of employees, management is ultimately responsible for individual failure on the job.

Regardless of the answer to Dr. Deming's counter-question, management must take action to correct problems with performance, fit and reorganization that are a normal part of doing business. An Outplacement program works together with a performance management system to deal with these inevitabilities and resolve these situations as constructively as possible.

The best way to help embolden managers to take responsible action when they have a bad fit with one of their employees is to create a culture where it is widely known that those who are asked to exit a company are given assistance to do so. The cost is nominal and the dividends huge.

MORE LESSONS FROM REAL LIFE

We will end this chapter with a pair of relevant tales from the front. The first concerns the practice of Job Posting and helps underscore why this program is such a beneficial companion piece to Catalytic Coaching. The second story recounts a coaching experience involving an EAP. As with earlier tales, each is based on actual events with real people. Minor details have been changed to preserve anonymity for those involved.

Monty's Irrefutable Logic

Job Posting systems are amazing. To senior managers who think they know their people, the introduction of Job Posting can be an eye-opening experience.

There was a job posted on the corporate Intranet of a large software company looking for a senior accountant in Plano, Texas. The HR representative in charge of filling the job had queried all her colleagues in other branches for logical candidates qualified for the position. The Headquarters office in San Francisco was the most desired location to draw from, but Geraldine, the HR coordinator there, reported that she had no candidates for the position. A week later Geraldine was surprised to learn that Monty, an accounting manager working down the hall, had applied for the position.

The HR rep in Plano called Geraldine to query as to whether Monty was having performance problems. She also wanted to double-check to make sure that Monty was aware of the fact that he had expressed interest in a position at a lower job grade. If granted his request, he would essentially be demoted.

Geraldine assured her colleague that Monty was, indeed, a good performer. She was curious as to why he had expressed interest in the move. Geraldine was only made more skeptical when advised by the Plano rep that in addition to being a demotion for Monty, they were not offering to pay for relocation. They tentatively agreed that Monty must be confused about the details of the posting, but Geraldine resolved to go speak with Monty directly.

When she met with Monty to set him straight on the situation, it was Geraldine who was in for the surprise. Despite being a high performer with an excellent track record as an accounting manager, Monty stated unequivocally that he was indeed interested in taking a step back to senior accountant. As it turns out, his parents had retired to a small town ten minutes from Plano, Texas. His father was in ill health. In addition, Monty had recently gone through an ugly divorce. He had no children and wanted to make a clean start in a new place with new friends. Being recently divorced, Monty was now renting an apartment and had very little to move. Therefore, a relocation package was of little concern to him. Because of the difference in the cost of living in the two areas, a reduction in pay was of minor consequence. Besides, he knew that normally in such situations the company did not reduce pay. Rather they usually just stopped giving increases for a while.

Monty desired to move to the Plano area so badly that he had recently contemplated resigning from the company without any firm employment prospects in hand. This job posting was perceived by him as a dream come true, an answer to his prayers.

Upon hearing of this incident, I couldn't help thinking about how the same situation would have been handled prior to the introduction of Job Posting. No one would have thought to consider Monty for the opening and he wouldn't have thought to ask. He'd probably have left the organization entirely to move back to live nearer his parents. They'd have lost an excellent employee and Monty would have had to start over somewhere else. Let's hear it for Job Posting!

THE "ZOMBIE" AUDITOR

Three months after giving Jerry a special recognition bonus, his boss and managing director were in the office of the Coach[2] asking for help with a serious performance problem. The Coach[2] was quite surprised. Jerry had twelve years experience with the company, and most of it was in this current capacity as an international auditor.

Jerry's bosses were apparently receiving repeated complaints from customers and others about Jerry's lack of initiative and failure to contribute to joint projects. The complainers said he was a "walking zombie" who made no real contribution to team audits. They had never heard this kind of complaint about Jerry before.

His managers entered with several competing theories as to the root of Jerry's sudden decline in performance. First and foremost, they were concerned that that he might be "burnt out." International auditing was very travel-intensive and Jerry had been on the road for years. Perhaps it was time to move him to a job involving less travel.

Complicating the situation were issues with respect to Jerry's personal life. He had a son in the Army Reserves who had been called into active duty for the Gulf War. And his nineteen-year-old daughter had recently left home with a boyfriend, against the wishes of both parents. Jerry told his boss that his wife was very distraught about both situations. In addition to the fears about her son and daughter, she had a general overall feeling of loss due to the newfound "empty nest."

All of these things had combined somehow to cause Jerry to come to work having had very little sleep. Furthermore, once at work he had a hard time concentrating on the task at hand. He had more pressing issues elsewhere.

His management team had great compassion for Jerry and had tried to cut him some slack. They adjusted his travel schedule as much as possible. They apologized to customers and audit partners and tried to explain his situation. Their assumption was that things would get better in a few weeks. After three months, however, things were only getting worse.

The first thing the Coach[2] suggested to the managers, and then ultimately to Jerry, was that they should seek professional help for Jerry with the Employee Assistance Program. When the Coach[2] began talking about the option with Jerry, Jerry was quick to ask about costs. As it turns out, he was also experiencing some rather serious financial problems on top of all the others. Jerry was relieved to know that the EAP did not cost him anything. Up to eight visits to the therapist were prepaid by the company.

Jerry was not overly concerned about confidentiality. In fact, he had told his supervisor everything he could about his problems. He was desperate to make corrections in his life and feel better. He knew he was failing at work and appreciated the care and concern of his management team. He left that day to begin seeing the EAP counselor.

Two months following his commencement of counseling, the Coach[2] thought things were going much better with Jerry. His supervisor had ordered him to "clean up his desk" and he had maintained an immaculate work area ever since. He had begun traveling again and we had no negative reports.

Then one day while Jerry was out of town someone called to inquire about an overdue bill. The caller claimed to be three months late in being paid. He said he had sent three different invoices to Jerry's attention. With Jerry out of the country, the boss went by his desk to look for the information the caller was describing. What he found was a shocker. Underneath Jerry's desk was a big cardboard box. In the box were dozens and dozens of unopened invoices and important communications. Jerry had taken the command to "clean up his desk" a little too literally.

The coach and Coach^2 confronted Jerry with the evidence and he denied nothing. Jerry said he simply could not muster the energy to deal with the paperwork. He felt horrible about it, but did not know what to do. His life was out of control. After a great deal of debate about whether they should fire Jerry, the company elected to put him on probation and issue a final warning. One more dropped ball and Jerry would be terminated—twelve years of excellent performance or not!

When the Coach^2 spoke with Jerry about whether he was continuing to seek counseling, Jerry said yes. The counseling was helping, but he still felt horrible. The Coach^2 then insisted that Jerry get a thorough medical examination. He had already been to see a general practitioner, but the company agreed to pay for Jerry to attend a university-sponsored clinic that ran a far more comprehensive battery of tests. As it turns out, Jerry was diagnosed as having a sleeping disorder—a very serious version of sleep apnea that was probably started by the various stresses in his life coupled with his smoking cigarettes, being overweight, etc.

When Jerry went to the sleeping clinic to be observed overnight they discovered that he experienced less than 30 minutes of REM sleep over an eight-hour period. With that little deep sleep for such a sustained period the doctor observed, "I am surprised you can still function at all."

Once Jerry's performance problems were determined to possibly have a medical origin, the company took him off probation. His supervisor modified his work schedule so that Jerry could get treatment and begin using a sleeping aid at night to get himself back in order. Almost immediately following the start of treatment for his sleeping disorder, Jerry's life changed. He became healthy again. He smiled and joked with people. *He no longer contemplated suicide.*

When things get put in proper perspective, it is almost an afterthought to me that Jerry became a productive employee again. One can only wonder what might have happened had his managers looked only at the facts and turned their backs on Jerry when he failed to measure up to the expectations at work. By using the full set of resources available to them (internal coaching expertise, Employee Assistance Program, medical services in the community) his management team not only salvaged a valued employee, but may have saved his life.

SUPPORTING SYSTEMS IN SUMMATION

There are many good programs to aid in people development. Those mentioned in this chapter were highlighted because they seem to provide clear synergies when included in an overall approach to people development that includes Catalytic Coaching. Nonetheless, they represent just a start. Many other good programs are available that should be considered in constructing the ideal working climate.

The point of this chapter is to stress that whatever people development programs you choose to offer make sure that they work well in conjunction with Catalytic Coaching. Too often in the past we have thrown together interesting programs and initiatives without enough thought about the interaction among these programs or the combined image we are creating and the capacity we are building. By looking more closely at synergistic relationships between strategic programs you will maximize benefit gained from the combined initiatives and minimize the cost.

One support system was deemed worthy of coverage on its own. Training and Development activities, which help an organization acquire coaching competencies are the subject of the next chapter.

Chapter 16

Acquiring Coaching Competencies Through Skills Training

> The great difficulty of education is to get experience out of ideas.
> —George Santayana, *The Life of Reason* (1905)

For Catalytic Coaching to bring about true cultural transformation and help a company get maximum benefit from system conversion, process participants must be given more than just a basic understanding of how the model works. Additional knowledge and skills are needed at two levels. Managers and supervisors must develop a basic set of coaching competencies, while those who coach the coaches, the Coach^{2}s (and in some cases Coach^{3}s), must develop more advanced capabilities. This chapter will explore some of the general competencies needed for maximum effectiveness and efficiency to be achieved.

Several good books have been written about how to coach. It is not the purpose of this chapter to try to somehow condense that wealth of knowledge into a *Reader's Digest* summary. Instead what we will do is highlight five key skill sets that are of significant value to those interested in using coaching as a foundation principle for a performance management system. In almost all cases, conversion from a system based on the prevailing paradigm to the Catalytic Coaching model would lead to an increased demand on these five competencies:

- Building Trust
- Listening
- Asking Questions
- Encouraging
- Diagnosing

We will review each of these competencies in this chapter. First, however, let's discuss the implications of converting managers and supervisors from bosses to coaches and talk about when coaching skills need to be utilized. Then we'll review each of the competencies and discuss the level of sophistication needed by coaches and those who guide them.

COACHING VERSUS COMMANDING

Most hierarchical organizations are built upon a military model. The hierarchical design insures that everyone is clear about who is in command. Those on top have been taught how to lead by telling those below what to do. Those on bottom look up for direction and do what they are instructed to. Appropriate responses to commands from a superior range from "Yes, sir. Right away, sir." to "How high would you like me to jump, sir?" Not much variety is required.

Teams and teamwork, the quality initiative, and now coaching have added new complexity to the manager/employee working relationship. Now, instead of barking out orders, bosses are supposed to be sensitive and figure out ways to motivate their people to want to do a good job.

Some catch on quickly. Some do not. One thing is clear, however. Changing someone's title from supervisor to coach does little to increase effectiveness of their working relationship with employees. Without an accompanying fundamental change in the way that these individuals interact with each other, the only true increases are likely to be in employee cynicism and management frustration.

WHEN TO USE COACHING SKILLS

The Catalytic Coaching model attempts to implant coaching practices into the formal process of discussing production capability. It places a large emphasis on a yearly conversation with subsequent quarterly dialogue involved in stewardship. Clearly, there is much additional to be gained from the more general practice of coaching on a more continuous basis. For an employee to truly consider a boss a coach, the more routine interactions that can occur literally every day need to take on the elements of coaching as well. Routine discussion about production issues, as well as those involving production capability, can benefit greatly from a use of this more empowering style of interaction. A wide body of literature attempts to make this point.

Foster and Seeker contend that "organizations that have made coaching an everyday part of employee development have realized many benefits." Among these they cite: "more exceptional employees, reduced turnover and improved interpersonal relationships."[1] Crane goes even further to state that an organization that uses coaching "as a predominant organizational practice creates a sustainable competitive advantage."[2]

Whitmore makes his perspective very clear. He feels that eventual conversion to a coaching-based paradigm for all employee-management interactions is almost inevitable: "Only when coaching principles govern or underlie all management behavior and interactions, as they certainly will do in time, will the full force of people's performance potential be released."[3]

Finally, Hendricks et al. argue that whether we realize it or not, managers of people are already de facto coaches. Anyone "expected to motivate, inspire, instruct, lead and correct the people who work for [them]" is already a coach, whether they realize it or not.[4] Their argument is that by building basic coaching competencies managers can perform better at a role they already have.

Each of the above-cited authors attempt to instruct managers and supervisors in how to perform the role of coach on a day-to-day basis. Suffice to say that much of what they teach effectively complements the Catalytic Coaching model and can lead to broader cultural change. Five elements that are essential to the execution of the model itself, however, are those listed previously and overviewed briefly below. These topics should be the subject of any training designed to help make Catalytic Coaching an effective part of an organization's culture.

BUILDING TRUST

Trust building is critical for Catalytic Coaching because an employee's confidence in his boss will have a tremendous influence over the way coaching feedback will be interpreted. Employees who feel uncomfortable with a coach or mistrust her motives are more likely to dismiss her message. Only by trusting the messenger is an employee likely to accept coaching feedback and take action on recommendations to change. Those coaches who have built solid foundations of trust are more effective at speeding the pace of meaningful behavioral change.

Quintero and Cripe have developed a coaching skills training program they call *REACH: Coaching for Performance Excellence.* In their two-day workshop, the very first topic is trust-building. They describe it as the first practice that distinguishes superior coaches from those that are less effective. They consider trust to be "the fuel needed for the coaching journey."[5]

Likewise, Hendricks et al. consider trust-building an essential competency. They describe trust as being built upon "critical foundation stones" which include: confidentiality, supporting team members, rewarding performance, honesty, consistency and encouraging communication freedom.[6] They include several assessment tools and role playing exercises that can be used to determine the level of trust that has been established and work to expand it.

Finally, Crane makes "coaching with heart" a central theme of his book. Acknowledging the personal element that is a part of work helps to build trust between the manager and employee, which can ultimately influence both behavior and results.

LISTENING

Effective listening skills are critical to the task of Catalytic Coaching. To be a good coach a manager must be able to clarify, interpret, expand and summarize what an employee has to say. She can do none of this if she has not listened effectively to what the individual has to say.

The Catalytic Coaching model attempts to build in critical listening into the process at Step One with the Employee Input Sheet. But listening skills are also vital in the face-to-face meetings that take place all year. And in most organizations these competencies are sorely lacking in our managers. They are usually better prepared to give opinions and instructions than to listen.

A large body of basic skills training is available to teach effective communications. Less is available which focuses specifically on listening. Less yet with a specific focus on coaching. Much of the literature and popular training is focused on "active" listening. This is differentiated from "passive" listening by stressing the role of the listener in making sure the speaker knows the message is being received. Quintero and Cripe take this concept a step further and describe what they call "reflective" listening.[7] Reflective listening places an even greater emphasis on insuring that a message is properly received. Techniques involve clarifying, summarizing, interpreting and expanding a given message. The goal of reflective listening is to insure that the message is received properly and to serve as a catalyst for providing insight to the person being coached.

ASKING QUESTIONS

Effective Catalytic coaches are almost always excellent at asking questions. They learn to adopt an almost Socratic method for allowing their employees to learn through the act of answering questions. Managers used to telling people what to do are often ill-equipped to assume the role of Socratic teacher. Training can assist them in moving further along the continuum from dependency to interdependence. The skilled questioner can help others develop insight to solve problems for themselves.

Whitmore feels the skill of asking questions is an essential coaching skill. He has two chapters in his book devoted to the subject. He also makes an excellent point about how questioning is different in coaching versus conventional settings. In conventional settings, questions are asked to obtain information for the questioner. To a coach that is of secondary importance. Whitmore feels that a coach's primary purpose for asking questions should be to provide the person being coached with insight. He contends that the coach's job is to raise awareness and accountability. Using a productive track of questioning is one of the most effective methods for helping someone realize and resolve her own performance problems.

ENCOURAGING

The act of providing encouragement to employees would seem to be a logical and natural supervisory practice. Unfortunately, it is not. Far too much energy is spent in business focusing on what's wrong. Goals and objectives, To Do Lists, Action Plans and Areas for Improvement dominate our lives. Accomplishments are quickly forgotten as the insatiable monster of business reality seems never to be satisfied.

Dale Carnegie and Stephen Covey training give some practical advice on these matters, but not specifically in the context of a true coaching relationship. Hendricks et al. address the importance of the coach's role in motivating and inspiring. They provide a number of exercises designed to help energize a coaching relationship.[8]

Quintero and Cripe suggest the use of a four-step model that is intended specifically to help a manager encourage her employee. The intent of their model is "to motivate, to communicate value, to enhance the other person's self esteem, and to reinforce positive behavior so that the coachee seeks to repeat those occurrences that are valued."[9] They stress the importance of giving positive feedback about desired behavior immediately after witnessing it and "anchoring" an image of the positive behavior such that it can later be repeated. They also give guidance on the subject of challenging

DIAGNOSING

Perhaps the most difficult competency to teach involves what we will call diagnosing. Despite the fact that we have attempted to make the Catalytic Coaching model as simple and straightforward as possible, the value of the coaching exercise can be greatly influenced by the individual doing the coaching. In no area are the skills of the coach more important in separating good experiences from bad than in the area of diagnosis.

Areas for Improvement in the Catalytic Coaching model are very subjective. Two different coaches might see and highlight different things. And frankly, some can put their finger on a problem much more easily and consistently than their colleagues. They must be both observant and insightful. They can "name that tune" in a way the employee and all involved recognize to be true. This is the skill and art form that is diagnosing.

After first converting to a Catalytic Coaching model and performing some initial training, a skill gap will emerge among coaches. Many will catch on quickly and seem to be making clearly stated, powerful diagnosis of how to help develop their employees. Others will struggle. Of those who struggle, the most frequent problem seems to be in their ability to see and articulate challenges and growth opportunities. This is where the Coach²s earn their keep. First, in making sure that the quality of all worksheets that go through the system is up to par. Second, in helping teach managers how to raise their ability to raise this vital competency for the future.

Foster and Seeker present several practical ideas for how to diagnose behavioral problems. They give tools and suggestions that are useful in training managers how to identify problems and reframe them as opportunities. In general, they help coaches trace perceived behavioral problems back to one of four sources: lack of knowledge, skill, motivation or confidence. Their guidance on how to resolve problems once diagnosed can also be usefully incorporated into the Catalytic Coaching process.

Competency in diagnosis is the single greatest area to emphasize when training $Coach^2$s and $Coach^3$s. To be of maximum value in their roles, those functioning as coaches to the coaches need to have advanced diagnostic skill sets. A $Coach^2$ should be able to sit with a perplexed manager and within an hour come away with a completed Catalytic Coaching Worksheet that the manager feels accurately portrays her feelings towards an employee. Especially in the early going when the process is new, $Coach^2$s must be counted on to provide this assistance. Early advanced training for those selected to play these vital roles will have a significant impact on the effectiveness of system conversion and the value obtained from the coaching experience.

INSTITUTIONALIZING SKILL DEVELOPMENT

We spoke in Chapter 11 of the critical role of $Coach^2$s for Follow-Up Coaching. These same individuals may also be utilized on a much broader scale to spread the technology of coaching and increase the base competencies being practiced by everyone.

Design and implementation of a comprehensive people-development process can be accomplished by contracting the work to an outside agent or agency. They can conduct your initial coaching skills training. Ongoing maintenance of that system, however, must normally come from inside. No matter how well you train your managers and supervisors to function as coaches, they will still need someone readily available to talk to for advice and counsel.

An individual or group within the organization should develop advanced skills in coaching and counseling to perform the ongoing task of maintaining the Catalytic Coaching system. We have referred to the people who perform this function as $Coach^2$s. In some large organizations, we have even introduced the concept of a $Coach^3$ who helps train and develop $Coach^2$s. These individuals teach supervisors, managers and even employees how to operate within the system. Ideally, they should be involved in its initial introduction.

Experienced $Coach^2$s should be qualified to conduct follow-up coaching for situations where that assistance is needed. They will work with the coach to make sure that all Job Threatening messages are properly worded and are cleared through the appropriate management and legal channels. They will work with employees receiving strong messages to make the sure messages are received as intended and progress is being made with the subsequent development plan. In cases where performance continues to fall below expectations, they will assist the coach in transitioning the employee out of the failed assignment.

Organizations must make sure that they have carefully selected and properly trained Coach^{2}s. They should also make sure that once trained, Coach^{2}s are given sufficient time to perform their assigned tasks properly. Where it is not possible or practical to have a full-time Coach^2, those assigned the responsibility should have an appropriate fraction of their jobs dedicated to providing ongoing support to other coaches. If this responsibility is treated as a mere addendum to responsibilities of those who have all-encompassing jobs already, results will be negatively affected.

To be an effective coach's coach requires a higher level of understanding of the basic competencies that all coaches should possess. In addition, Coach^{2}s must have the ability and desire to teach the five basic competencies outlined in this chapter. Trained properly, they should be able to raise the skill levels of coaches at the same time that they help them resolve specific challenges.

CLOSING THOUGHTS ON SKILLS TRAINING

Being a boss is a function of position and authority. Being a coach is a function of activity. While it is possible for an organization to announce that they are changing the formal job titles of all managers and supervisors to "coach," the act itself conveys does nothing positive. Quite the contrary. If the company remains rooted in the classic paradigm of evaluation and grading, and uses a command and control style of management, a change in titles can be seen as almost insulting.

For employees to regard their bosses legitimately as coaches, the bosses must work with employees in fundamentally different ways. They must interact both formally and informally in ways that fit a coaching model. And this requires training. It requires the development of some basic competencies in several skill areas that distinguish coaching behavior from traditional management/employee interactions.

In the end, however, training itself will not do it. Managers and supervisors must change the way they interact with employees and put in practice the training they receive. Only then will employees perceive a change in titles as legitimate and worthwhile. Only then will conversion to Catalytic Coaching pay maximum dividends.

Specific advice on how to change the way managers act with a variety of employee types is the subject of Chapter 17. In that chapter we will discuss special case coaching.

Chapter 17

Special Case Coaching

Go, call a coach, and let a coach be called;
And let the man who calleth be the caller;
And in the calling, let him nothing call,
But coach! coach! coach! Oh, for a coach, ye gods!
— Henry Carey, *Chrononhotonthologus*, act II, scene 4 (1734)

In addition to understanding the model and developing general coaching skills, specific knowledge on how to apply the Catalytic Coaching model is critical for all who wish to function effectively as coaches. More specifically, coaches must learn how to use the model in a variety of different kinds of situations. In this chapter we will look at six different types of common coaching challenges, which we will call "special cases." While there are probably dozens of special cases that could be examined, these were selected because they occur frequently and each poses a very different coaching challenge.

We will examine what it takes to handle each of the following special cases:

- *The Climber*—Good Performer with High Potential and/or Aspirations

- *The Problem Performer*—Individual Failing to Meet Expectations

- *Unreliable*—Good Performer When S/he's (Sometimes) There

- *The Rebel*—Good Performer but Radical Nonconformist

- *The Leaper*—Good Performer Nonexempt Employee Wanting Exempt Status

- *Typecast*—Good Performer Held Back by Past Reputation

You will note that only one of the six we have selected to profile is what might be called a "bad performer," meaning someone with some kind of skill or knowledge deficiency. With the exception of the so-called Problem Performer all others are labeled as "good performers," meaning they have sufficient knowledge or skills, and yet each poses a specific type of coaching challenge.

Pure "bad performers" are relatively easy to deal with. Once you learn to confront them directly with your list of required changes, they either change their behavior such that their overall contribution is positive, or you remove them from their positions. If they are forced to exit, it is typically without much regret on the part of the organization.

Losing a good performer is another story. Whether it is because they cannot overcome a specific issue, like an Unreliable or Rebel, or because they never make it to their true potential, like a Climber, Typecast or Leaper, the loss hurts. These are cases where advanced coaching skills can make a critical difference. Let's begin our study of types by concentrating on one of the organization's most prized commodities. An individual with the skills and capabilities to assume higher office that we will call the Climber.

THE CLIMBER—GOOD PERFORMER WITH HIGH POTENTIAL AND/OR ASPIRATIONS

Having responsibility to coach a Climber is a good problem to have. Employees with the capability to ultimately assume higher levels of responsibility are the lifeblood of an organization. They are its future. Nonetheless, Climbers require more time and energy to properly coach than perhaps any other type of employee.

Employees with high achievement and high aspirations typically want lots of feedback on their performance. Climbers are feedback sponges. They work very hard, deliver a lot and want to know that they are appreciated. Because most are ambitious, they want confirmation that they are making progress on their journey toward their goals.

It is easy to take Climbers for granted. They seem to work very hard and do a great job with minimal supervision. After a few weeks or months on the job they can operate with almost no direct guidance or direction on routine matters. And since this is not the case with so many others, energy can easily be diverted to those in need of more direct daily contact. It is quite common for the poor and modest performers to dominate a supervisor's time and attention.

Another common problem with coaching Climbers comes from traditional evaluation systems. If the system is set up to provide a rationale for salary increases, then paperwork tends to focus on the current job. This normally means it is filled with nothing but superlatives. While the Climber appreciates this information, and the resulting salary impact, it does little to aid her in her ultimate goal of making career progress. What she really wants and needs goes beyond fair and reasonable salary treatment. She needs to talk about what she can do to promote development and increase competitiveness for advancement. At minimum a supervisor should supplement a traditional evaluation-based system with something like the Catalytic Coaching Worksheet form to give Climbers more frank feedback on issues impacting their advancement potential. Ideally, they will be able to use this process without the burden of a more conventional evaluation-based system.

Assuming one has in place a performance management system like that described in this book which focuses on development instead of evaluation, a supervisor/manager has the proper tools to function as a true coach. For the rest of this example, we will assume that one is using the Catalytic Coaching model in interactions with the Climber.

A critical component of effectively coaching a Climber is to review carefully her Coaching Input Sheet. Make sure she fills it out conscientiously and thoughtfully. Challenge her to reflect on her true aspirations for career advancement. If this is a young person with little perspective on the organization, more time may need to be invested in dialogue to help her begin to think beyond her early and limited perspective. Ask her to take time to sit with potential mentors or role models in other areas.

When a Climber comes forward to discuss her aspirations in the formal interview, listen carefully. Ask tough questions. Make sure she realizes the implications of her desired future path. For example, let's assume the Climber is a Senior Accountant in a Headquarters assignment who aspires to be CFO. Is she ready to accept a field assignment to broaden her perspective? Is she aware that the last three Corporate Controllers (a required position for all CFOs) moved in and out of field assignments twice before being named to that position. If she is not prepared to relocate now, when will she be? What are the implications if relocation is never possible?

These are difficult questions, but they need to be addressed and Climber needs to address them. After all, it is her career, not the manager's and not the company's. The burden of responsibility for career development must remain with her.

Almost every organization that actively develops employees for succession has faced dilemmas similar to the example cited above—relocating for development purposes. It is not always a woman who is reluctant to move for family reasons. Men frequently struggle with the same choice. The point is, it doesn't matter whether the person is male or female, white or black, 21 years old or 59.

If they don't or can't accept a broadening assignment that mandates relocation, how are they going to demonstrate they are competitive for the office to which they ultimately aspire? By effective coaching, you help the Climber take ownership of this challenge. Let it be her problem to struggle with. The coach's job is to help the Climber consider options and to reconcile obvious inconsistencies between aspirations and actions.

Once the coach has a firm grasp of the Climber's aspirations and has helped her deal with the realistic implications, it is time to provide feedback. When completing the Catalytic Coaching Worksheet on a Climber the coach needs to be writing to a clearly defined audience. Who is the form being completed for? The file? the coach's boss? Human Resources? or the Climber?

If the answer is as it should be (the Climber), the message will be focused on the future, and discussion will be calibrated against aspirations as well as current job expectations. Strengths should be discussed in this manner. How do the Climber's strengths, as determined from observing behavior in current and previous jobs, sound with respect to the jobs to which she aspires?

If a young engineer is perceived as having "excellent initiative" and being a "great self-starter," a coach might speak of how that bodes well for the general management position she covets. If a research scientist is perceived as "extremely well organized" and "excellent at managing large scale projects," the coach might reflect on how those attributes might serve someone well who aspires to move into strategic planning.

In short, compare the strengths to the aspirations and discuss those openly with the employee during the coaching session. If she is not perceived as strong in areas that normally correlate highly with success in a particular position or job path, that is of interest too. These should be discussed as Areas for Improvement.

Areas for Improvement for most true Climbers, almost by definition, seldom have Job Threatening elements in them. In fact, once they've had a position for any length of time, they tend to evolve into issues that are skewed more toward Potential Enhancing than Performance Impacting. In other words, they're doing a great job at their current level. On the other hand, almost all need to work on certain things to continue the path up the ever narrowing ladder to the top.

The most significant contribution a coach can make in the quest to help a Climber is to help her discover what might be holding her back. Assuming she really wants to take on more responsibility and move up the organization, she needs to hear the straight scoop. What are people saying about her behind her back?

Sunset for Sonny

Sonny was a Climber for a Big 8 accounting firm. He was young, handsome, totally driven and exceptionally bright. He had graduated valedictorian from a leading black university. Not only did he hit the ground running at the firm, he left a trail of scorched track behind him. Sonny had his sights set on the top.

Sonny's accounting firm used a conventional performance management system. Once a year they called him in and reviewed a formal evaluation sheet with him. After three years of getting nothing but superlative reviews full of nothing but accolades, and with three years of continuous almost double-digit percentage base salary increases, Sonny abruptly resigned. In fact, he made the decision to leave on the spot during the course of his third performance review.

"I was tired of hearing how great I was. I knew I had a ton left to learn, but they were just way behind me. I was focused on three levels up and they spent all their time discussing the job I was in that day," he said. "I wanted to work someplace where people would tell me I had a lot to learn, so quit and started my own business." He was a millionaire in five years.

Had the company engaged Sonny more actively in his own career development, they might of learned of his need for more challenging feedback. Certainly if they had talked with him about his current skill set compared with the positions he ultimately desired, the list of improvement areas would have been more substantive. As it was, Sonny lost interest and went in search of more growth-oriented challenges. The corporation lost a significant investment in a person that might have been able to contribute at significantly higher levels.

The Story of Carey

Carey was a geologist who everyone loved. He was the darling of the entire Geology department and appeared to be highly regarded throughout the entire corporation. Carey seemed to always come out on top of every rank list.

Based on all the adulation and praise, Carey assumed his ascension into general management would come quickly. It did not. Carey was passed over repeatedly for jobs he coveted. Looking at his evaluations full of nothing but praise did little to console him. Almost ready to quit, Carey came to Gail in Human Resources in search of explanation and guidance.

When Gail (assuming the role of a Coach[2]) helped Carey track down the root of his dilemma, it was kind of alarming. The fact is, Carey was perceived as "too nice a guy." Executives at the top questioned his ability to make the tough decisions that they felt had to be made at the highest levels. Could he, for example, make a decision to lay off people, if that's what the business seemed to require? Not having any examples of tough decisions Carey had previously made, they opted to go with those who had shown toughness in the past.

Confronted with this information, Carey became very angry. Why didn't they just tell him this was a concern? Perhaps he could have done something about it much sooner. He immediately began working on his image to display more "toughness."

Gail worked with Carey and his manager to develop an aggressive Personal Development Plan. It included getting Carey appointed to an ad hoc team that was looking at some very difficult problems with information management. Ultimately the team recommended outsourcing most of the company's information management function. The plan also called for Carey to reduce his involvement in United Way and teaching team-based management. He had already proven himself capable in these areas, and they wanted to combat the image that he was inclined only toward the upbeat activities.

Carey also made a commitment to work performance problem cases with members of his group in a manner that few other supervisors had nerve enough to tackle. All told, he attempted to demonstrate to those above him that he had the skills and attributes desired for higher office. Within a year he was promoted to one of the positions he coveted.

The key learning with both the above examples, of course, is that a coach must give Climbers aggressive feedback. They don't need to hear endless renditions of how wonderful they are at doing what they are doing. Their focus is UP. They need to be given help in seeing themselves compared to their aspirations. They value most the coach who is brutally honest with them and challenges even the best to improve.

THE PROBLEM PERFORMER—INDIVIDUAL FAILING TO MEET EXPECTATIONS

One of the biggest challenges facing any supervisor, and for many the most intimidating and unpleasant aspect of their jobs, is in dealing with Problem Performers. Individuals who, for one reason or another, do not meet expectations in their current assignment. While there are many different variations on this theme, we will concentrate on two different types of performance issues in this section. The individual who it appears *can't* perform up to standards and the individual who it appears *can but doesn't*.

The words connoting tentativeness in the previous paragraph were chosen carefully. It is important for a coach to begin with the assumption that he may not have all the facts about a given performance situation. Even when it is demonstrably clear to a supervisor that his direct report is not meeting concrete goals and objectives, there are sometimes circumstances he may be unaware of that affect that individual's ability to produce.

The coaching exercise should be used as a dialogue to discuss perceptions and establish the proper facts and circumstances. After all, we know from systems theory that individuals operate within complex environments of functional interdependence, and it is easy to interpret a system failure as an individual one. We must demonstrate to the individual being coached that we are being more than fair in our interpretation of their individual contribution. Investigations of this type are when the general coaching competencies outlined in the previous chapter pay their dividends. Building trust, listening and questioning are critical components of an effective investigation.

Despite these words of caution, it is still possible and, indeed, necessary to confront an individual on perceived failings. Over time in many cases one can even make direct attribution of responsibility to the employee. To do this effectively with maximum impact, however, one must follow clear and logical processes built into the Catalytic Coaching method.

Before confronting an individual about a performance issue, it is important to keep in mind the objective of all coaching interactions. The business purposes may vary slightly by company, but as we've discussed, most contain at least these three essential elements:

- Change behavior in a positive manner.
- Motivate the employee to work hard.
- Minimize legal exposure.

When an employee is perceived to be making a contribution below acceptable standards, it is the supervisor's responsibility to get him to change. This means a confrontation must take place. They must talk. And it must be a formal discussion, not something casual. In terms of the Catalytic Coaching process, the step that is of significance here is the downward feedback segment—Step Two. Unless the perceived problem surfaces precisely in concert with the regularly scheduled coaching cycle, an intervention-style coaching session should be conducted off-cycle.

Performance problems of any significant size should be dealt with when they occur. Problems should not be allowed to fester and ferment until the advent of the annual review. They should be dealt with whenever they become apparent. And here is a cardinal rule: A Catalytic Coaching Worksheet should be completed and delivered to an employee in a formal interview as soon as a coach perceives even one aspect of the employee's behavior to be Job Threatening.

Most organizations mandate that all such messages be cleared by an appropriate Human Resources or Legal expert before formal discussion takes place. If no internal resources are available, or the situation is perceived as highly risky, an outside expert may also be consulted. Requiring that a boss/coach must seek external help when handling a person whose job is at risk, should in no way suggest that line management is incapable of conducting difficult interviews without oversight. Rather, this step of involving a second coach utilizes a team approach to improve effectiveness and safety. Using a Coach^2 provides objectivity, expertise and helps minimize legal exposure.

It is commonly understood in psychological circles that even the best therapists need outside counseling for difficult situations in which they themselves are active participants. The Coach^2 contribution (as we have described it earlier in Chapter 11) provides an objective perspective that is impossible to have when one is personally engaged.

A frustrated supervisor or manager coming to a Coach^2 for the first time will sometimes express interest in firing a poor performer immediately, on the spot. Quite frequently, however, they have not gathered the necessary information or taken the steps the organization requires for a dismissal to taken place. They are just fed up with the sub-optimal level of performance they've witnessed for years. In many instances (especially those involving classic evaluation-based performance management systems), they have never actually told the employee directly that his job was at risk.

Once a manager makes a decision that an employee is "not worth fixing" it is natural to want him removed immediately. The reality of business says this is neither fair nor safe, however. What a manager needs in times like these is someone who can help him do the right thing for both the employee and the company. That involves working in concert to produce an orchestrated act of confrontation.

For an off-cycle Catalytic Coaching session, no Coaching Input Sheet is required. The coach and his advisor should review the last submitted form but need not request that another be completed. In some cases where there is no Input Sheet on file, it makes sense to request one. However, this is the exception rather than the rule.

Key things to examine on an existing Coaching Input Sheet are the employee's perceptions about his current assignment and contribution as well as his aspirations for the future. Sometimes there are clues about work he might find more appealing. He may demonstrate awareness of his performance deficit on the form. On the other hand, he may show that he's simply oblivious to perceived problems.

Jim's Downward Spiral

An international salesman named Jim made a pitch to his management during the annual coaching cycle that he should be promoted and transferred to another accounting function. On his previous Coaching Input Sheet Jim described himself as "tired and burned out" after seventeen years of extensive travel. In fact, he attached a note formally requesting a transfer to a position that involved less travel.

The problem was Jim had let his performance slip so visibly that his once very positive reputation was being sullied almost daily. No one wanted him in other parts of the organization because he was perceived as "damaged goods." He had quit working hard and no one had a high-level position to offer someone that seemingly wanted to coast.

Bottom line, his managers felt they had to confront Jim with the cold, hard fact that he had to improve performance *in his current job* to keep from being *fired*. A Coach[2] assisted the manager in completing a Catalytic Coaching Worksheet on Jim featuring two areas for improvement that were Job Threatening. These were described as "Quantity of Work Produced" and "Follow Through with Customers." Jim was told that no transfer (even to a lower grade) would be approved until he brought his work back up to acceptable standards. They did, however, begin to talk to him about other opportunities that might one day exist if Jim returned to his previous form.

The coach and Coach[2] set a target of three months to make the next formal review of Jim's status. Weekly meetings were held with his coach/manager (fifteen minutes each) for Jim to present evidence of work produced and insure that he was sticking to his Personal Development Plan. The Coach[2] made himself available to Jim as a second level counselor.

In three sessions with Jim, the Coach[2] was able to help him see that the company was not trying to "run him off," as Jim suggested might be the case immediately following his first session with his supervisor. Jim's theory was quite typical. He was an older worker who had earned his way to high salary. His new young supervisor was trying to justify terminating him so he could hire other youngsters he could pay less to do the same work.

Accepting this logic Jim did not have to change. If his supervisor was truly biased, Jim's termination was inevitable. He was better off taking lots of notes and hunting around for a good lawyer. As a defender of the company's interest, the Coach[2] found this to be an interesting but inaccurate and dangerous line of reasoning. He reinforced the manager's message and helped Jim develop a plan to demonstrate the rebuilding of his previous good reputation.

Two parts of the process helped save Jim. First, it was hard for Jim to reconcile his conspiracy theory with the strengths his manager listed on the Catalytic Coaching Worksheet. Among other things, Jim was cited for having "Intimate Knowledge of Key Customers" and being the "Resident Expert in International Sales." Several examples were given to justify each descriptor. If Jim's supervisor was just trying to fire him, why would they say such positive things? The answer was clear to him. His boss said those things because they were true. He considered them both accurate and fair.

The second factor that helped Jim decide to recommit to the organization was their offer to invest in him. The manager suggested that Jim attend a highly regarded outside training course in hopes that it might help him regain some enthusiasm about his work. He offered to pay the $2,100 fee if Jim would take the course at night on his own time. In order to complete the course, his supervisor also had to allow Jim to arrange his travel schedule so that he was in town consistently for the fourteen weekly sessions. Clearly, this was not something the company would do to someone they were merely trying to "run off."

Jim bought the logic, he took the course, he changed his attitude and he saved his job. It took about a year, but eventually Jim was able to bid successfully for a position outside international sales. It seems his intimate knowledge of key customers and familiarity with the international market made him a strong contender for a position in new product development.

The case of Jim represents the operational definition of win/win/win. In this case the supervisor won by increasing productivity from his work unit. The company won by salvaging a valuable employee and avoiding a potentially ugly and costly lawsuit. And Jim won by getting a new and exciting job and finding a way to feel good about his contribution again. In the world of coaching and counseling, it doesn't get any better than this.

Jim is obviously a case of an individual who *can* perform at an acceptable level, despite the fact that he *wasn't*. Other cases involve individuals who just *can't* do the work. Gerald, an oil field maintenance worker, was one such example.

Gerald Can't Cut It

Gerald was a maintenance worker operating out of a field office in Canada. He had been with his company for three years when his supervisor and manager decided he needed to be let go. They called their headquarters HR representative (Coach[2]) to discuss how to release him for poor performance.

Gerald's primary performance problem was that he had never grown to a point where he could perform routine maintenance functions on his own. As the number of personnel allocated to the field office was were slowly reduced due to deteriorating economic conditions, it became impossible to send someone more capable with Gerald on every assignment. They could no longer afford this inefficiency.

The only thing preventing a quick release of Gerald was that his file was full of nothing but positive comments. To put it diplomatically, his local management, using the performance evaluation system in place at the time, had been very "optimistic" about the way they described Gerald. Each year Gerald had been described as an "Effective" (average) performer with no glaring deficiencies.

By way of explanation, his managers stated that they were trying to protect Gerald's salary treatment in case he began making improvements and they determined he was actually salvageable. They were concerned that if they rated him aggressively on the form that no money would be placed in the budget for him and if he improved they would have no way of rewarding him for the miraculous increase in performance. They also preferred to deal with the problem themselves and felt a negative performance label would attract too much "help" from Headquarters. Regardless of their logic, Gerald never made the improvements and now they just wanted to be done with him.

Gerald on paper was a far cry from the Gerald they described to the Coach[2]. Despite the fact he was with the field office only a short period of time, company lawyers felt that the paperwork represented a potential liability. They had never documented any concerns about Gerald's performance deficiencies. The paperwork completed to date could only hurt the company in court.

The Coach[2] asked Gerald's supervisor and manager to develop a clearer message by completing a Catalytic Coaching Worksheet. They then used the form in an immediate coaching intervention. On the CCW, Gerald was described as "Dependable, Hard Working and Excellent at Following Instructions." Nonetheless, he was told that he must learn to "Troubleshoot Pumps, Diagnose Production Problems and Calibrate Gauges" all *"without direct supervision."*

On Gerald's Personal Development Plan, he was given additional time to retake training modules at work. He was offered a new mentor to ride with him for six weeks. He was informed of the business reason for having to change the job requirements.

Before the six weeks were concluded, Gerald came forward to ask his management for a severance package, as provided by Canadian law. It was not very large, but Gerald concluded that he could not do the required work without supervision. He did not want to pose a safety threat to himself or others now that the job required him to function on his own. Gerald left the company and took a job teaching physical education in a local high school. He has remained friends with his former work colleagues. He still plays on their hockey team.

Common Factors

Despite moments of anguish and inner turmoil, both Performance Problem cases concluded with a productive solution. They share an honesty and fairness that is not typical of performance confrontations using most evaluation-based systems. Again, here the secret is focus and ownership.

Changing behavior and motivating people to work hard requires active participation on the part of the individual whose behavior needs to be changed. He must perceive that he is being treated fairly if you expect to get positive results. He must perceive your communications to be as honest as possible when describing his shortcomings. Most importantly, he must feel that you are aware of him as a person. When these conditions are present, the odds of producing a positive outcome are maximized for all parties.

UNRELIABLE—GOOD PERFORMER WHEN S/HE'S (SOMETIMES) THERE

Attendance and punctuality are issues that plague many supervisors of lower level employees. What do you do about the receptionist who delights her customers but has developed a habit of missing work and showing up late? What about the Computer Help Desk Analyst who has missed three Mondays in a row but is revered by the people who use her services? Does it change the picture any if you have experienced massive turnover in these jobs and have a local unemployment rate below 4%?

The Unreliable worker is a problem precisely because her performance is good. If she were consistently tardy and missing lots of days while also being a marginal contributor, the path toward resolution would be much more direct. It's the good ones that make life difficult.

In preparing for engagement with an Unreliable, the first thing to examine is the job she's occupying. Is this job artificially rigid in its definition? Is it possible for someone to perform the functions of this position successfully without working the hours that you are rigidly trying to enforce? If so, perhaps some of the employee's lack of discipline comes from a knowledge that she can still get all the work done without being obsessive about start and stop times.

Justifying the rigid hours merely by saying that the same rules apply to everyone and you can't demonstrate flexibility for this person may be interpreted as arbitrary to the Unreliable. This is especially true if she has what she feels to be a good reason for her occasional tardiness or excessive use of sick days. For example, taking care of sick children, parents or animals.

It is not our purpose here to lecture anyone on the merits of flex-time or telecommuting. Nonetheless, it is important to prepare yourself for an inevitable argument with the Unreliable if your reasons for enforcing rigid attendance standards are arbitrary or merely represent a long-standing tradition. Young employees, especially those who have grown up in a world of plentiful work opportunities, may well challenge your rules. So also may long-term employees who are going through temporary off-work problems.

Assuming no reasonable flexibility exists for the current job, one must next ponder possible explanations for the repeated absences. Has the employee informed you as to what the root problem may be? Are there any signs of a medical condition that might justify the absences? The answers to these questions should serve as background information. They do not prevent you from confronting the employee but merely color the manner in which you do so.

Most HR or Employee Relations specialists have encountered many situations that have elements of medical problems and many that do not. They know about situations involving child care, the use of alcohol and drugs and, in recent years, gambling problems. Seeking counsel from an experienced HR person will normally help a supervisor think through all these possible explanations in advance of the meeting. Patterns of absences will be examined. Potential avenues of assistance can be readied.

As with the Problem Performer, the key tool for confronting the Unreliable is the Catalytic Coaching Worksheet. It should be completed whenever it is appropriate for the strong counseling to take place. Normally this will be off-cycle from the annual review. Care should be taken to be fair in completing the CCW. The objectives of changing behavior and motivating the employee to work hard should be foremost in the coach's mind. Next in line is the necessity to minimize legal exposure.

A true Unreliable has strengths that make that person worth spending time to help. If they struggle with fundamental aspects of the job as well as attendance and punctuality, they should be treated as a Problem Performer.

It is important with an Unreliable to give fair treatment to the discussion of Strengths. Make sure you list at least four of them and give at least three good examples of each positive attribute. Make it very clear that they are appreciated for the good work that they do.

When describing Areas for Improvement it is generally not necessary to indicate that "Attendance" and/or "Punctuality" issues are Job Threatening in the first interview. Rather, classify them as Performance Impacting while noting that they are very serious in nature and can grow to be Job Threatening very quickly if performance does not change. In other words, give the Unreliable the proverbial "shot over the bow."

The fact that a good performer is being called in for a serious performance discussion off-cycle is a pretty big message. Most see this as a *huge* issue and may even overreact. They frequently need to be assured that they are still held in high esteem and that this is not the end of their career. As their coach, it is your job to talk to them about their performance *before* it becomes an issue that will damage their careers.

Tough but Fair

In explaining the problem to the Unreliable, it is important to get her to understand the business reasons for the confrontation. This is not personal. This is related to fulfilling the department's duties to the corporation.

The receptionist needs to understand the problems encountered by the company when she fails to report to work on time or repeatedly calls in sick. Customers don't get taken care of. Others must abandon their jobs and cover for her. The coach is not expecting her to live a life void of illness. She should generally be expected, however, to provide more than ten minutes notice when she is forced to take a sick day.

One technique to reduce tension when confronting an Unreliable is to make an issue of the fact that the discussion is being conducted off-cycle. Being off-cycle means the Catalytic Coaching Worksheet does not necessarily have to be sent through formal channels. It makes improvement areas noted ''supervisory issues'' which, if dealt with successfully, may never have to be become part of a central personnel file.

In fact, a coach and Coach[2] can make an agreement with an employee nervous about the status of her ''official personnel file.'' If the employee completely corrects the problem behavior in question within six months, for example, the CCW documenting the conversation will be removed from her central personnel file. For some people this can be a highly motivational tactic.

It should be made clear to an employee that a working copy of the incident will remain on file somewhere in the company. This can be with the Coach[2], in a legal file or with the supervisor only. The incident cannot be removed from history. Certain issues were discussed as problems and those could be put into evidence if there was ever a repeat performance of substandard behavior. On the other hand, removing the form from the active general file makes it unavailable for anyone to note who is not already in the loop. Should the person post for a job in another department, the manager making the employment decision would not find record of the corrected situation in the file sent for her to examine.

Outside assistance may also be useful in helping an Unreliable. In terms of Development Recommendations, sometimes it is appropriate to recommend the use of an Employee Assistance Program to an Unreliable. If the reason for the pattern of absences is personal or family in nature, sometimes an outside counselor can be very helpful. If there are drug or alcohol issues that have not fully surfaced, the EAP counselor can frequently get the employee to consider treatment. If there is concrete evidence of dependency problems, professional guidance is a must.

It is helpful if in the Development Recommendations a coach can demonstrate some degree of flexibility. Even if it is only to give the employee her home phone number with a request that she call when it looks like she might miss work the next day. Allowing a compromise start-time one day a week or putting the employee in charge of coordinating acceptable back-up coverage for desired absences works even better.

Unreliables can often be cured of performance problems quite rapidly. Most frequently problems linger far too long because supervisors fail to confront them in a formal, organized fashion. Failure to directly address a problem of this sort soon after it is first recognized can allow a minor irritation to grow into an ulcerated wound. Once a supervisor has successfully coached an Unreliable through a process of change, she normally moves more proactively to confront similar problems from developing with other employees in the future.

John's Wake-Up Call

John was a computer help desk operator who was highly valued by his clients. He'd worked with the company for four years when his pattern of attendance started to slip. After being late or absent on twelve days in a four-month period, John's manager called a Coach[2] for assistance. Neither could find a consistent reason for John's absences and tardiness.

The Coach and Coach[2] proceeded to complete an off-cycle Catalytic Coaching Worksheet on John. They indicated to him that his attendance and punctuality were Performance Impacting, but borderline Job Threatening. Despite having several informal discussions with his supervisor before this, John was stunned to see something in writing that confronted him on negative behavior. He considered himself a very valuable, high-performing employee. His only explanation for the pattern of absences was that he thought the rules were "stupid and arbitrary." He felt it would be much wiser for him to be allowed to do much of his work by telecommuting from home.

The coach explained to John that, while this was a very interesting notion, it was not possible to do it at this time. And he reminded John that he had been given clear instruction that he was needed in the office at a certain time. During the conversation John disclosed to his coach that he was seriously considering taking a job offer with another company. This led into a dialogue about what John really wanted to do with his career.

To make a long story short, both sides made a decision to recommit to the relationship. The company wanted John to stay and was willing to work with him on transitioning to a position more in line with his aspirations. For his part, John immediately returned to his previously reliable attendance pattern. The off-cycle CCW was removed from his file after six months. John was promoted and transferred within nine. He later served on a task force that investigated methods of allowing computer professionals to work from their homes.

Memorable Loss

Not all stories turn into win-win situations, of course. Unfortunately, it is not uncommon to have to terminate someone who is capable but unwilling to meet the requirements of a job. One case of this sort involved an employee who developed severe gastro-intestinal problems.

Rebecca was a 21-year-old receivables clerk whose life was turned upside down by Krohn's disease. When her illness struck, her attitude and priorities changed. Her entire management team felt bad forcing her to leave, but she had become so unreliable and uncooperative that they could not afford to keep working with her.

Even before the American's with Disabilities Act the company went out of its way to accommodate Rebecca's illness, but to no avail. After six weeks of focused coaching she just stopped coming to work one day. From a company perspective, Rebecca left without severance. They did not deny her unemployment claim but were not sued. With no fear of litigation, they were able to immediately begin searching to fill her position with someone who would perform the job reliably.

From a human perspective, her coach and Coach[2] felt confident they had treated Rebecca fairly. The turmoil in her life simply changed her priorities and she moved on to other things. They had performed their duties responsibly but were also able to wish Rebecca well in her quest to reconstruct her life and find inner peace.

THE REBEL—GOOD PERFORMER BUT RADICAL NONCONFORMIST

Have you ever worked with someone who is a great performer but has a giant, seemingly suicidal, flaw? Welcome the Rebel. He's the executive wannabe who wears a Pee Wee Herman costume to work on Halloween. Or the top performer you'd like to grant a special bonus to who insists on pinning down visiting senior executives with extremely controversial questions in public meetings. Or the one who works 70-hour weeks but refuses to be there consistently when normal office hours start.

Again, the dilemma here only holds if this is a good performer. A poor performer who is a radical nonconformist is not normally a long-term player. The excellent performer with what otherwise appears to be upward potential who intermittently commits these attention-grabbing, jaw-dropping gaffes is another matter.

In dealing with a Rebel, perhaps the first thing you should do is look in the mirror. Often what they appear to be doing is challenging traditional thinking on the ultimate implications of the offending behavior. Perhaps your gregarious colleague, by wearing the controversial costume, is trying to inject a bit of levity in an otherwise uptight work environment. He may have gone too far in making his point, but is it possible the work environment is perceived as stifling to others as well? Is he alone in his point of view or is he pointing to something important?

Think through the consequences of such behavior. In your company, does a display of such behavior necessarily eliminate him from the management promotion list? If no, relax and enjoy the show. If so, and the reality of this cannot be changed, then you definitely need to talk with him. On a similar tact, does arriving at inconsistent start times really propel the organization into chaos, or might it display some level of compassion and flexibility to accept and embrace such an arrangement on a negotiated basis?

Assuming you have quickly arrived at a decision that the behavior is, indeed, at least potentially damaging to the employee, you owe it to him to have a discussion. As with the Unreliable, it is often less threatening to conduct such conversations off-cycle. If the Rebel is concerned about what you put on paper and agrees to work to minimize or eliminate the offensive behavior, you can then structure a deal to pull the CCW from the file at an agreed-upon future date. This assumes, of course, that there is a noted improvement.

Here's the ultimate truth about this kind of situation. Most upwardly mobile Rebels appreciate when a supervisor provides counsel on how their behavior impacts promotability. They may or may not change their behavior, but they will at least be aware of the potential consequences of continuing down their chosen path. The key is to be brutally honest and let them know what others are saying about them.

The Surfing Supervisor

Sometimes subtlety and general announcements don't get the job done. When Internet access is granted to employees of large corporations, employees are normally blanketed with caveats about what it's okay to look at and when. The expectation is that responsible people will heed this warning and conform. Most do.

Reggie was a bit of a Rebel. He was a well-regarded senior professional who worked in quality control for an international engineering company. He traveled a lot and worked many nights and weekends. Reggie was also very computer literate and liked to keep in touch with what was going on outside the workplace. He did so by surfing the Internet.

Unfortunately, Reggie surfed some areas that the company felt were nonwork-related. *Very* non-work related. He did this using company equipment *during* work hours. He was very surprised when confronted on his specific pattern of use by his manager along with the Vice President of Human Resources. They presented him with a Catalytic Coaching Worksheet that described this type of behavior as Job Threatening. Reggie was given another chance but was clearly and unequivocally informed that one more such incident would result in his termination. He was also told that it represented an error in judgment that could affect his promotability. Nonetheless, his career was not yet ruined. He just needed to quickly shape up.

Reggie's management team had every confidence that he would make an immediate and sustained turnaround. He was terribly embarrassed and apologetic when confronted for his indiscretions. He vowed to never use company equipment or work time to engage in this type of behavior again. He expressed contrition, asked for forgiveness and thanked his management for the second chance.

Six weeks later Reggie's secretary was looking for a file in his desk drawer when she discovered a hardcore pornographic magazine. Reggie was terminated the next day.

The story of Reggie is important because it reminds us that we can't win them all. Even the best coach has to fire a few players. If the Rebel's negative behavior pattern is deeply ingrained and if it goes beyond acceptable limits, the only recourse is to sever ties. Reggie's coach and Coach² created a clear, well-documented set of expectations. The CCW was unequivocal in stating the behavior he must change to keep his job. Because of this, company attorneys felt minimal exposure in terminating Reggie for cause and gave him no severance.

There are many examples where people with behavior just as deeply ingrained can be coached into making dramatic changes. One of the most remarkable involves an individual named Ken.

Commander Ken

Ken was the manager of Corporate Relocation for a financial company. He was also a tyrant. Or at least his direct reports thought so. In a word, they loathed him. He was demeaning, demanding and demotivating. He sucked all the energy from his people and left them lifeless or bitter. Ken has been labeled a Rebel because he knew about his reputation as an extreme authoritarian but didn't seem to mind. It was an idiosyncrasy that, for a long time, seemed to be tolerated by the organization. It felt comfortable to Ken.

Ken's new boss learned of this problem on the first day she started work for the company. Three of Ken's seven direct reports came to her independently pleading for relief. A month later the most experienced person in the work group abruptly resigned, three years short of obtaining her pension. She reported that she could not take it any more. Her immediate mental health was more precious to her than a lifetime of paid medical benefits and a few more dollars in the bank. Ken had lost or run off three others in the last eighteen months.

The irony of all this is that Ken was perceived as a fine performer by most of those higher up in the organization. He was cordial and responsive and always bailed executives out of problems when they needed help. He was the backbone of the department and had been considered, but ultimately denied, the Director position. Nonetheless, he quickly ingratiated himself with the new Director, who saw his technical skills as invaluable.

In confronting Ken about the need to change, his coach and Coach[2] started with the notion that Ken had been passed up for promotion in large part because of the perceptions of him as a poor people manager. If Ken still aspired to a Director position at some time in the future he would have to improve the way people felt about working for him.

His boss did an off-cycle coaching session using a Catalytic Coaching Worksheet. It listed specific people management skills as Performance Impacting. Void of significant change in this area, a promotion could not be recommended. In fact, if he could not improve his ability to work with direct reports, the issue was significant enough to eventually merit relieving Ken of people management responsibilities. The key for Ken lay in the area of Development Recommendations. Ken's coach and Coach[2] recommended three key actions for him to take.

First, they asked him to consider a facilitated upward feedback session where his direct reports gave him specific suggestions on what they'd like him to do differently to be a better boss. Second, they offered to send him to a highly regarded week-long workshop focused on improving management style at The Center for Creative Leadership in North Carolina. Third, they provided him with a copy of the book *Zapp!* by Byham and Cox and offered a mentor to help him integrate some of their empowerment strategies.[1]

To say Ken took the feedback seriously is an understatement. Despite the fact he had previously displayed a cavalier attitude about being labeled an authoritarian, he quickly concluded that his reputation needed to change. Ken accepted all three of the recommendations and proceeded to lead the follow-up effort in each area.

While I would love to conclude this story by reporting that Ken later was promoted to the Director level, that has not happened. While he did improve his working relationship with direct reports, he still struggles to be a good boss. During a reorganization Ken was stripped of some of his staff responsibility. Ken's coach and Coach[2] currently forecast that he will never make Director. Perhaps now, however, he has a better indication of why. Perhaps also he has lengthened his ultimate stay with the organization and postponed forced early retirement.

Choices

The short course on Rebels says they need to be given information and choices. Some choose to change. Some can; some can't. Some elect not to change. Conformity makes some careers and kills others. Like breaking a bronco, Rebels are fun and challenging to coach. They provide lots of action and adventure and never a dull moment.

THE LEAPER—GOOD PERFORMER NONEXEMPT
EMPLOYEE WANTING EXEMPT STATUS

Perhaps the most difficult promotion to obtain in a traditional business organization involves the leap from nonexempt to exempt status. Even those who have ascended to the highest ranks of the nonexempt ladder normally find the transition to the lowest ranks of the exempt ladder very difficult. In this section, we will refer to the individual seeking to make this precipitous jump as a Leaper.

In its purest form, "nonexempt" is a technical term. It signifies someone who gets paid overtime if they work more than the standard work day or week. "Exempt" employees, very simply, are those that are not paid overtime. By this logic, it would stand to reason that (assuming equal base salaries) one would be better off being classified nonexempt than exempt. If nonexempt status provides extra income or guarantees a 40-hour workweek, why fight it? Why are people frequently willing to take a total earnings decrease in order to make the leap from nonexempt to exempt?

The answer is simple. There are two reasons: status and future pay. There is a big divide between exempt and nonexempt status in an organization. In most settings, it is no longer acceptable to refer to exempt employees as "professionals." Doing so suggests that nonexempt employees are somehow "nonprofessionals" or "support staff" who passively assist exempt employees in accomplishing real work. Times have changed such that top nonexempt positions frequently function in a manner almost indistinguishable from their lower level exempt counterparts. Nonetheless, in many companies the perceived status differential between "professional" and "nonprofessional" jobs persists.

Beyond perceptions of status is pay. Despite the fact that there is normally some overlap between the two ladders, ultimately the exempt ladder is always much higher and richer than the nonexempt ladder. Once on top of the nonexempt ladder there is nowhere else to go—without changing ladders. Hence the attraction. The best of the best nonexempts frequently aspire to leap to exempt status.

To understand how to effectively coach a Leaper one must understand about the nature of the leap. The coach must come to grips with not just the immediate exempt position coveted by the Leaper but also the whole system the coveted position operates within. Some coaches become very frustrated that they can't gain organizational support for a Leaper to make the jump. Often this experience comes from a failure or unwillingness to recognize or accept the bigger picture. Perhaps it is easiest to explain with an example.

Sally's Lack of Sponsorship

Sally was a fourteen-year Human Resources Senior Administrative Assistant in a large industrial corporation working in a 2,000-person field organization. Sally handled all the Benefits and Payroll issues for the entire factory workforce.

In doing so, she coordinated the administrative work of seven others. Sally was regarded by almost everyone in the organization as the "go to" person in Human Resources. Executives in the firm used Sally as their personal liaison. They trusted her to handle even the most difficult and sensitive problems quickly, efficiently, accurately and confidentially.

Sally was a supervisor's dream. In fact, she had trained many of her bosses to move up and out of the local organization and on to bigger things. In the process, she had been rated very highly and always given top salary and promotion consideration. After fourteen years, however, she had reached the summit of both pay and level. Because she was at the very top of her salary range, Sally could no longer be given a base salary increase. Instead, the organization recognized her continued outstanding performance by giving her a cash award (lump sum) at evaluation time.

Hoping to overcome the salary cap obstacle, Sally's supervisor made what he thought would be an easy case to promote her to the exempt ranks. To her supervisor's surprise, however, Sally was denied promotion. The logic used to make the denial hit him very hard. The supervisor was informed that Sally could only receive promotion to exempt ranks if the HR group was willing to forgo another exempt employee. They would have to hire a support staff person in place of the MBA they were currently allocated to acquire.

Despite her talent at doing the job, Sally, only had a high school education. She started night school at a local college a few years earlier but had to drop out because of the grueling hours she was putting in at work. When being considered to fill an exempt position, Sally was being compared with the best and the brightest that could be hired on campuses at the finest schools across the country.

Even though everyone knew Sally could outperform any new campus hire in an entry-level exempt position, who had the greater likelihood of promotion from there? One of the key criteria in filling the entry-level exempt positions was to feed the succession planning system. MBAs were hired based on the perception that they could one day serve as Directors or Vice Presidents. If they did not appear to have this aptitude, they were simply not hired.

Most felt Sally was already outperforming many of her lowest-level exempt counterparts. Likewise, they conceded that many of hot shot newcomers would never make the managerial level, let alone make it to Director or above. Nonetheless, they were reluctant to "waste a draft pick" on Sally.

From a coaching standpoint, the challenge was more clear. For Sally to be promoted to exempt status, she must be perceived to have potential to run an HR department one day. In an effort to begin testing this premise and making this case, the coach and Coach[2] obtained permission to change Sally's job. They did not classify her as exempt, but the duties were clearly parallel. Sally became the executive compensation coordinator, if not in title, then in function. She took over the duties of a Stanford MBA who had done well in the job before her. He, in turn, had taken over duties from the most senior HR manager in the company who had performed this function for almost twenty years. Technically, the Section Manager had the formal responsibility for these activities, but he made it clear that Sally was the one doing the work.

Over the next eighteen months, Sally had an opportunity to work one-on-one with the most senior officials in the organization on issues of tremendous personal interest to them (their own pay, perquisites and bonuses). She put in new systems and procedures to help them organize their portfolios in a way that surpassed any service they'd had before. And she was able to show them first hand what tremendous potential she had.

Although it was not possible or practical during the eighteen months to get Sally back into night school, they did manage to get her off to some very powerful comprehensive general management training. The reputation of the schools (University of Michigan, Harvard) helped enhance Sally's attractiveness on paper.

In short, after eighteen months of focusing on the key issue of demonstrating potential for advancement, Sally was promoted to the exempt ranks. In the ensuing years she has continued to climb the exempt ladder, has been moved to corporate headquarters and remains a highly valued contributor of the corporation.

Perhaps one of the lessons we learn from the case of Sally is that a good coach sometimes resembles a political campaign manager. Sally's manager helped her run a successful race for entry into the exempt ranks. He helped her discover the issues that defined her campaign and design a plan to prove herself. If Sally had not have an effective coach serving as intermediary it is likely that she would have never understood the root of her dilemma. Nor would she have been afforded the opportunity or had the proper mindset to effectively demonstrate the competencies that were key to winning election to higher office.

To be sure, not all employees can or should be allowed to make the leap from nonexempt to exempt status. There is nothing sadder than seeing an outstanding performer in one class promoted to mediocrity in another. A close second, however, may be the individual intelligently denied promotion who fails to understand the decision-making process.

An effective coach gives the straight scoop to Leapers. She helps those who have the skill and determination mount effective campaigns. She helps those who lack key ingredients for advancement get comfortable with their status as top contributors in the nonexempt ranks. Either situation can be defined as a success by a caring leader and a self-aware employee.

TYPECAST—GOOD PERFORMER HELD BACK BY PAST REPUTATION

If any situation involving a good performer is more challenging than coaching a Leaper, it has to be coaching a Typecast. A Typecast will be defined here as a good performer who is held back by a bad history or reputation.

Organizations have very long memories. If you have ever coached or supervised someone who at one time was labeled a poor performer, you will know what this means. "Once a bad performer, always a bad performer" seems to be the operative mentality. When the transition from poor performance to good performance comes with a change in supervisors, even more skepticism can be aroused. Accusations that the new supervisor is an "easy grader" or "nice guy trying to ingratiate himself with the troops" can surface quite quickly.

All these problems are compounded if you have a system that calls for distributing performance grades either by ranking or along a bell-shaped curve. While there is seldom a problem moving a person significantly down a rank list, moving a person even micrometers up a list can create all sorts of resistance from other managers who don't want their people to get bypassed.

Earlier chapters have covered in depth the inherent problems of competitive rating and ranking systems. For the purpose of this discussion, suffice to note that the use of labels and grades and rankings magnifies problems that exist for a Typecast. These systems make it very difficult to change the way someone's performance is formally perceived.

From a coaching perspective, when an individual has made a marked improvement in performance, it is very helpful to be able to reflect that in his formal performance discussion—both orally and on paper. Noting these improvements goes a long way toward validating change efforts made by the Typecast. It helps solidify, or lock in, the desired behavior.

Systems that artificially restrict the amount of progress that can be credited can discourage an employee and lead her to believe that no effort will be great enough to overcome the weight of history. In that case, why try? Since change is painful, why not just stay the way she was and at least avoid the discomfort?

Lighting Demitrie's Fire

Demitrie was a 30-year-old clerk in a large file room. Her main job was to file and retrieve maps and engineering drawings. Demitrie had done this job for eleven years without a single promotion. In fact, she had come close to being fired a year earlier for gross misconduct.

The critical incident for Demitrie involved stuffing more than a week's worth of filing arbitrarily into the bottom drawer of her desk the week before she left for vacation. She had apparently not been keeping up with her work and didn't want to stay late, so she crashed a load of it in her bottom drawer and forgot about it. She returned from vacation to face a week suspension. She was given a final warning. Her managers did not expect her to last out the year.

But she did. In fact, she did fine, especially after there was a change in her supervision. Demitrie liked her new boss, and he found a way to really get through to her that no one ever had. He challenged Demitrie and inspired her to work at a higher level. He started using a team process with the group and, to everyone's surprise, Demitrie emerged as the star. In a creative environment, she was a different person, a bright light of energy.

Over time, the supervisor began changing the role Demitrie played in the group. In fact, given all her experience in the file room and her newfound skills in working with people, she began serving as an informal coordinator for the rest of the eight file clerks.

While Demitrie was making rapid progress in her contribution within the department, her status in the organization had not really changed. In fact, when her supervisor went to the annual ranking session to assign competitive grades to all employees, he was totally and completely rebuffed. The only upward movement Demitrie experienced on the rank list was in relation to the others within the supervisor's own rank group. His peers blocked any other upward movement on the combined division and organization-wide rank lists.

They did not endorse his recommendation for promotion and openly questioned his judgment as a manager. "Your predecessor would have fired her if she had the courage. And now you think she should be promoted. You guys need to get your stories together," they chided.

Fortunately, Demitrie had low expectations. After eleven years, she didn't expect to ever be promoted, no matter how well she did. Nonetheless, she continued on her new course of working hard and doing well within her work group. In addition, Demitrie's peers nominated her to serve as departmental representative in a team training exercise that the organization sponsored. In that setting Demitrie had the opportunity to display her new skills and positive attitude to dozens of people outside her own work area.

The supervisor (coach) could not have been more surprised the next year when he came to the annual rank session. He had prepared several pages of documentation to justify raising the performance label for Demitrie and hoped again to appeal for promotion. He was prepared to fight a ferocious battle in the name of fairness and justice.

To his amazement, almost before he spoke the first words in Demitrie's defense, another manager spoke up and noted what a wonderful job Demitrie had done for him over the past year. Another added that she had been an excellent facilitator in team training. Finally, a third offered to move her into the "Very Effective" performance rating category, even if it meant displacing one of his own employees.

Soon after the ranking session, four of these managers came to Demitrie's promotion party to recognize her for the progress she had made. When downsizings and layoffs swept the company the following year and the staff of the file rooms was cut by over half, Demitrie received a promotion and was placed in charge of all file rooms for the company. Several managers literally competed to obtain her services.

Showcasing Talent

One of the key strategies for helping Typecasts overcome imperfect pasts is to help showcase their talent. Slowly but steadily the Areas for Improvement that helped create the negative images must be demonstrated as no longer an issue. Unknown or unrecognized Strengths can then be displayed until they get the widespread recognition they deserve.

The Catalytic Coaching process helps you do these things, but the reward systems (pay and promotion) must work in harmony. All these systems must work together guide to transform Typecast into a high performing, appropriately valued employee.

CONCLUSION: THE TRUE REWARDS OF GREAT COACHING

The true rewards of great coaching are both personal and professional. Few aspects of a supervisory position are as personally satisfying as helping someone once thought of as a poor performer redefine herself in a positive light. There is a great deal of satisfaction that comes from knowing you were a critical catalyst in an employee's successful effort to grow, develop and win.

Professionally, the rewards extend well beyond any public relations coup for getting someone who works for you higher marks. It stems from a knowledge of the true business implications of facilitating such a transformation.

A poor performer who feels slighted is a lawsuit waiting to happen. Even cleanly terminating a troubled employee involves cost and represents a trauma to the organization. Then there is the downtime and expense associated with recruiting and orientation/training for the replacement.

Some may view the act of converting a negative performer into a positive as the equivalent of making a diamond from a lump of coal, or wine out of water. But clearly, it is more than that. The coal and water had at least some positive value before their transformation. A negative performer is at best a drain and at worst a serious liability.

Helping someone resurrect their career and become a valued asset is an act of creation. In addition to all the good business reasons to help coach for a transformation in performance, it also makes you feel great as a human being to help someone else succeed.

Chapter 18

Walking the Talk:
Leaders as Role Models

While managers appraise their subordinates, subordinates also appraise their managers. The test they use is a simple one: Does my leader practice what he or she preaches?
—James M. Kouzes and Barry Z. Posner, *The Leadership Challenge*[1]

The third essential ingredient in making Catalytic Coaching work involves commitment to the process on the part of the organization's leaders. As depicted graphically in Figure IV-1, this activity may be even higher on the impact pyramid than building either competencies or infrastructure. The best way to demonstrate commitment is not for leaders to publicly sponsor the improvement of others. It is for them to openly utilize the methodology to improve themselves.

Teach, preach, and talk all you want, but people in organizations watch closely what their leaders do. When they hear one thing but see evidence of another, they usually trust their sight to be more accurate. The purpose of this chapter is to help you, as a leader, learn to be an effective recipient of Catalytic Coaching. We will discuss the importance of modeling desired behavior and five key characteristics of an effective coaching recipient. We will conclude the chapter with a final tale from the front. Throughout the chapter the theme is clear. By embracing this process as an enthusiastic recipient of Catalytic Coaching, not only will you learn and grow, you will influence others to follow suit.

MODELING DESIRED BEHAVIOR

We begin this inquiry with a very simple but powerful axiom. To get others to follow your advice, make sure you follow it yourself first. If you want your staff members to be open to feedback and work actively to improve, nothing is more influential than modeling those behaviors yourself. As Crane observes, "Successful coaches are their messages."[2] Asking others to change—take risks and adopt new behaviors that are uncomfortable to them—is easy. Showing them how it is done is hard.

We are not talking here about modeling specific behavior. In other words, showing a subordinate how to delegate effectively is wonderful. It is a fine form of mentoring. Unless "Delegating" is one of *your* Areas for Improvement, however, it is not a courageous act of leadership. The challenge here is to demonstrate willingness to face personal shortcomings and muster the courage to attempt to correct them. You must acknowledge your own limitations and show resolve in addressing those.

This does not mean you have to be perfect. Far from it. It means you have to be both a student and a teacher. When your students see you working hard to learn and change and grow, they will be more inclined to follow suit. Beyond the obvious benefits you derive from your own personal transformation, you will gain additional credibility and effectiveness as a Catalytic Coach.

CHARACTERISTICS OF AN EFFECTIVE COACHEE

To be an effective recipient of coaching one has to do several things:

- Find a coach (or coaches)
- Take ownership of the change process
- Think deeply and honestly
- Listen actively and objectively
- Be willing to experiment with new behavior

Find a Coach (or Coaches)

Almost everyone has a boss. Some have two or three. In this modern age, some even report to teams. With the possible exclusion of someone who owns a small business, most of us have somebody to look up to that would like to influence the way we behave. The President of the United States probably wishes he had a boss. It would be a lot easier to get feedback from one person than from over 266 million.

Some may react to this advice with frustration: "But I don't trust my boss. She is a lousy judge of character. She doesn't really know about the work that I do. She hasn't liked me from the start. She likes Carol and Charlie more than me. Etc."

Whether or not these statements are true, your boss (almost by definition) has more control over your immediate future in business than any other individual on the planet. It is normally a pretty good idea to know for certain where he or she is coming from.

If you find your boss's perspective intolerable and the relationship incurably toxic, you probably need to initiate a move. If you can't move within the company, then consider a move out. Waiting for someone you cannot trust or respect to leave or retire is a very costly prospect. It can impact your mental and spiritual well-being as well as your career.

Those who want to survive and prosper in most businesses generally find a way to make even the least effective boss tolerable as a coach. In those instances when you are not a great believer in your boss's perspective or skill, try to at least understand it. Give the boss every benefit of a doubt and supplement her guidance, if necessary, with that obtained from other sources. Often it is possible to receive stronger insight and growth ideas from mentors and others you can enlist as supplemental, informal coaches.

Whenever possible, use data gathered from supplementary sources to influence the boss's thinking on how to shape you. It does not always work, but if you make a decision to stay in a toxic relationship with a boss you do not trust as a coach, it may be the best path available. And in many cases, a poor people manager is quite happy to get help coming up with suggestions for how to deal with her charges. She may gladly embrace your suggestions and adopt them as her own.

Whether or not you have a boss who you consider a trustworthy source of coaching, you will almost always benefit by seeking supplemental input to help shape your development. No one says you must limit coaching input to the person who signs your check. The formal system may operate that way, but you are always free to supplement it.

Others besides your immediate boss can also provide excellent coaching input. Employees who work for you can help you learn to be a better supervisor, manager or executive. Peers and associates can give you advice on how to become a better team player. Senior staff members can coach you to become a better professional.

The challenge is to find people you trust who know something about both you and the areas that you need most to improve. Wherever possible, start with your boss and then supplement that input with input from others who are capable and willing to help.

Take Ownership of the Change Process

We have stated repeatedly that the ultimate purpose of Catalytic Coaching is to help people change behavior in a way that has a positive impact on the business. Catalytic Coaching is not about giving feedback. Nor is it about documenting company files. It is about helping the person being coached change her behavior and improve her impact on the business.

The only way to do that successfully is for the recipient of the change effort to take ownership of the process. Coaching is not *about* you, it is *for* you. If you don't actively engage in the process and take ownership of your own development, then everyone is really wasting their time.

From the perspective of an organization looking at an employee who elects not to be coached, what it sees is what it gets. With no concerted development effort, it's what it can expect to be getting for a long time to come. If that's acceptable, you get to stay. If not, the organization will start taking steps to ask you to leave whenever your performance drops below the threshold of pain.

If you're not interested in getting any better, why should someone else be interested in spending valuable time trying to coach you? If you work for a family business and your boss is a parent, she may have little choice. She probably won't fire you. Indifference on the part of most employees is a dangerous profile, however. The boss may elect to "cut bait" rather than continue to fish in a dry hole.

As a coach yourself, you know that what you want to see in a coachee is ownership and passion. You want to work with people who don't like deficiencies and aren't content to be less than their ideal best. Anyone trying to run and grow their business has a need for talent. Talent, almost by definition, is best displayed by people who are motivated to do their best.

Think Deeply and Honestly

For coaching to be more than superficial, the individual being coached must know what she wants to do or become. If work-related aspirations for an average performer are relegated to survival in the current job until retirement, the value of a coach is nominal. The importance of the coaching process escalates along with the aspirations of the incumbent. To determine these aspirations one must think deeply and honestly.

On the side of my grandmother's bed when she died was a thick, scripture-laden book entitled "Know Thyself." She liked to read western novels and spy thrillers, too, but that book was a constant in her life. Although I was only in my teens when she died, I always had this sense about my grandmother that she really knew who she was and what she was put on this earth to do. She seemed to have found her niche in life and from that flowed happiness and joy. I like to think that that book and the introspection it implied had somehow helped her become and stay that way.

My grandmother was a homemaker and survivor. Most people reading this book are not. Some of you may be working because you have to. Most, like me, would be empty without work. While few of us have options that allow us *not* to work, most of us do have options in terms of what type of work we must pursue. In large companies, for people with general background and eclectic aptitude, the choices can be staggering.

Even the most talented learn at an early age that while they may possibly be able to do anything, they most certainly can't do everything. Life forces us to make choices. A good coach can help you match your skills, capabilities and interests with opportunities available in a firm. It is helpful, however, if you can do some of the preliminary sorting yourself. Start by figuring out what you *don't* want to do.

Sometimes these choices get taken away over time. If you get used to earning a $100,00 a year, it is hard to cut back to $50,000. That makes it difficult to open a bait and tackle shop on a small lake if you are a Director of Manufacturing for a large firm, or leave an international sales position to work in a dance studio, or direct the ski patrol in Aspen when you are a Controller in Des Moines.

Life can make it difficult, seemingly impossible, to live your dreams. That's assuming you've even stopped long enough to have any. Don Marquis once said, "Ours is a world where people don't know what they want and are willing to go through hell to get it." Hard work without adequate analysis can be very unproductive.

Have you ever answered some of the really tough questions seriously? For example: "If you were independently wealthy, what would you do with your time? Would you still work? Would you still work here?" Or how about the same question from a different angle: "What would you do if you won the lottery?" A favorite remains, "What do you want to be when you grow up?"

A facilitator used the last question as an icebreaker once for a newly formed accounting team. Out of twelve people in the room, nine said that if money were no object they'd ideally like to teach school. These were bright, relatively young, hard-working CPAs making an average of $30,000 a year. The state was Louisiana, ranked dead last in terms of school performance. While it certainly seemed inappropriate to help these people figure out a way to pursue their dreams by leaving the company to teach school, something seemed wrong with this picture. Surely there must be some way to allow them to get in closer alignment with their dreams.

In the book *What Color Is Your Parachute?* Richard Bolles describes a two-step transformation process. It goes something like this. Joe is currently an auditor for a clothing manufacturer in Milwaukee, but his dream is to be in Public Relations for the Milwaukee Brewers. Joe has a tremendous love of baseball and an intimate knowledge of Brewers team history. Nonetheless, if the Brewers have an opening in Public Relations, Joe is not likely to get very far in the interview process. What should Joe do? The two-step transformation process suggests two options. Step One could go one of two ways.

Option A, Joe could seek a transfer in his current company to the Public Relations Department. Since they already know Joe and his capabilities as an international auditor, they may be willing to give him a chance in a new field. Here he would have to sell his tremendous desire and aptitude for the field of public relations.

Option B would be to seek employment with the Brewers as an accountant or auditor. His love of the game and knowledge of team history might serve to differentiate him from others applying for such a job.

Step Two would come two years later as he tried to make the transition into PR for the Brewer organization. If he is already with the Brewers but in Accounting, he might be able to demonstrate his aptitude for PR by volunteering to help coordinate special events or serve on a PR-related team. If he is with his former company in the PR function, he can now apply for a job with the Brewers having had the requisite background. Now his intimate knowledge of baseball and the team can be used to his advantage.

Bottom line, a coach can be more effective in helping someone who has done some thinking about who he is and to what he aspires. While a good coach can assist in this process of discovery, however, it helps to have a subject for coaching who has done his homework.

Listen Actively and Objectively

Coaching is a partnership that involves a great deal of communication. Despite the admonition to "know thyself," it is also critical to be open to new data. With any luck your coach will provide you with things you did not already know and a perspective that you may have missed. To obtain these critical insights, a good subject of coaching will try very hard to control defensive thoughts and actions.

You must be willing to work hard to understand the message that the coach is trying to send. This involves silencing that inner voice that likes to argue. It means leaning forward in the chair and asking clarifying questions. It means making sure that you understand the message that is being given. It means understanding and accepting the examples the way the coach is trying to use them.

The ideal coaching subject does not roll over and play dead when given what appears to be incorrect information. Neither does she argue and fight. She searches for the key point being made by the coach. She examines the examples being given as evidence of an Area for Improvement. She tries to understand the perspective of the person providing the feedback.

A Director of Technology named Rodney was given an AFI that he felt was completely incorrect—180 degrees out of phase. In fact, by the time his boss sat down with him on the information she had written a month earlier on the Catalytic Coaching Worksheet she knew she had blown the call.

The Area for Improvement was not extremely negative. It was just not applicable to Rodney and it made no sense for him to use the AFI as a benchmark to improve. After talking about it for a while, his boss agreed. Together they came up with an AFI that was a much tougher challenge for Rodney than the one originally assigned. As it turned out, it would have been a lot easier for Rodney to work on the one his boss gave him originally . . . but then he would not have experienced as much real growth. Only the paper version of the progress report would have looked nicer.

Be Willing to Experiment with New Behavior

As we have said before, the Catalytic Coaching process is only complete when it results in positive behavioral change that impacts the business. Coaching activities that result in lots of nicely documented files and engaging conversation are of no real value without positive behavioral change.

Insanity, as popularly defined, is expecting change while doing nothing different. A good subject of coaching, therefore, must enter the process of self-improvement anticipating the need to make some modifications in behavior.

Despite the fact that most of us are comfortable with our current activities (or we would already have changed them), a good subject of coaching is willing to experiment with new behavior. She knows this is the only logical path to self-improvement and is willing to sacrifice temporary discomfort in order to see what positive gains might come from it.

Ralph Waldo Emerson said: "Do not be too timid and squeamish about your actions. All life is an experiment." You must look for opportunities to try new behaviors if you want to get different results.

A teenage girl quit the neighborhood swim team recently because the swimming coach had asked the novice swimmers to stand on the side of the pool and make what the teenager considered silly swimming gestures in the air on dry land. "That looks stupid," she reported to her parents that night after refusing to do the exercise. She wanted to be on the team and compete in matches, but did not like some of the things they asked her to do at practice. She did not see the connection between the exercises and learning to swim competitively. So she quit. Two months later, some of those kids who put up with the silly on-land exercises were winning swim tournaments. The self-conscious teenager probably never will.

In contrast, some coaching subjects are willing to try almost anything that a coach asks them to do. Even if it is awkward or the purpose is unclear to them, they try something new at the earliest suggestion. Sometimes the experiments work, sometimes they don't. The best coachees sometimes fail over and over again and still come back for more. They care so deeply about the issue they are trying to change that it is worth several failed experiments to ultimately get it right.

There is a popular expression about change that is repeated over and over again in the general population. "You can't teach an old dog new tricks" is the theme. This is baloney. The dog just has to be willing to try. She has to allow herself to make lots of mistakes and look silly. But if she tries long enough and wants it bad enough, smart money is on the old dog.

Adults often marvel at the progress of a young child who has recently taken up playing a musical instrument. "Oh, honey, I wish that I had learned to play the piano when I was your age,'' says the 60-year-old woman. ''Why don't you learn now, grandma? You could take lessons with me,'' says the child. ''Oh no, sweetheart. Grandma is too old for that. Children your age learn much more quickly.''

This viewpoint should be challenged. There is a basic problem with the logic. To illustrate, imagine putting Grandma and her grandson in head to head competition. Give them the same beginner piano class. Have them work on the same material and practice the same number of minutes a day. You'd be best off to bet on Grandma. The problem is our expectations. Grandma would not be filled with near as much pride hearing herself play a flawless rendition of ''Three Blind Mice.'' Yet, she was delighted when her grandson played the tune. Grandma somehow thinks that because she's older, she should be able to play Chopin in the first month or two. Her grandson will get to Chopin in three years. Grandma will still not have started.

The same principle applies to people at work. Computers in the office are everywhere, but not everyone has figured out how to use them. In fact, many of the most senior members of the workforce (at the top of the organization) are the least capable of taking advantage of their many benefits. They hire new ''kids'' every day who have grown up with computers and can really make them sing.

Executives are too embarrassed to take beginning computer classes. They somehow think because they are so highly ranked that they must be able to perform sophisticated functions right away. Because they can't, they write off computer work as just something they're not good at. In so doing, they reduce their effectiveness and cut themselves out of the mainstream.

What's missing? Permission to experiment. Time to absorb the basics. Willingness to confirm to others that you need their help to get better. Willingness to admit you're not the best at everything.

Consequences? Three to five years later the technology gap looks more like a chasm. Better start pondering early retirement.

The willingness to experiment with new behavior is a tremendous asset to an individual in this rapidly changing world. It is an absolutely essential characteristic of the ideal coaching candidate. If you want to show others how to be one, you've got to be willing to experiment a bit yourself.

The Volunteer

Our final tale from the front is about someone who personifies the best in coachability. Few could better exemplify the spirit of self-improvement displayed by the man it depicts.

Todd was an Organization Development consultant who had been working with the leadership team of a small manufacturing operation for several weeks. His task was to work with the leadership team to implement a new team-based management system. While they had only held one initial orientation session with a small group of supervisors, the word was spreading fast that change was coming. The goal of the program was to establish a new way of working together that stressed empowerment and teams. The old "command and control" management style would soon be on its way out.

One evening after a meeting with the leadership team Todd received a surprise visit from John, the plant's Operations Superintendent. John was a long-serviced employee who had worked his way up through the ranks to a position of great prominence. He was well known to Todd by reputation, but Todd had never met him personally. In fact, stories of John's tyrannical leadership style were legend at the plant and had been discussed in management meetings as the type of behavior they were trying to eliminate with change in culture. John was a brilliant but intense man who scared people just by being in the same room.

John introduced himself as he walked into Todd's temporary office and closed the door. "I know we've never met, but you've probably heard of me," he said with a knowing smile as he stood above Todd's chair. "I've heard about some of the things you've been teaching my bosses and I have just one question for you." John paused as Todd took a deep breath, still stunned at the sudden meeting. "Do you think I could learn to do things this new way?"

To say Todd was shocked was an understatement. After quickly collecting himself, he responded with some questions of his own, "Why do you want to know, John? Why is it important to you?"

"For two reasons," said John. "One, cause I figure that guys who get things done the way I get them done are gonna be on the endangered species list in a few months and I'm not ready to retire. Two, because I don't want to be remembered forever as a mean S.O.B."

"John, I don't know if you can change," Todd said after a brief pause to absorb his statement, "but I'm very encouraged that you've asked the question." He continued, "Changing habits for a guy like you who's been operating like you have for so many years will be very challenging. But if you are willing to give it 100% effort, I'd be willing to try to teach you a different way to manage."

"I'd be much obliged," said John as he put back on his hard hat and left the room.

What happened next was the start of a very intensive Catalytic Coaching exercise. It included some very frank and hard-hitting upward feedback sessions with all of John's direct reports and a few of his peers. Todd facilitated a series of meetings in which the group told John how difficult he was to work for and how much pain he had caused both them and their families. They also told him he was technically brilliant and would be first person they would look to for leadership in a crisis.

John apologized for his past behavior and explained that he was doing what he was taught to do by others before him. He told his team that he wanted to change and asked for their help. He committed to making four major improvements and shared with them his Personal Development Plan.

Over a nine-month period John made more fundamental changes in his management style than anyone Todd had ever worked with before or since. He went to classes and read books. In fact, he used his famous "intensity' " in this search for a better way to operate. In follow-up meetings with his feedback group, they noted the tremendous progress he was making and thanked him for making their lives better.

It would be nice to report that the story had a perfect ending with John being nominated for "Boss of the Year" or some other high accolade. Unfortunately, it was not to be. Despite the dramatic improvements John had made over the course of a nine-month period, during a reorganization the company saw fit to relieve him of his supervisory duties. They moved him to a parallel post where he oversaw technical aspects of the operation, but did not have responsibility for the people. He simply had done too much damage in the past 27 years to overcome his reputation in nine months.

Because of his tremendous attitude and the demonstrated growth in people skills, John was not asked to retire. Todd had no doubt that had John stayed on his previous path, he would have been forced out of the organization. Instead, because of his courageous willingness to engage in the coaching process and accept change, John earned the right to continue his work and retire in his own time. John and the organization were both winners in the end.

FINAL WORD ON DEMONSTRATING COMMITMENT

Walking the talk is good exercise. Those with the courage and strength to lead by example will benefit in many ways. They will grow and prosper themselves. They may even live up to their ultimate potential. This would be a lofty achievement for anyone. More importantly, however, leaders who effectively demonstrate personal commitment to the coaching process encourage others to do the same. By so doing they can produce dividends that extend far beyond the scope of their individual achievements. They put to use the power of the modern organization at its best.

Chapter 19

Conclusion

No man ever undertakes an art or a science merely to acquire knowledge of it. In all human affairs there is always an end in view—of pleasure, or honor, or advantage.

—Polybius, *Histories*, III (ca. 125 B.C.)

This book was written to help people and the organizations that employ them. It proposes a paradigm shift in the manner in which supervisors formally interact with employees on the subject of job performance. It fills the void left by Dr. Deming's bold assertion that doing nothing is better than doing something that does harm.

Few of us in industry felt comfortable with complete abandonment of formal performance reviews, and very few stopped doing them. Our previous systems may have, as Dr. Deming contends, done more harm than good, but we felt lost without them. Despite the fact they were unpopular and many questioned their value, we knew they were designed with the best of intentions. Very few large companies tossed their systems entirely.

Instead, we tried to repair them, to patch them up and make them work. We tweaked them by modifying basic components and procedures. Or we supplemented them by adding entirely new features. And a few brave souls even dared substitute the traditional system with something else entirely.

Because we have lacked a true understanding of the paradigm we were attempting to improve, the results of our change initiatives seldom resulted in real improvements. They made our systems different but seldom truly better. Three years after any given change initiative the same problems resurfaced and we began looking for ways to change the system again. Those who suffered through these changes could only roll their eyes in mock disbelief. Customers of our performance management processes could be assured of only two things. The new system would not solve their problems. More changes would inevitably follow.

By looking at performance management from a systems perspective, clearly defining our desired outcomes in terms of business objectives and prioritizing a short list of key customers, we were able to see the roots of our dilemma. We were able to clearly identify the prevailing paradigm and understand why it cannot be salvaged. We were able to recognize the components of the system that must be eliminated if a replacement system is to have a chance at being more effective and efficient.

With this insight we were able to start again and construct a new performance management system, one that was vastly simpler and far more effective in generating meaningful behavioral change. That systemic, integrated approach we labeled "Catalytic Coaching."

Catalytic Coaching is systemic because it introduces a new process along with accompanying infrastructure. It calls for creation of new competencies and requires a demonstration of commitment from organizational leaders.

The Catalytic Coaching methodology explained in this book reduces the burden and bureaucracy inherent in most traditional performance management systems. It does so by minimizing the number and length of forms that need to be completed and the time it takes to complete them. It abandons the chaff in order to give the grain total attention.

Catalytic Coaching completely changes the perspective on supervisor–direct report discussions. No longer are forms completed *by* the supervisor *to* the employee *for* the file with a focus on *compliance*. Instead, they are completed *by* the supervisor *to* the employee *for* the employee with a focus on *development*.

Responsibility for employee development in traditional systems is shared by Human Resources and senior management. Catalytic Coaching places responsibility for development on the person being developed. It challenges individuals to identify growth aspirations and discuss these openly with supervisors and management teams. It helps them not only achieve better performance in their current jobs but make progress toward the type of jobs they ultimately aspire to obtain.

Changing the role of the employee also changes the role of the manager. She becomes coach. Instead of criticizing, critiquing and grading, she is charged with giving honest feedback about performance in the current job in context with the individual's own growth objectives. The higher the objectives and aspirations, the more direct and challenging the feedback. She must learn to say *to* the employee what she used to say *about* the employee to her bosses and peers.

Because Catalytic Coaching is geared toward helping people grow and not justifying salary treatment, the level of honesty can escalate. Good performers are helped because they can be given more honest feedback. It is possible to

tell someone she must resolve fundamental performance issues to become competitive for advancement while simultaneously giving her a salary increase well
above average. Salary treatment is understood to be market driven and annual
increases are not expected to have more than an indirect correlation with annual
performance.

Poor performers are told frankly and directly what they must do to improve.
They are given praise for contributions they make that are positive but clearly
instructed on any specific issue that places their job at risk. They are given an
opportunity to speak with a third party and both coach and employee are assisted
by a Coach[2] until the performance issue is either resolved or the employee has
been removed from the position. Because of the focus, clarity and demonstrable
fairness of this process, legal exposure is minimized.

The paradigm shift from evaluation to coaching produces dramatically different responses on the part of the process customers. In contrast to the dread
people feel when anticipating traditional performance evaluations, both employees and supervisors often look forward to participating in the Catalytic Coaching
process. Conducted properly, these sessions often feature the most meaningful
exchange of ideas and energy that a boss and employee will share all year. As
a consequence, Catalytic Coaching can re-ignite the human spirit that traditional
evaluation systems had all but extinguished.

This is not to claim that everyone eagerly awaits her annual Catalytic Coaching session in organizations that have adopted this format. On the other hand,
very few dread the exercise and many coaches as well as coachees find the
experience truly energizing.

Conducted properly, feedback and counsel presented in the Catalytic Coaching process is a gift. A gift that is tailored to an employee's specific needs and
aspirations and not some arbitrary set of standards. A gift that is truly honest
and straightforward about real issues and concerns. A gift crafted carefully for
that person in a way that conveys deep understanding and empathy. A gift that
thanks the employee for what she has done and inspires her to work harder to
achieve even more.

Using the Catalytic Coaching process, it is not uncommon to leave a coaching
session on such an emotional high that you have a hard time sleeping twelve
hours later. Knowing that you have helped someone clearly understand for the
first time what she must do to end career stagnation is a powerful experience.
Especially when she looks back at you with tears in her eyes and says, "I can
do that. I'm *going* to do that. I'm going to *show* you that I can perform in that
way." It sends a chill up your spine.

Despite the many words, tables and formulas set forth in this book to try to
demonstrate business impact of a performance management system that works,
it is hard to definitively calculate the value of the interaction described immediately above. It is likely impossible for social scientists to isolate enough variables to empirically demonstrate the ultimate contribution of good coaching on

performance. As Dr. Deming was fond of repeating, "The greatest gains and losses are often unknown and unknowable."[1]

Suffice to say that having an employee thank you sincerely and repeatedly for conducting an annual performance discussion is a unique experience for most managers. For the majority, it has probably never happened. Using the methods outlined in this book, it is possible to learn to inspire each one of your direct reports to feel this kind of appreciation. More importantly, by substituting Catalytic Coaching for a traditional performance evaluation system, an organization can relieve all its supervisors, managers and employees of a tremendous burden and give them an opportunity to experience some of the same joy.

Appendix A

Catalytic Coaching
Employee Input Sheet

CATALYTIC COACHING EMPLOYEE INPUT SHEET

Employee: _____   Job Title: _____

Department/Division: _____   Time in Position: _____

Date: _____   Time w/ Supervisor: _____

1. WHAT I'VE DONE FOR YOU LATELY.

ACCOMPLISHMENTS

-
-
-
-

DISAPPOINTMENTS

-
-
-

2. WHAT I'VE DONE FOR <u>ME</u> LATELY.

PERSONAL GROWTH

- NEW SKILLS (COMPETENCIES) I'VE ACQUIRED:

- IMPORTANT EXPERIENCE I'VE GAINED:

- RELATIONSHIPS I'VE BUILT THAT AID MY PRODUCTIVE CAPABILITY:

3. WHAT I'D LIKE TO BE WHEN I GROW UP.

CAREER ASPIRATIONS

- NEXT YEAR OR TWO:

- FIVE YEARS:

- TOP JOB I ASPIRE TO:

4. OTHER IMPORTANT THINGS I'D LIKE YOU TO KNOW AS MY COACH.

OTHER BACKGROUND DATA

- MOBILITY ISSUES:

- PAY OR BENEFITS ISSUES:

- QUESTIONS/CONCERNS:

Employee: _____ Date Submitted: _____

Coach: _____ Date of Discussion: _____

Appendix B

Catalytic Coaching Worksheet

CATALYTIC COACHING WORKSHEET

Employee: _____   Job Title: _____

Department/Division: _____   Time in Position: _____

Date: _____   Time w/ Supervisor: _____

STRENGTHS

-
-
-
-

AREAS FOR IMPROVEMENT

Performance Impacting	Potential Enhancing	Job Threatening	
			•
			•
			•
			•

DEVELOPMENT RECOMMENDATIONS

-
-
-

Immediate Supervisor: _____   Human Resources: _____

Reviewing Supervisor/s: _____   Employee: _____

274

DEFINITION OF TERMS

STRENGTHS

Characteristics or attributes regarded as noteworthy in a positive manner. Strengths should be clearly tailored and specific to each individual.

AREAS FOR IMPROVEMENT (AFI)

Characteristics or attributes regarded as places to concentrate improvement efforts to achieve optimum benefit to the individual and Company. AFIs do not necessarily imply deficiency. In keeping with our theme of continuous improvement, everyone has numerous areas in which to get better. Selecting 3 to 5 AFIs per individual per counseling period helps focus attention on areas the supervisor perceives to be of highest priority. Each AFI should be classified in one of the following ways, based on the primary message that management is trying to convey. If an AFI is considered to have two equally weighted messages, two boxes can be checked.

- Performance Impacting
  This AFI describes performance that, if improved measurably, may result in an increased contribution in the current assignment. It does not necessarily imply deficiency. At minimum, however, it represents an opportunity to enhance an employee's personal impact or organizational productivity. Importance for improvement in this area may range from helpful to important.

- Potential Enhancing
  This AFI describes performance that, if improved measurably, may result in increasing an employee's potential for advancement to higher levels within the corporation. Improvement in this area does not necessitate promotion so much as enhance the likelihood of being competitive for one, should the opportunity exist.

- Job Threatening
  This AFI describes performance below an acceptable level. If an employee does not improve this aspect of his/her work significantly for a sustained period of time, it may result in his/her removal from the current job assignment through transfer, demotion or termination of employment. Importance for improving this area requires immediate attention.

DEVELOPMENT RECOMMENDATIONS

The supervisor and Human Resources are prepared to help the employee improve in the areas noted above. This can include providing training or classroom instruction, mentoring or coaching, or exposure to different work experiences. It can also include regularly scheduled follow-up coaching, counseling and feedback sessions.

Appendix C

Sample Catalytic Coaching
Worksheets

CATALYTIC COACHING WORKSHEET

Employee: *High Potential Employee*   **Job Title:** *Field HR Coordinator*

Dept / Div: *Employee Relations / HR*   **Time in Position:** *2 years*

STRENGTHS

- *Judgment: Recommendations Made with a Keen Eye for What Is Appropriate and Inappropriate in any Given Situation.*

- *Interpersonal Skills: Ability to Interact with Management and Employees of All Levels in a Pleasant and Persuasive Manner.*

- *Mastery of Technical Detail: Deep Understanding of Processes, Policies and Procedures.*

- *Quantity/Quality of Work Produced: Large Volume of High Caliber Work Produced.*

AREAS FOR IMPROVEMENT

PI   • *Sr. Management Advice & Counsel: Aggressively Pursue Ideas to Help Refinery Management Improve Their Ability to Work With and Through People.*

PI/PE • *Develop Support Staff: Train Local Contact to Perform Essential Functions of Field HR Liaison. Delegate as Much as Possible. Help Establish Realistic Maximum Capacity.*

PE   • *Employee / Management Development: Continue to Develop Skills in Interacting with Management and Employees to Improve Performance and Develop Key Personnel.*

PE   • *Speaking & Training Skills: Continue to Hone Skills as Designer and Provider of Training Services. Increase Poise & Confidence Speaking in Front of Groups and Working on Teams.*

DEVELOPMENT RECOMMENDATIONS

- *Participation in Plant TQM Initiatives.*

- *Consider Working w/ Dale Carnegie as a Graduate Assistant.*

- *Participation in Hillsdale College Leadership Seminar.*

- *Continued Coaching, Counseling and Mentoring by Supervisor.*

CATALYTIC COACHING WORKSHEET

Employee: *Employee w/ Attendance Problem*   **Job Title:** *Computing Analyst*

Department/Division: *Info Systems Help Desk*   **Time in Position:** *8 Months*

STRENGTHS

- *Tenacious—Staying with the problem through complete resolution.*

- *Resourceful and creative regarding training responsibilities.*

- *Willingness to take on new projects/assignments.*

- *Positive impact on field organizations as contributing team member.*

AREAS FOR IMPROVEMENT

Potential Enhancing	Performance Impacting	Job Threatening	
		X	• *Reduce time away from work* *(shown progress in this area since discussion on 12/30/97)*
	X		• *Listen and respond non-defensively*
	X		• *Increase technical knowledge in MS-Office applications*
	X		• *Increase number of help desk tickets resolved*
	X		• *Improve management of multiple priorities*

DEVELOPMENT RECOMMENDATIONS

- *Bi-weekly review with supervisor of progress (incl. coaching on priority mgmt.)*

- *Employee Assistance Program*

- *Dale Carnegie course in interpersonal relations*

- *Customer service communication training*

CATALYTIC COACHING WORKSHEET

Employee: *Strong Performance Message*   **Job Title:** *Sr. Admin. Partner*

Dept / Div: *Marketing*   **Time in Position:** *3 Years*

STRENGTHS

- *Outgoing Personality*
- *Communication Skills*
- *Self-Confidence & Poise*
- *Willingness/Eagerness to Take on Difficult Challenges*

AREAS FOR IMPROVEMENT

- *Follow Through on Assignments: Need to pursue projects without prompting and constant reminders. Several incidents of assigned work falling through the cracks or being delayed indefinitely. Need to make sure someone else picks up responsibilities when you must be gone and follow through on assigned duties when you return to work. [Performance Impacting]*

- *Attendance and Punctuality: Need to be in the office more. Several medical and family emergency situations in 1994 and 1995 led to extensive excused absences. Need to minimize unplanned absences so that those you support can rely on your services more dependably. [PI]*

- *Personal Time Management: Need to prevent delegated tasks from falling into "black holes." Assigned work is not getting done. Reduce time spent on phone discussing personal issues and talking with employees about non-work issues. [PI]*

- *Support for Managers: Aggressively look for ways to reduce bureaucratic responsibilities of Managers. Seek ways to organize and systematize paper flow, scheduling issues, etc. [PI]*

DEVELOPMENT RECOMMENDATIONS

- Planning participation in ????

- Meet weekly to discuss progress; prepare new CCW in 6 months if improvements are made.

- Provide access to Steven Covey's tape series on time management: "First Things First."

280

CATALYTIC COACHING WORKSHEET

Employee: *Job Threatening Message* **Job Title:** *Buyer*
Dept/Div: *Purchasing* **Time in Position:** *3 ½ Years*

STRENGTHS

• *Knowledge of tubulars and related services.*

• *Familiarity with suppliers.*

• *Knowledge of Company drilling operations.*

• *Tenacity in pursuing adjustments from suppliers.*

AREAS FOR IMPROVEMENT

Performance Impacting
• **_Following Instructions:_** *Significantly improve responsiveness to projects delegated by supervisor or manager and accept priorities they establish. Follow through on direct orders from supervisor and manager to perform tasks.*

Performance Impacting
• **_Willingness to Accept Change:_** *Accept adjustments in work duties and responsibilities in a courteous and professional manner without arguing or complaining. Participate constructively in team-based efforts to improve departmental effectiveness.*

Job Threatening
• **_Keeping Management Informed of Your Whereabouts_**: *Make sure that you inform Department Secretary when leaving the 27th floor. On several occasions in the past, failure to notify us of your whereabouts has greatly inconvenienced fellow workers and run the risk of costing the Company money.*

Performance Impacting / Potential Enhancing
• **_Financial Analysis:_** *Increase capability to analyze and present financial data in order to make recommendations for decision making.*

DEVELOPMENT RECOMMENDATIONS

• *Weekly meetings with supervisor to review status of work load.*

• *Provide training opportunity in spreadsheet analysis and presentation.*

• *Supervisor will provide coaching on financial analysis.*

CATALYTIC COACHING WORKSHEET

Employee: *New to Position*   **Job Title:** *Field HR Coordinator*

Dept/Div: *Human Resources*   **Time in Position:** *6 Months*

STRENGTHS

- *Superior Work Ethic*

- *Quantity of Work Produced*

- *Follow Through on Assigned Tasks*

- *Organization Skills*

AREAS FOR IMPROVEMENT

Performance Impacting:
- *Performance Improvement Coaching & Counseling:* *Continue to build skills in assisting management in the process of promoting positive behavioral change. Increase knowledge of available schools, books, tapes, etc. that serve as benchmarks in the training & development process (Covey, Carnegie, Deming, Scholtes, etc.).*

- *Identifying ER Issues and Recommending Strategies:* *Proactively pursue ways to help improve employee morale, teamwork and organizational effectiveness.*

- *Team Facilitation:* *Increase knowledge and comfort level operating in a team environment using established techniques.*

Potential Enhancing:
- *Knowledge of Compensation:* *Need to increase familiarity with the job classification, salary system, bonus system, and stock option plans. Also need to understand these practices from a theoretical or industry-wide perspective.*

DEVELOPMENT RECOMMENDATIONS

• *Continued Coaching, Counseling and Mentoring by Supervisor and HQ HR staff.*

• *Dale Carnegie Course in Effective Speaking & Human Relations.*

• *Authorize funding of local audiotape library ($200/year).*

Appendix D

Personal Development Plan

CATALYTIC COACHING
PERSONAL DEVELOPMENT PLAN

Name: _____   Job Title: _____

Department/Division: _____   Time in Position: _____

Date: _____   Time w/ Supervisor: _____

IMPROVEMENT GOALS   This section sets forth an action plan for my personal development and itemizes steps I am going to take to address no more than three Areas for Improvement from my Catalytic Coaching Worksheet or from the development needs highlighted by the 360° Feedback Process.

Goal 1 _____

•

•

Goal 2 _____

•

•

Goal 3 _____

•

•

STRENGTHS   This section is an attempt to help me capitalize on my strengths and contains a goal based on one of my strengths as listed in my Catalytic Coaching Worksheet and/or my 360° Feedback Process.

Goal 1 _____

•

•

Employee: _____   Date Submitted: _____

Coach: _____   Date Approved: _____

Appendix E

Sample Personal Development Plan

CATALYTIC COACHING
PERSONAL DEVELOPMENT PLAN

Name: **Sally Service**   Job Title: **Restaurant Manager**

Department/Division: **Store #123**   Time in Position: **4 Years**

Date: **1/13/1999**   Time w/ Supervisor: **2 Years**

IMPROVEMENT GOALS	This section sets forth an action plan for my personal development and itemizes steps I am going to take to address no more than three Areas for Improvement from my Catalytic Coaching Worksheet or from the development needs highlighted by the 360° Feedback Process.

Goal 1   Reduce Turnover of Key Staff

- *Work with HR to identify and meet salary and benefit needs of top performers.*

- *Attend Dale Carnegie Course on Effective Management & integrate motivational techniques.*

- *Clarify needs and wants of each supervisor and complete coaching process to assist each in developing a personal development plan aimed at helping them achieve their career objectives.*

Goal 2   Produce More Bench Strength

- *Spend 30 minutes a week personally training and mentoring each shift supervisor.*

- *Conduct quarterly half-day training sessions for all non-supervisory staff.*

Goal 3   Improve Familiarity with Key Customer Base

- *Personally greet each customer group at some point during their meal. Distribute three free hors d'oeuvre cards each evening to our most frequent repeat customers.*

- *Compile list of top 50 customers and learn to greet them by name. Take digital picture of each couple while dining and provide them a copy before they leave the restaurant. Use other copy to memorize names.*

STRENGTHS	This section is an attempt to help me capitalize on my strengths and contains a goal based on one of my strengths as listed in my Catalytic Coaching Worksheet and/or my 360° Feedback Process.

Goal 4   Estimating Optimum Inventory

- *Conduct seminar for peer Restaurant Manager group on my system of Inventory Management.*

- *Document algorithm used to stock special food items for featured items and advertised specials.*

Appendix F

Sample Stewardship
Documentation

First Quarter Update (4/15/99)

CATALYTIC COACHING
PERSONAL DEVELOPMENT PLAN

Name: **_Sally Service_**   Job Title: **_Restaurant Manager_**

Department/Division: **_Store #123_**   Time in Position: **_4 Years_**

Date: **_1/13/1999_**   Time w/ Supervisor: **_2 Years_**

IMPROVEMENT GOALS	This section sets forth an action plan for my personal development and itemizes steps I am going to take to address no more than three Areas for Improvement from my Catalytic Coaching Worksheet or from the development needs highlighted by the 360° Feedback Process.

Goal 1   **Reduce Turnover of Key Staff**

- ~~Work with HR to identify and meet salary and benefit needs of top performers~~.   *Completed 2/1/99*

- Attend Dale Carnegie Course on Effective Management & integrate motivational techniques. *Scheduled for 5/3/98*

- *Clarify needs and wants of each supervisor and complete coaching process to assist each in developing a personal development plan aimed at helping them achieve their career objectives .*   *In progress. ETA 5/2/99*

Goal 2   **Produce More Bench Strength**

- Spend 30 minutes a week personally training and mentoring each shift supervisor. *4 Sessions to Date. Meeting Bi-weekly.*

- Conduct quarterly half-day training sessions for all non-supervisory staff. *Postponed to second quarter.*

Goal 3   **Improve Familiarity with Key Customer Base**

- Personally greet each customer group at some point during their meal. Distribute three free hors d'oeuvre cards each evening to our most frequent repeat customers. *In progress.   Working great!*

- Compile list of top 50 customers and learn to greet them by name. Take digital picture of each couple while dining and provide them a copy before they leave the restaurant. Use other copy to memorize names. *Got camera.   33 Pictures to date.*

STRENGTHS	This section is an attempt to help me I appraise the my strengths and accumulate a good head on some of my strengths as listed in my Catalytic Coaching Worksheet and/or my 360° Feedback Process.

Goal 4   **Estimating Optimum Inventory**

- ~~Conduct seminar for peer Restaurant Manager group on my system of Inventory Management.~~   *Completed 2/25/99*

- ~~Document algorithm used to stock special food items for featured items and advertised specials.~~ *Completed 1/15/99*

Appendix G

Performance Management System Cost Metrics Calculation Tool

PERFORMANCE MANAGEMENT SYSTEM COST METRICS*

To determine the approximate operating cost of a Performance Management System, provide your best estimate of the following seven variables. Then use these data to complete the equations listed below.

A. _____ # Hours/Year Spent on Performance Management by the Average *Employee*
   _____ Form Completion & Preparation for Formal Discussion
   _____ Discussion with Supervisor/Manager
   _____ Stewardship and Follow-Up

B. _____ # Hours/Employee/Year Spent on PM by the Average *Supervisor/Manager*
   _____ Form Completion and Preparation for Formal Discussion
   _____ Review & Approval Process with Senior Management
   _____ Discussion with Employee
   _____ Stewardship and Follow-Up

C. _____ # Hours/Employee Spent on PM by *Senior Management*
   _____ Review Time Per Employee
   _____ Average Number Senior Managers Involved

D. _____ # Hours/Year Spent on PM by the *Administrative Staff*
   _____ Preparation/Communication/Oversight
   _____ Discussion Assistance
   _____ Stewardship and Follow-Up

E. _____ # Employees Who Receive Annual Reviews

F. $_____ Average Hourly Salary Burden for All Employees Subject to the PM System
   (Please note: In most cases this will include supervisors and managers.)

G. $_____ Average Hourly Salary Burden for Supervisors/Managers

H. $_____ Average Hourly Salary Burden for Senior Management

I. $_____ Average Hourly Salary Burden for Administrative Staff

METRICS:

$((A + B + C + D) \times E)$ = Total Annual Hours Invested Per Year
((___ + ___ + ___ + ___) x ___) = _____

$((A \times F) + (B \times G) + (C \times H) + (D \times I)) \times E$ = Total Annual Monetary Investment
((___ x $___) + (___ x $___) + (___ x $___) + (___ x $___) x ___) = $_____

Appendix H

Sample Performance Management System Cost Metrics Calculation

EXAMPLE: XYZ CORPORATION

PERFORMANCE MANAGEMENT SYSTEM COST METRICS*

To determine the approximate operating cost of a Performance Management System, provide your best estimate of the following seven variables. Then use these data to complete the equations listed below.

A. __7__ # Hours/Year Spent on Performance Management by the Average _Employee_
   - __3.5__ Form Completion & Preparation for Formal Discussion
   - __1.5__ Discussion with Supervisor/Manager
   - __2.0__ Stewardship and Follow-Up

B. __7__ # Hours/Employee/Year Spent on PM by the Average _Supervisor/Manager_
   - __3.0__ Form Completion and Preparation for Formal Discussion
   - __0.5__ Review & Approval Process with Senior Management
   - __1.5__ Discussion with Employee
   - __2.0__ Stewardship and Follow-Up

C. __4__ # Hours/Employee Spent on PM by _Senior Management_
   - __0.5__ Review Time Per Employee
   - __8.0__ Average Number Senior Managers Involved

D. __1__ # Hours/Employee Spent on PM by the _Administrative Staff_
   - __0.50__ Preparation/Communication/Oversight
   - __0.25__ Discussion Assistance
   - __0.25__ Stewardship and Follow-Up

E. __1,000__ # Employees Who Receive Annual Reviews

F. __$30__ Average Hourly Salary Burden for All Employees Subject to the PM
   (Please note: In most cases this will include supervisors and managers.)

G. __$40__ Average Hourly Salary Burden for Supervisors/Managers

H. __$50__ Average Hourly Salary Burden for Senior Management

I. __$20__ Average Hourly Salary Burden for Administrative Staff

EXAMPLE: XYZ CORPORATION

PERFORMANCE MANAGEMENT SYSTEM COST METRICS*

METRICS:

$(A + B + C + D) \times E$ = Total Annual Hours Invested Per Year
$(7 + 7 + 4 + 1) \times 1000 = 19,000$

$((A \times F) + (B \times G) + (C \times H) + (D \times I)) \times E$ = Total Annual Monetary Investment
$((7 \times \$30) + (7 \times \$40) + (4 \times \$50) + (1 \times \$20)) \times 1,000 = \$710,000$

Appendix I

Performance Management System Assessment Tool

	Customer					
	1. _____ _____	2. _____ _____	3. _____ _____	4. _____ _____	Total	
Outcome	Weighting: __	Weighting: __	Weighting: __	Weighting: __	#	%
A. _____ _____ _____ Weighting: __						
B. _____ _____ _____ Weighting: __						
C. _____ _____ _____ Weighting: __						
D. _____ _____ _____ Weighting: __						
Weighted Total # %						

System Being Evaluated: _____

Date System Was Installed: _____

Date Of Evaluation: _____

PERFORMANCE MANAGEMENT SYSTEM ASSESSMENT TOOL FORM COMPLETION PROCEDURES

1. Determine each customer of the process and place names in boxes 1 to 4.

2. Determine the four most important outcomes of the process and place process names in boxes A - D.

3. Weight each customer in terms of importance, dividing a total of ten points between all customers. (For example, if each of four customers is of equal importance, each would receive 2.5 points.) Place weighting beside the appropriate column.

4. Weight each outcome in terms of importance, distributing a total of ten points between all outcomes. (For example, if there are three differently valued outcomes, Outcome 1 might be given five points, Outcome 2 three points, and Outcome 3 two points.)

5. Have each customer (or customer group) rate the PM system capability for satisfying each desired outcome using the five point scale as listed below.

> 5 = Significant Positive Impact
>
> 4 = Minor Positive Impact
>
> 3 = Neutral Impact
>
> 2 = Minor Negative Impact
>
> 1 = Significant Negative Impact

6. Multiply performance scores by the appropriate weightings and place the end result in each box. Add rows and columns to determine totals for each customer, outcome and the system as a whole.

Appendix J

Sample Performance Management System Assessment (Without Weighting)

Outcome	Customer				Total	
	1. Employee	2. Manager/ Supervisor	3. Executive Management	4. H.R./ Legal	#	%
A. Positively Change Behavior	3	3	4	3	13	65%
B. Increase Career Potential	4	4	4	4	16	80%
C. Enhance Motivation	2	3	3	2	10	50%
D. Prevent Lawsuits	3	3	3	2	11	55%
Total #	12	13	14	11	50	
Total %	60%	65%	70%	55%		63%

System Being Evaluated: *ABC Corporate Evaluation System*

Date System Was Installed: *October 1989*

Date Of Evaluation: *January 1999*

Appendix K

Sample Performance
Management System Assessment
(With Weighting)

Outcome	Customer 1. Employee Weighting: 5	2. Manager/ Supervisor Weighting: 3	3. Executive Management Weighting: 1	4. H.R./ Legal Weighting: 1	Total #	Total %
A. Positively Change Behavior Weighting: 5	3	3	4	3	13	
	5	3	1	1		
	5	5	5	5		
	75	45	20	15	155	62%
B. Reward for Performance Weighting: 2	2	2	3	2	9	
	5	3	1	1		
	2	2	2	2		
	20	12	6	4	42	42%
C. Plan for Succession Weighting: 2	2	3	3	2	10	
	5	3	1	1		
	2	2	2	2		
	20	18	6	4	48	48%
D. Provide Input For Training Weighting: 1	3	3	3	2	11	
	5	3	1	1		
	1	1	1	1		
	15	9	3	2	29	58%
Weighted Total #	130	84	35	25	274	55%
Weighted Total %	53%	56%	70%	50%		

System Being Evaluated: _XYZ Corporate Evaluation System_

Date System Was Installed: _October 1992_

Date Of Evaluation: _December 1998_

Notes

PREFACE

1. This quote was taken from a live presentation made by Dr. Deming in New Orleans, La., on March 10, 1993. He made this comment as part of his discussion on the management of people, which is outlined in Chapter 6 of the notebook used to accompany his famous four-day course titled "Quality, Productivity, and Competitive Position."

2. See W. Edwards Deming's *Out of the Crisis* (Cambridge, Mass.: Massachusetts Institute of Technology, 1992) for a thorough account of most of the Quality concepts attributed to Deming in the Preface and throughout this book. Two other excellent resources for learning more about Dr. Deming's management philosophy are Mary Walton's *The Deming Management Method* (New York: The Putnam Publishing Group, 1986) and William Latzko and David Saunders' *Four Days with Dr. Deming* (Reading, Mass.: Addison-Wesley, 1995). The former gives a broad overview of his philosophy and explains each of his Fourteen Points in detail. The latter gives a first-person accounting of his famous "Four Day Seminar."

3. Dr. Deming's "Fourteen Points" and "Seven Deadly Diseases" have changed over time. The version quoted here was from the time period when I attended his Four Day Seminar in March of 1993, one of Dr. Deming's last programs.

4. Ibid.

CHAPTER 1

1. Scott Adams, *The Dilbert Principle: A Cubicle's-Eye View of Bosses, Meetings, Management Fads & Other Workplace Afflictions* (New York: HarperBusiness, 1996), p. 101.

2. This statistic and several others were reported by Chris Lee in "Performance Appraisal: Can We 'Manage' Away the Curse?" *Training*, May 1996, pp. 44–59. The 70 percent estimate was attributed to the *Wall Street Journal*. Lee also summarized the William Mercer study findings.

3. Ibid.

4. This survey was conducted in 1997 by Aon Consulting for the Society of Human Resource Management.

5. These two studies were conducted by the Institute of Management and Administration, Inc. They were part of the 1997 and 1998 annual surveys reported in a series of issues of the *Pay for Performance Newsletter*.

6. John Whitmore, *Coaching for Performance: The New Edition of the Practical Guide* (London: Nicholas Brealey Publishing, 1996), p. 8. Whitmore's book is an excellent treatise on the general nature of coaching and its application in a business setting.

7. Thomas Crane, *The Heart of Coaching: Using Catalytic Coaching to Create a High-Performance Culture* (San Diego: FTA Press, 1998), p. 12. Crane's book provides a deeply passionate portrayal of how to use various coaching techniques to bring out the best in others.

8. Dave Ulrich, *Human Resource Champions: The Next Agenda for Adding Value and Delivering Results* (Boston: Harvard Business School Press, 1997). Ulrich redefines the role of HR in clear and authoritative terms. He challenges HR leaders to assume four critical roles: strategic business partner, administrative expert, employee champion and change agent. This should be required reading for anyone in Human Resources who aspires to work as a full business partner. It is also an excellent resource for the senior executives who interface with them.

PART I

1. Data reported by Towers Perrin in a seminar for business leaders entitled "Performance Appraisal Doesn't Have to Be a Dirty Word! (Does It?)." I attended this workshop in New Orleans, La., in January 1993.

2. 1998 Pay for Performance Strategies Survey conducted by the Institute of Management and Administration, Inc. See note 5 in Chapter 1 above.

CHAPTER 2

1. Fred Nickols is Executive Director, Educational Testing Service, and a highly respected performance improvement consultant. This quote came from Nickols, "Don't Redesign Your Company's Performance Appraisal System, Scrap It!" *Corporate University Review*, May–June 1997.

2. See Jonathan Segal, "Evaluating the Evaluators," *HR Magazine*, October 1995. Interesting article written by a lawyer on the common problems with completion of conventional evaluation forms. In addition to clearly describing the phenomenon of grade inflation, he reviews recurring problems like inconsistency, failure to focus on behavior, and lack of specificity or explanation. Unfortunately, Segal's only advice is to do more training to teach supervisors how to minimize these errors.

3. Ulrich, *Human Resource Champions*, p. 189.

CHAPTER 3

1. W. Edwards Deming, as quoted by Latzko and Saunders in *Four Days with Dr. Deming*, p. 123. See note 2 in Chapter 1.

CHAPTER 4

1. See Steven Kerr, "On the Folly of Rewarding A While Hoping for B," *Academy of Management Journal*, Vol. 18, No. 4, 1975, pp. 35–46. This is a classic article that helps explain the inherent problems of tying pay directly to evaluations of performance. It is reported to be the most frequently requested article for reprint in the history of the journal.

2. Peter Block, *Stewardship: Choosing Service Over Self-Interest* (San Francisco: Berrett-Koehler Publishers, 1993), p. 168. A great book on the subject of responsibility in governing. Block looks deep at our values and helps us see that sometimes doing the right thing is also the smart thing.

3. Ibid., pp. 162–163.

4. Ibid., p. 169.

5. See Chapter 10 for a more complete explanation of this phenomenon.

CHAPTER 5

1. See Chris Lee, "Performance Appraisal," for a reference on this figure and summary of the Mercer study.

CHAPTER 6

1. See H. L. Mencken (ed.), *A New Dictionary of Quotations on Historical Principles from Ancient & Modern Sources* (New York: Random House, 1978), p. 1033.

2. Nickols, "Don't Redesign Your Company's Performance Appraisal System, Scrap It!"

3. Gina Imperato, "How to Give Good Feedback," *Fast Company*, September 1998, p. 147. A good quick read on the changing modern practices in performance management.

4. See R. Zacks "Welding Wounds," *Technology Review*, Vol. 101, No. 6, 1998, pp. 72–76. This is a fascinating article that gives a wonderful glimpse of a paradigm shift in a benchmark procedure in the field of medicine.

CHAPTER 7

1. See Mencken, *A New Dictionary of Quotations*, p. 774.

2. This quote was taken from a 1995 working paper by Fred Nickols entitled "Cost/Benefit of Performance Appraisal." To my knowledge this has never been published. At the time of this writing it was available online at http://users.aol.com/hrmbasics/perf-cost.htm.

3. While this specific quote is taken from page vii, Ulrich's entire work, *Human Resource Champions*, is about redefining the role of Human Resources in a way to make it more of a value-added function. It recognizes the potential of Human Resources to make a strategic contribution to the business but lays out several challenges that must be met for this potential to be realized. *Human Resource Champions* should be required reading for anyone intending to make a career in the field of Human Resources.

4. Jac Fitz-enz, *How to Measure Human Resources Management* (New York: McGraw-Hill, 1995), p. xii. The work of Dr. Fit-enz and the Saratoga Institute is rela-

tively unique. They are attempting to develop a standard series of measures by which to measure the discipline of Human Resources. They have assembled an enormous database that can be used to benchmark many key HR practices.

5. Ibid., p. 21.

6. In addition to the benchmarking efforts of Fitz-enz and the Saratoga Institute, noted above, see the work of William Tracey as a prime example. His book *Human Resource Development Standards* (New York: AMACOM, 1981) is still a classic. It offers a very detailed methodology for assessment of the results produced by HR systems. The work of Jack Phillips is also noteworthy. He argues persuasively for the critical need for a results-based approach to HR management and gives numerous examples of how to do this in a book entitled, *Accountability in Human Resource Management* (Houston, Tex.: Gulf Publishing Company, 1996).

7. Fitz-enz, *How to Measure Human Resources Management*, p. 36.

CHAPTER 8

1. Latzko and Saunders are quoted here (from page 123 of their text) speaking with what they call the "executive's voice." This quote was their way of describing a typical reaction felt by participants attending Dr. Deming's famous "Four Day" seminar.

2. Peter Scholtes wrote a series of position papers and articles trying to explain and expand upon Deming's discussion about the perils and pitfalls of performance assessment. Three of his pieces are listed in the bibliography.

3. This quote was taken from page 1-24 of a notebook provided by Peter Scholtes for a course entitled: "Performance Appraisal: Developing Management Alternatives." The material was copyrighted in Madison, Wis., by Joiner Associates Inc. in 1992.

CHAPTER 9

1. See Mencken, *A New Dictionary of Quotations*, p. 700.

2. Stephen Covey, *The Seven Habits of Highly Effective People* (New York: Simon & Schuster, 1989), p. 15. A benchmark work on values. Most organizations have already internalized his teachings and committed this work to memory.

3. Some might argue that this question is not reflective of enlightened thinking—that is, it implies that the corporation owns the employee. We have continued to use it in most cases because it creates such a lasting impression on the part of the process participants. Realistically, they know they "owe" the company something and this takes care of that obligation quickly and directly. In order to be memorable, we have run the risk of being only slightly provocative.

4 Covey, *The Seven Habits of Highly Effective People*, p. 54.

5. Peter Senge, *The Fifth Discipline: The Art and Practice of the Learning Organization* (New York: Doubleday, 1990). A difficult read but an enlightening perspective on what it takes to survive and thrive as a business in an information-based economy.

6. Ibid., p. 4.

CHAPTER 10

. John-Roger and Peter McWilliams, *Do It! Let's Get Off Our Butts* (Los Angeles: de Press, 1991), p. 102.

2. Please see the Chapter 17 on Special Case Coaching for a more detailed analysis on how to handle this specific type of problem. Suffice to say at this point in our discussion, "Attendance and Punctuality" can become an *AFI* that merits a *Job Threatening* categorization.

3. Jack Walsh, President, Columbian Chemicals Company. Jack is a voracious reader and strong supporter of higher education but has even greater belief in the benefits of learning on the job.

CHAPTER 11

1. Henry David Thoreau, *Walden: or Life in the Woods* (Boston: Ticknor and Fields, 1845).

CHAPTER 12

1. John-Roger and McWilliams, *Do It!*, p. 266.
2. John-Roger and McWilliams, *Do It!*, p. 340.
3. Stephen Covey, Roger Merrill and Rebecca Merrill, *First Things First: To Live, to Love, to Learn, to Leave a Legacy* (New York: Simon & Schuster, 1994), p. 27. This book expands on the bedrock principle of time management advocated in *Seven Habits*. It contains lots of practical wisdom and advice.

CHAPTER 13

1. John-Roger and McWilliams, *Do It!*, p. 420.
2. John-Roger and McWilliams, *Do It!*, p. 142.

CHAPTER 14

1. John-Roger and McWilliams, *Do It!*, p. 360.
2. John-Roger and Peter McWilliams, *Wealth 101* (Los Angeles: Prelude Press, 1992), p. 52.
3. From the Alan J. Pakula–directed Warner Brothers Film, *All the President's Men*, released in 1976. The movie was based on the Carl Bernstein and Bob Woodward book of the same name. The second edition of *All the President's Men* was published in New York by Touchstone Books in 1994.
4. See the discussion in Chapter 4 on compa-ratios and salary ranges.
5. As described in the previous section, this means that the employee has been formally notified that his or her job is at risk based on one or more performance deficiencies. Being given a Job Threatening message does not necessarily mean an employee will be terminated, if improvement is not forthcoming. Transfer or demotion are other options that might be available in some cases.

CHAPTER 15

1. Statistics on current and projected unemployment rates were taken from the report on *The Economic and Budget Outlook: Fiscal Years 1999–2008* submitted by June E.

O'Neill (Director of the Congressional Budget Office) to the United States Senate on January 28, 1998. They range from a low of 4.8 in 1998 to a high of 5.9 in years 2004–2008.

2. An informative perspective on this trend is provided in a report released by the Conference Board in April of 1998. "Transforming the HR Function For Global Business Success" is based on a survey of 516 senior executives representing 373 global companies headquartered in 33 countries. The study was sponsored by William M. Mercer Limited Companies LLC.

3. Zandy Leibowitz, Caela Farren and Beverly Kaye, *Designing Career Development Systems* (San Francisco: Jossey-Bass, 1986). A very useful book for those wanting to take a systemic approach to people development. Contains great advice on getting people involved in the design of their own continued evolution.

4. Robert Haskell, *Reengineering Corporate Training: Intellectual Capital and Transfer of Learning* (Westport, Conn.: Quorum Books, 1998). Deep thinking on the importance of making sure that training and development activities are meaningful and purposeful.

CHAPTER 16

1. Bill Foster and Karen Seeker, *Coaching for Peak Employee Performance: A Practical Guide to Supporting Management Development* (Irvine, Calif.: Richard Chang Associates, 1993), p. 12. Nice basic book on how to coach. It is very straightforward with lots of practical exercises and worksheets.

2. Thomas Crane, *The Heart of Coaching: Using Catalytic Coaching to Create a High-Performance Culture* (San Diego: FTA Press, 1998), p. 12.

3. John Whitmore, *Coaching for Performance*, p. 5.

4. W. Hendricks et al., *Coaching, Mentoring and Managing: Breakthrough Strategies to Solve Performance Problems and Build Winning Teams* (Franklin Lakes, N.J.: National Press Publications, 1996), preface.

5. This quote was taken from page 2.9 of a workbook for a training program developed by Carlos Quintero and Ed Cripe. It is a two-day workshop entitled *REACH: Coaching Performance Excellence* (Atlanta: Sales Effectiveness Inc. & Merit Performance, Inc., 1998). The program is structured around five key principles: Respect, Educate, Aim, Collaborate, and Heart. Highly interactive format.

6. Hendricks et al., *Coaching, Mentoring and Managing*, pp. 73–81.

7. Quintero and Cripe, *REACH*, Module 3.

8. Hendricks et al., *Coaching, Mentoring and Managing*, pp. 98–102.

9. Quintero and Cripe, *REACH*, Module 5.

CHAPTER 17

1. William Byham and Jeff Cox, *Zapp! The Lightning of Empowerment* (New York: Harmony Books, 1988). This is a great book for use as developmental. *Zapp!* is written like a novel and couches its teachings on empowerment and employee involvement very productively. It is a quick and enjoyable read. Feedback from those who have been asked to utilize the book to gain insight on becoming more open and inspiring leaders has been positive.

CHAPTER 18

1. James M. Kouzes and Barry Z. Posner, *The Leadership Challenge: How to Get Extraordinary Things Done in Organizations* (San Francisco: Jossey-Bass, 1987), p. 11. An excellent resource for executives and managers looking for practical advice on how to display more inspirational leadership. Emphasis on process perspective and service-driven organizations.

2. Crane, *The Heart of Coaching*, p. 186.

CONCLUSION

1. Dr. Deming attributed the original form of this original statement to Dr. Lloyd S. Nelson, the Director of Statistical Methods for Nashua Corporation. See *Out of the Crisis* (Cambridge, Mass.: Massachusetts Institute of Technology, 1992), p. 20.

Bibliography

Adams, S. *The Dilbert Principle: A Cubicle's-Eye View of Bosses, Meetings, Management Fads & Other Workplace Afflictions.* New York: HarperBusiness, 1996.

Belasco, J. A. and Stayer, R. C. *Flight of the Buffalo: Soaring to Excellence, Learning to Let Employees Lead.* New York: Warner Books, 1993.

Block, P. *Stewardship: Choosing Service Over Self-Interest.* San Francisco: Berrett-Koehler Publishers, 1993.

Byham, W. C. and Cox, J. *Zapp! The Lightning of Empowerment.* New York: Harmony Books, 1988.

Carnegie, D. *How to Win Friends and Influence People.* New York: Pocket Books, Simon & Schuster, 1986.

Conway, W. E. *The Quality Secret: The Right Way to Manage.* Nashua, N.H.: Conway Quality, 1992.

Convey, S. R. *The Seven Habits of Highly Effective People.* New York: Simon & Schuster, 1989.

Convey, S. R., Merrill, A. R. and Merrill, R. R. *First Things First: To Live, to Love, to Learn, to Learn to Leave a Legacy.* New York: Simon & Schuster, 1994.

Crane, T. G. *The Heart of Coaching: Using Catalytic Coaching to Create a High-Performance Culture.* San Diego: FTA Press, 1998.

Crow, R. "You *Cannot* Improve My Performance by Measuring It." *Journal for Quality and Participation*, January–February 1996, pp. 62–64.

Daniels, A. C. *Bring Out the Best in People.* New York: McGraw-Hill, 1994.

Davis, B. L., Skube, C. J., Hellervik, L. W., Gebelein, S. H. and Sheard, J. L. *Successful Manager's Handbook: Development Suggestions for Today's Managers.* Minneapolis, MN: Personnel Decisions International, 1992.

Deming, W. E. *Out of the Crisis.* Cambridge, Mass.: Massachusetts Institute of Technology, 1992.

Fitz-enz, J. *How to Measure Human Resources Management.* New York: McGraw-Hill, 1995.

Foster, B. and Seeker, K. R. *Coaching for Peak Employee Performance: A Practical Guide to Supporting Management Development.* Irvine, Calif.: Richard Chang Associates, 1993.

Gutteridge, T. G., Leibowitz, Z. B. and Shore, J. E. *Organizational Career Development: Benchmarks for Building a World-Class Workforce.* San Francisco: Jossey-Bass, 1993.

Haasen, A. and Shea, G. F. *A Better Place to Work: A New Sense of Motivation Leading to High Productivity.* New York: American Management Association, Membership Publications Division, 1997.

Hammer, M. and Champy, J. *Reengineering the Corporation: A Manifesto for Business Revolution.* New York: HarperCollins, 1993.

Haskell, R. E. *Reengineering Corporate Training: Intellectual Capital and Transfer of Learning.* Westport, Conn.: Quorum Books, 1998.

Head, C. W. *Beyond Corporate Transformation: A Whole Systems Approach to Creating and Sustaining High Performance.* Portland, Ore.: Productivity Press, 1997.

Hendricks, W. et al. *Coaching, Mentoring and Managing: Breakthrough Strategies to Solve Performance Problems and Build Winning Teams.* Franklin Lakes, N.J.: National Press Publications, 1996.

Imai, M. *Kaizen: The Key to Japan's Competitive Success.* New York: McGraw-Hill, 1986.

Imperato, G. "How to Give Good Feedback." *Fast Company,* September 1998, pp. 144–156.

Kaplan, R. S. and Norton, D. P. *The Balanced Scorecard: Translating Strategy into Action.* Boston: Harvard Business School Press, 1996.

Kerr, S. "On the Folly of Rewarding A While Hoping for B." *Academy of Management Journal,* Vol. 18, No. 4, 1975, pp. 35–46.

———. "Risky Business: The New Pay Game." *Fortune,* July 22, 1996, pp. 94–96.

Kouzes, J. M. and B. Z. Posner. *The Leadership Challenge: How to Get Extraordinary Things Done in Organizations.* San Francisco: Jossey-Bass, 1987.

Kram, K. E. *Mentoring at Work: Developmental Relationships in Organizational Life.* Glenview, Ill.: Scott, Foresman and Company, 1985.

Lancaster, H. "Performance Reviews: Some Bosses Try Fresh Approach." *Wall Street Journal,* December 1, 1998, p. B1.

Latzko, W. J. and Saunders, D. M. *Four Days with Dr. Deming.* Reading, Mass.: Addison-Wesley, 1995.

Lee, C. "Performance Appraisal: Can We 'Manage' Away the Curse?" *Training,* May 1996, pp. 11–59.

Leibowitz, Z. B., Farren, C. and Kaye, B. L. *Designing Career Development Systems.* San Francisco: Jossey-Bass, 1986.

McGregor, D. "An Uneasy Look at Performance Appraisal." *Harvard Business Review,* May–June 1957.

Nadler, L. *Corporate Human Resources Development: A Management Tool.* New York: Van Nostrand/American Society for Training and Development, 1980.

Nichols, F. "Don't Redesign Your Company's Performance Appraisal System, Scrap It!" *Corporate University Review,* May–June 1997, pp. 54–59.

Patton, A. "How to Appraise Executive Performance." *Harvard Business Review*, January–February 1960, pp. 93–100.

Peck, M. S. *The Road Less Traveled*. New York: Simon & Schuster, 1978.

Peters, T. *The Circle of Innovation*. New York: Alfred A. Knopf, 1997.

Phillips, J. J. *Accountability in Human Resource Management*. Houston, Tex.: Gulf Publishing Company, 1996.

Quintero, C. and Cripe, E. *REACH: Coaching Performance Excellence*. Training workshop in coaching skills marketed by Sales Effectiveness Inc. and Merit Performance, Inc., Atlanta, GA., 1998.

Ricciardi, P. "Simplify Your Approach to Performance Measurement." *HR Magazine*, March 1996, pp. 98–106.

Rosen, R. H. *Healthy Companies: A Human Resources Approach*. New York: American Management Association, Membership Publications Division, 1986.

Rummler, G. A. and Brache, A. P. *Improving Performance: How to Manage the White Space on the Organizational Chart*. San Francisco: Jossey-Bass, 1995.

Sashkin, M. "Appraising Appraisal: Ten Lessons From Research for Practice." *Organizational Dynamics*, Vol. 9, No. 3, 1981, pp. 37–50.

Scholtes, P. R. "An Elaboration on Deming's Teachings on Performance Appraisal." *Working Paper*. Madison, Wis.: Joiner Associates, 1987.

———. "Performance Appraisal: Developing Management Alternatives." *Workshop Notebook*. Madison, Wis.: Joiner Associates, 1992.

———. "Total Quality or Performance Appraisal: Pick One." *National Productivity Review*, Vol. 12, No. 3, Summer 1993, pp. 349–364.

Scholtes, P. R., Joiner, B. L. and Streibel, B. J. *The Team Handbook*, 2nd ed. Madison, Wis.: Joiner Associates, 1996.

Segal, J. A. "Evaluating the Evaluators." *HR Magazine*, October 1995.

Senge, P. M. *The Fifth Discipline: The Art & Practice of the Learning Organization*. New York: Doubleday, 1990.

Senge, P. M., Kleiner, A., Roberts, C., Ross, R. B. and Smith, B. J. *The Fifth Discipline Fieldbook: Strategies and Tools for Building a Learning Organization*. New York: Doubleday, 1994.

Sherman, S. "Stretch Goals: The Dark Side of Asking for Miracles." *Fortune*, November 13, 1995, pp. 231–232.

Souerwine, A. H. "The Manager as Career Counselor: Some Issues and Approaches." In D. Montross and C. Shinkman (eds.), *Career Development in the 1980's*. Springfield, Ill.: Thomas, 1981.

Sprague, L. "The High Costs of Personal Transitions." *Training and Development Journal*, October 1984, pp. 60–62.

Tracey, W. R. *Human Resource Development Standards*. New York: AMACOM, 1981.

———. *Human Resources Management & Development Handbook*. New York: AMACOM, 1985.

———. *Critical Skills: The Guide to Top Performance for Human Resources Managers*. New York: AMACOM, 1988.

Ulrich, D. *Human Resource Champions: The Next Agenda for Adding Value and Delivering Results*. Boston: Harvard Business School Press, 1997.

Waldrop, J. and Butler, T. "The Executive as Coach." *Harvard Business Review*, November–December 1996.

Walton, M. *The Deming Management Method*. New York: The Putman Publishing Group, 1986.

Whitmore, J. W. *Coaching for Performance: The New Edition of the Practical Guide*. London: Nicholas Brealey Publishing, 1996.

Zacks, R. "Welding Wounds." *Technology Review*, Vol. 101, No. 6, 1998, pp. 72–76.

Index

About the Author

GAROLD L. MARKLE is a founding principal of Energage Incorporated, a consulting firm based in Marietta, Georgia. Gary and his associates help business leaders provide coaching, training, and consulting services that produce superior business results through people. Markle is also a Chairman of The Executive Committee in Atlanta, Georgia, and he lectures frequently as an active member of the Georgia Speakers Association and the National Speakers Association. Markle has served in senior-level human resource management and executive positions for the four different, globally prominent companies, including three listing among the *Fortune* 100. His most recent position was Vice President of Human Resources and member of the executive leadership team for an international chemical company.

CPSIA information can be obtained
at www.ICGtesting.com
Printed in the USA
LVOW13s0224110718

583038LV00003BA/3/P